Other Books by Dan Kurzman

*Fatal Voyage: The Sinking of the USS Indianapolis**
A Killing Wind: Inside Union Carbide and the Bhopal Catastrophe
Day of the Bomb: Countdown to Hiroshima
Ben-Gurion: Prophet of Fire
Miracle of November: Madrid's Epic Stand 1936
The Bravest Battle: The 28 Days of the Warsaw Ghetto Uprising
The Race for Rome
Genesis 1948: The First Arab-Israeli War
Santo Domingo: Revolt of the Damned
Subversion of the Innocents
Kishi and Japan: The Search for the Sun

*Published by Pocket Books

LEFT TO DIE

The Tragedy of the USS *JUNEAU*

Dan Kurzman

POCKET BOOKS

New York   London   Toronto   Sydney   Tokyo   Singapore

POCKET BOOKS, a division of Simon & Schuster Inc.
1230 Avenue of the Americas, New York, NY 10020

Copyright © 1994 by Dan Kurzman

Library of Congress Cataloging-in-Publication Data

Kurzman, Dan.
    Left to die : the tragedy of the USS *Juneau* / Dan Kurzman.
       p.   cm.
    ISBN 0-671-74873-4
    1. *Juneau* (Antiaircraft cruiser) 2. Shipwrecks—South Pacific
Ocean. 3. Shipwreck victims—United States. 4. World War,
1939–1945—Search-and-rescue operations. 5. United States. Navy—
Search-and-rescue operations. I. Title.
D774.J86K87 1994
940.54′5973—dc20   93-26082
                                                         CIP

First Pocket Books hardcover printing March 1994

10 9 8 7 6 5 4 3 2 1

Printed in the U.S.A.

For my dear wife, Florence—

whose spirit brightens every page

even as the ocean roars its rage

Contents

CONTENTS

Acknowledgments

I am deeply grateful to my wife, Florence, for her indispensable collaboration in the preparation of this book. She helped to edit it, rewriting passages and offering invaluable advice on bringing to life the characters portrayed.

My warm thanks are also due Paul McCarthy, my editor at Pocket Books, and Julian Bach, my agent, for their splendid editorial suggestions.

I wish to express my appreciation as well to the following people for their generous help in facilitating my research:

Pat Alling—librarian, Waterloo, Iowa, Public Library

Billie Bailey—director, Grout Museum of History and Science, Waterloo, Iowa

Richard Boylan—archivist, Suitland Reference Branch, National Archives, Washington, D.C.

Mary Catalfamo—librarian, Nimitz Library, U.S. Naval Academy, Annapolis, Maryland

Bernard F. Cavacante—director, Operational Archives Branch, Naval Historical Center, Washington, D.C.

Rebecca Christian—free-lance writer

Col. Elliot V. Converse III—Historical Research Center, Maxwell Air Force Base, Alabama

Deb Cue—office of the president, Citibank

Capt. George Cully—Historical Research Center, Maxwell Air Force Base

Dan Dundon—city editor, *Waterloo Courier*

Dick Gamma—Historical Research Center, Maxwell Air Force Base

Susan Graves—daughter-in-law of Vice Adm. Robert B. Carney

Father Donald Hawes—pastor, St. Mary's Church, Waterloo

ACKNOWLEDGMENTS

John Hodges—Naval Historical Foundation, Washington, D.C.

Scott Johnson—scientist, Naval Ocean Systems Center, San Diego, California

Robert Kemp—USS *Juneau* researcher

Yuko Kubota—interpreter from Japanese

Jim Lee—Naval Historical Foundation

Kenneth Lyftogt—professor, University of Northern Iowa

Michael Magee—researcher, Sullivan family

Jean Max—*Time* magazine

John C. Reilly, Jr.—Ships Histories Branch, Naval Historical Center

Saul Shapiro—editor, *Waterloo Courier*

Hiromi Shinobu—translator from Japanese

Seiichi Soeda—coordinator, media assistance, Foreign Press Center/Japan, Tokyo, Japan

Paul Stillwell—editor, *Naval History*, U.S. Naval Institute, Annapolis, Maryland

Jan Taylor—librarian, Grout Museum of History and Science

Richard A. von Doenhoff—naval historian, Military Reference Branch, National Archives

Mike Walker—archivist, Operational Archives Branch, Naval Historical Center

Cherie Watson—Ships Histories Branch, Naval Historical Center

Harold Woodruff—official, Army-Navy Country Club, Arlington, Virginia

Mary Zlabek—librarian, *Waterloo Courier*

Among the persons kind enough to grant me interviews were:

William Anderson—crew captain, PBY rescue plane

James Baird—officer, USS *Helena*

Hazel Ball (Peterson)—sister of Bill Ball, the Sullivans' friend

William R. Barnett—officer, USS *Helena*

Roswell Bosworth, Jr.—newspaper publisher, Bristol, Rhode Island

ACKNOWLEDGMENTS

William Bunker—officer, USS *Helena*

Wyatt Butterfield—*Juneau* survivor

Charles L. Carpenter—officer, USS *Helena*

Orrel Cecil—sailor, USS *Juneau*

John L. Chew—officer, USS *Helena*

Richard L. Cochrane—officer, USS *Helena*

William Cole II—son of captain, USS *Fletcher*

Charles Cook, Jr.—officer, USS *Helena*

Edward Corboy—officer, USS *Atlanta*

G. Bowden Craighill, Jr.—officer, USS *Atlanta*

Murray Davidson—son of Genevieve Sullivan

John Draude—friend of Sullivan brothers

William R. Entrikin—radioman, B-17

Arthur Friend—*Juneau* survivor

Adelaide Fullenwider—friend of Captain Swenson

Victor Gibson—sailor, USS *San Francisco*

Robert L. Gill—pilot, B-17

Lilyan Grycky (Steciw)—sister of John Grycky

Leo Harrington—friend of Sullivan brothers

Lucy Hartney—wife of Joseph Hartney

Allen Heyn—*Juneau* survivor

Dr. Willis Hoch—colleague of Charles Wang

Alfreda Holmgren—mother of Frank Holmgren

Frank Holmgren—*Juneau* survivor

Gilbert Hoover, Jr.—son of Captain Hoover

Beatrice Imperato (Ferreri)—fiancée of Madison (Matt) Sullivan

Margaret Jaros (Woods)—fiancée of Joseph (Red) Sullivan

William W. Jones—officer, USS *Helena*

Steve Katalinich—friend of Sullivan brothers

Eileen Koch—friend of Alleta Sullivan

James Latta—friend of John Grycky

Ruth Leet (Roe)—girlfriend of George Sullivan

Laura Swenson McIntire—sister of Captain Swenson

William David McIntire—friend of Captain Hoover

Robert Metcalfe—friend of Joseph Hartney

Katherine Miller—daughter of Captain Hoover

John J. Mitchell—friend of Charles Wang

Albert Mixdorf—friend of Sullivan brothers

ACKNOWLEDGMENTS

John Mrzlak—foreman at Rath plant, Waterloo
Tsukuo Nakano—crew member, submarine *I-26*
Joseph Nevins—colleague of Captain Swenson
James Rogers—brother of Patrick and Louis, *Juneau* victims
Joseph Rogers—brother of Patrick and Louis
John Rooff—cousin of James Sullivan
Leo Rooff—uncle of John Rooff
Claire Schonland—wife of Herbert E. Schonland, acting
   commander, USS *San Francisco*
Richard Schultz—friend of Sullivan brothers
Stanley Steciw—husband of Lilyan Grycky
Eugene R. Stephens—friend of Sullivan brothers
James Sullivan—son of Albert Sullivan
Robert Swenson—son of Captain Swenson
Forrest C. Tanner—naval officer aboard B-17
Rev. Delbert W. Tildesly—friend of Captain Hoover
Michael T. Tyng—officer, USS *Helena*
Gene Francis Wagner—friend of Sullivan brothers
George Walker—navigator, B-17
Marie Wang—wife of Charles Wang
Richard M. Wang—brother of Charles Wang
Ellery Watson—Army Air Corps flier
Dr. James Welsh—colleague of Charles Wang
Lawrence B. Williamson—pilot, PBY rescue plane
Ann Wood—daughter of Captain Hoover
Joseph C. Wylie—executive officer, USS *Fletcher*
Lester Zook—*Juneau* survivor
Frank Zubak—friend of Sullivan brothers

LEFT
TO DIE

Prologue

ON THE BRIGHT TROPICAL MORNING OF NOVEMBER 13, 1942, Capt. Gilbert C. Hoover stood on the open bridge of the cruiser USS *Helena* as it plowed southward off the coast of Guadalcanal and contemplated with a sense of wonder the tranquil, virtually waveless South Pacific waters that washed the shores of the Solomon Islands. After emerging from one of the wildest, most destructive sea battles in history, he could hardly believe there still existed a world so peaceful, so infinitely peaceful, reaching, it appeared, even beyond the barely perceptible horizon, where sea and sky blended into one seamless mantle of blue.

Suddenly, Hoover's battle-glazed eyes focused on a streak of white foam that ripped across the ocean surface like the cut of an invisible knife. A torpedo! And it seemed headed toward his ship! Normally, Hoover was cool in a crisis, and once he even casually blew smoke rings after he had seen a submarine periscope poking out of the water nearby and ordered evasive action. Now, however, shaken and helpless, and hardly with time to gather his thoughts, he could envisage only the smoke that was about to coil from his "doomed" vessel.

But as Hoover chillingly braced for disaster, fate abruptly reversed course. The torpedo sped harmlessly past the stern of the *Helena*. Before Hoover could fully recover from his shock, the ship trembled from the impact of a tremendous thunderclap nearby. He looked around and saw a plume of white water soar a thousand feet into the sky, to be swallowed by a steaming brown cloud that stretched for more than half a mile across the ocean. Like an evil star hurled by some mad demon, a huge 5-inch gun mount flew leisurely over the *Helena*. Other pieces of lethal shrapnel rained down on the sea with a steely persistence that led some American ships in the area to sound an air-raid alert.

Hoover turned to an officer beside him and gasped, "My God, I can't believe it!"

The torpedo that had streaked past his ship had blasted into another on his starboard quarter. It was the most awesome explosion Hoover had ever seen. And when the smoke finally cleared, he saw, with even greater dismay, nothing at all. The light cruiser USS *Juneau*, with almost seven hundred men aboard, had been limping along wounded and powerless when it suddenly vanished like a face in a dream.

Hoover's consternation was all the greater since he had only hours earlier assumed command of the shattered remnants of a thirteen-ship task group that had survived a deadly night battle in which most of the ships—American and Japanese—were sunk or damaged, and the top U.S. commanders killed. Hoover, though a mere captain, was now the most senior officer alive and had thus become the new task group commander. Almost before he could absorb the full impact of the burden thrust upon him, he found himself faced with a dilemma that might have stumped Solomon: Should he search for survivors and try to knock out the submarine that had launched the torpedo, or should he flee with his ships before the submarine struck again?

Hoover sounded a general alarm calling all members of his crew to their battle stations, then paused to reflect on the *Juneau*'s seven hundred men, who had, in a few seconds, simply disappeared. The ship's commander, Capt. Lyman Knut Swenson, was an old classmate from the Naval Academy—dear old "Swens." Suddenly, he was gone. And there were the five Sullivan brothers, who had made headlines because they insisted on sailing together—even if they had to die together. Now surely they had.

Could there be any survivors? Of his battered flotilla of two cruisers and two destroyers, only one destroyer, the USS *Fletcher*, was undamaged and had the sound equipment and depth charges necessary to protect itself while searching for survivors and enemy submarines. A third destroyer, the *O'Bannon*, had been sent away so it could radio headquarters a report of the night battle without revealing the task group's position.

But as Hoover scanned the sea with his binoculars, all he could see was a calm, glassy surface free of floating debris— human or otherwise. His lookout men, too, failed to detect any sign of life. Hoover hurriedly met with his top officers, who worshiped him as a brilliant skipper and a warm, down-to-earth human being. The captain's rosy, usually animated face was now pale and impassive.

"I do not see how anyone could have survived," he said. But should he send a destroyer to search—just to make sure?

No, his officers responded, no one could possibly be alive after such an explosion. The *Juneau* had split in two and disintegrated in seconds—there was no time for anyone to escape. And even if by chance a few men did, they would have to be sacrificed, for should the *Fletcher* be sent on this mission, the rest of the flotilla would be unprotected against another submarine strike. Had not headquarters sent word earlier that three enemy submarines were thought to be lurking in the area?

Hoover listened, then concluded that it didn't make sense to risk another attack and the lives of hundreds more men.

It was just like the skipper, his officers felt. Always thinking about how to save lives.

And so the wisest option, all agreed, was to steam away as swiftly as possible.

Anyway, they could radio headquarters to send help, someone suggested.

No, Hoover replied, his task force was operating under radio silence, and the rule was very strict. He would not break the silence. As a captain suddenly thrust into an admiral's boots, he was not about to disobey orders. The commander of the submarine, of course, already knew where the task group was, but perhaps he had not yet notified his headquarters.

Any qualms Hoover may have had about his decision were apparently dispelled when a B-17 darted into view. Let the pilot of that plane break radio silence! Hoover ordered a signalman to notify the pilot with blinkers that the *Juneau* had been sunk and that he should radio for help. With his conscience now at ease, Hoover signaled the *Fletcher,* which was already racing toward the scene of the disaster, to turn back, and he ordered all his ships to retreat rapidly from the area and continue cruising toward Nouméa, New Caledonia, his headquarters.

No man could have survived that explosion, Hoover repeated to his officers. He was doing the right thing—saving lives. Still, he wondered with gnawing uncertainty, would his superiors agree?

Whatever their reaction, about one hundred and forty men would not—the survivors of the *Juneau.* Bloody and hysterical, many without arms or legs, they clung to bits of debris and watched in agonized disbelief as the ships receded into the hazy distance, leaving them to the sharks and other terrors of the sea.

CHAPTER

· 1 ·

Seed of Doubt

EIGHT MONTHS EARLIER, IN MARCH 1942, CAPT. SWENSON HAD RE-
alized his dream. He proudly stood on the bridge of the newly
commissioned *Juneau*, the commander of a cruiser at last. But
by May, as his sleek antiaircraft vessel was about to set out for
its baptism of fire, reality had already tempered his elation. The
night before his ship was to sail out of American waters for the
first time, he went to see Adelaide Fullenwider, the widow of
a fellow naval officer who had been his dearest friend.

Swenson and the Fullenwiders had been close since the early
1920s when the two young officers served on the USS *Tennes-
see* together. In the early 1930s, they shared adventures along
the Yangtze River in China, where Swenson was commander of
the USS *Isabel*, a river gunboat.

Adelaide congratulated her guest, expecting to find him jubi-
lant over his new command, especially since he had an ebul-
lient nature and usually found humor in even the harshest
realities of life. It was his ultimate defense against adversity, to
which he was no stranger. And now, finally, at fifty, he had
reason to feel joyous, and it seemed he was not.

Swenson had changed. His straight-backed, lanky physique,
nurtured on the basketball court, in the swimming pool, along

the bridle path, and on other sporting grounds, seemed slightly hunched, and his piercing gray eyes lacked the familiar fire and ironic twinkle. Even his firm, determined jaw could not hide the look of a man in doubt.

"Adelaide," Swenson said, "I'm proud of my ship, but if we get into a battle, we're goners. We have no armor because we must carry heavy antiaircraft guns and move rapidly. The ship is poorly designed, and all we're really good for is convoying."

Adelaide was startled by Swenson's uncharacteristic gloom. Yet she could understand his deep concern. The war was just a few months old and the United States was losing battles. Washington needed combat ships after losing much of its fleet at Pearl Harbor, and it wasn't likely to keep a new cruiser out of enemy range no matter how vulnerable it was.

Actually, Swenson was worried not only because he felt his ship was unsuited for combat, but because he thought most of his men were unready for it. They were new recruits untested in battle and inadequately trained in the little time given them before their dispatch overseas. He was especially disturbed because the Navy, despite his protests, had assigned to his vessel all five Sullivan brothers, as well as the four Rogers brothers. If his ship went down, it would bear the stigma of having lost multiple family members—and this was not the fame he sought for it. When Swenson complained about this, the Navy simply replied that it was good public relations for so many members of the same family to serve on the same ship. Swenson was enraged. A captain had enough on his mind without having to worry about a mother losing all her sons in one fell swoop.

But Swenson's troubles stretched beyond his ship and his men. The captain was plagued as well by tormenting personal problems. He was divorcing his second wife, Lauretta, and his case had been weakened by his long absence at sea. And now he would be sailing off again—and might never come back. If his wife became a widow, she would claim much of his estate, and he wanted to leave almost all his money to his two children from his first marriage.

In fact, Swenson had an obsessive need to serve his children—to make up for those tragic lost years. . . .

* * *

■ 6 ■

LEFT TO DIE

Tragedy stemmed from a tempestuous first marriage with a beautiful San Francisco socialite, Milo Abercrombie, whom Swenson had wed in 1917, a year after graduating from the Naval Academy. Milo's family had struck oil in Texas years earlier, and she now lived with her mother in a forty-two-room mansion. A spoiled, neurotic young woman who had been divorced from a German count, Milo demanded that her reluctant husband move into the house and mingle with the Nob Hill crowd, though he felt ill at ease at their cocktail parties amid gossipy dowagers and debutantes who utterly bored him.

Swenson's roots were not in the silken swank of a pseudopatrician society, but in the sacred soil of a pious one. His father had come from Denmark in 1856 armed with the Bible of Mormonism and settled in Pleasant Grove, Utah. Here he bought a hundred-acre farm, where he lived with a large family of brothers, sisters, and their brood in one harmonious community. When young Lyman was not studying Mormon doctrine, he eagerly worked the salty earth of Utah, which, to many Mormons, was almost a religious experience in itself, since salt, the Bible says, has "power to be the seasoning, savoring, preserving influence in the world."

Swenson's labor outdoors strengthened him not only spiritually but physically, and in school he excelled in sports. He also excelled, according to the Naval Academy yearbook of 1916, "as a breaker of hearts." The charm of "lovable old Swens" lay not only in his infectious laugh, his gentle manner, and his refusal ever to utter an unhappy thought, but in his tactlessness, which gave him a reputation for complete honesty and sincerity that would follow him into the Navy. To his officers and men, he was still "lovable old Swens," though they treated him with the by-the-book respect due a military superior.

Milo found Swenson lovable, too—until he refused to live indefinitely in her mansion together with a mother-in-law who appeared to feel that the blood of a Navy ensign was not quite blue enough to flow through the veins of her exclusive social set. Finally, after several years of marriage, Swenson packed his bags and moved out of the house, suing his wife for divorce and demanding custody of their two children.

When the court began leaning in Swenson's favor, Milo became desperate and charged that her husband had molested their five-year-old daughter, Cecilia. After a bitter battle that graced the local newspapers with screaming headlines, the court rejected the charge and gave Swenson custody of his son and daughter. But Milo kidnaped them and, constantly moving around the country, managed to elude the father, though he feverishly searched for them.

While shattered by the loss of his children, Swenson further agonized over the slander of his character, which, despite his court victory, seriously damaged his career. He had served with distinction on a submarine in World War I and had commanded one after the war, but it was years before the Navy, which had been dismayed by the publicity the "scandal" generated, agreed to promote him again.

Finally, Swenson, tipped off in 1937 by one of Milo's relatives, found his family in New York. He knocked on the door and, when it opened, stared into the startled eyes of a fifteen-year-old boy. They both knew instantly and fell into each other's arms. But Cecilia shied away. For years, Milo had tried to poison the minds of her children against their father, and though the son, Robert, never believed her, Cecilia apparently did, perhaps, according to Swenson's friends, after being led to fantasize events in her childhood.

A few years later, when World War II erupted, Swenson proudly saw his long-lost son through the Naval Academy and once even sailed the *Juneau* into the port of Annapolis just so Robert and his fellow midshipmen could visit him aboard the vessel. But Cecilia refused his money and his company. Pathetically, he pleaded for a reconciliation, but to no avail.

Swenson married a second time in 1929, but this marriage also crumbled when a dozen years later it grew clear that Lauretta had reneged on her promise to be a "mother" to his children. Selfish and extravagant, she was, once they were found, usually too busy to see them, Swenson's friends say.

Despite all the tragedy, the heartache, and the humiliation, Swenson fought relentlessly to conquer misfortune. And though still tormented by his daughter's rejection of him and the snail-paced divorce proceedings, he had largely triumphed. His son was devoted to him, and the Navy had let him command the destroyer squadron that took President Franklin D. Roosevelt to his historic meeting with Prime Minister Winston Churchill off the coast of Iceland in 1941, then had entrusted him with a cruiser, however belatedly, and promoted him from commander to captain.

But he was so tired, so emotionally drained. And if he had gained a son of his own, how many other sons might be sacrificed aboard his "papier-mâché" ship? Yet he loved his ship—his ship—as a father might love a handicapped child.

When Swenson left to rejoin his crew, Adelaide noted that his expression was unchanged. The burden of his enormous responsibility was still etched in his tensely lined face. She knew his concern was not for himself, but for his men, who did not suspect that their ship might soon be sailing into battle with the odds of survival pitifully low—and whole families at risk.

CHAPTER

· 2 ·

The Five Sullivan Brothers

DECEMBER 7, 1941, WAS A TYPICAL WINTRY DAY IN THE SLEEPY town of Waterloo, Iowa. Few people tramped the snowy streets in the bitter cold, and those who did were probably heading for the homes of relatives or friends, where they might savor a hearty meal of sausages or corned beef—perhaps processed by their own hands. For many of the townspeople worked in the giant Rath Packing Company that, with the Illinois Central Railroad and John Deere Tractor Company, dominated the economy of Waterloo.

Among the hungry residents inhaling the intriguing scents wafting from a kitchen that afternoon were four brothers, who, as they did every Sunday, lazily lounged in the simply furnished living room of a white frame house at 98 Adams Street. This was the home of Thomas Sullivan, a freight conductor on the railroad, who lived here with his wife, four of his five sons, his daughter, and mother-in-law. While the women prepared dinner, Tom sat silently listening, occasionally nodding, as his sons engaged in animated conversation, trying to compete with the shrill sound of music emanating from a static-plagued radio and the tinny sound of pots and pans rattling on the kitchen stove.

Usually the family chatted about the mundane domestic problems of the day—the electric light that wouldn't go on, the garbage can blown over by the wind—or about the latest local baseball scores, the stupidity of the foreman at the Rath plant, where all five boys worked, the tattoos that decorated the arms of George, twenty-eight, and Francis (Frank), twenty-six. The two brothers proudly displayed the rippling anchors that had been indelibly ingrained in their skin while they were serving a four-year hitch in the Navy, which had ended a few months earlier, in June 1941. George, however, did not dare relate how he happened to be tattooed. On one shore leave, he had enough money either for a tattoo or a prostitute. So he flipped a coin, and the tattoo won.

Though George, a gunner's mate second class, and Frank, a coxswain, had glimpsed life along the coasts of mysterious islands and distant continents, the family's world seldom stretched beyond the boundaries of Iowa. But on this Sunday, the family talk reached to the shores of Europe and Asia, for the gathering war clouds could cast a long shadow over their lives. The headlines were shouting that the Japanese were greasing their guns. If war struck, not only would George and Frank be recalled, but two younger brothers, Joseph (Red), twenty-three, and Madison (Matt), twenty-two, would soon be at the front. Even the youngest, Albert, twenty, the sole married brother and the father of a one-year-old son, James, might be pulled into the struggle. Al was to join the group later in the evening.

Also, the brothers had many friends now in the service and were especially worried about Bill Ball, their closest buddy. He was aboard the battleship USS *Arizona* anchored in Pearl Harbor, together with his brother, Masten, and if war broke out, the Japanese might well attack that port. Before he joined the Navy in 1938, Bill, a farmer from nearby Fredericksburg, came into Waterloo every Thursday to join the Sullivan boys, their sister, Genevieve, and often their mother for an evening out at the Electric Park Ballroom. This was the highlight of the week for all of them, and an inexpensive way for the Sullivan boys to cavort with the girls.

There were plenty of girls to choose from, and each hoped to draw the brother wearing the single pair of Sunday shoes that the five young men could afford and thus shared. It was not easy prancing around with someone who seemed almost glued to the floor with work shoes or clodhoppers. Meanwhile, Bill monopolized Genevieve, a frail, attractive, soft-spoken girl who relished dancing with so handsome a partner, a natural athlete who aspired to become a professional baseball player. So close was Bill to the family that sometimes Genevieve, twenty-four at the time, couldn't quite decide whether he was more like a sixth brother or a first boyfriend. . . .

And so now, on Sunday, December 7, 1941, with war imminent, the brothers talked, and worried, about Bill. A night out at the Electric Park Ballroom just wasn't the same without him.

Suddenly, the music on the radio stopped, and a voice tersely announced: "The Japanese have bombed Pearl Harbor!"

The family was stunned. Bill was there—on the *Arizona*. What had happened to him? Everyone sensed that the joy of youth, of life, in Waterloo would soon seem like a distant dream.

It was fun to be born in Waterloo in the first quarter of the twentieth century. For the railroad was fun. It hired, together with Rath, most of the able-bodied men in town, especially those who lived on the east side of the blue-green Cedar River, which crept indolently through the municipality. Here the railroad yard stretched along the narrow avenues of garden-garnished wooden homes that housed the engineers, conductors, signalmen, and others who made the trains run.

The Sullivans lived in one of these homes. The day always started right for the five sons, for what young boy would not enjoy waking to the sound of the long, whining whistle of a train rumbling by, and watching through the window the magic smoke that curled into odd forms as it rose with measured transparency into the blue morning sky. Almost every child in Waterloo aspired to become an engineer, the man who blew the whistle, arousing fantasies of far-off places full of adventure, mystery, and danger.

Many mornings, Tom Sullivan might just have debarked from the train, for normally he made the night run from Waterloo to

Dubuque and back. The Illinois Central was the major freight carrier chugging between Chicago and Omaha, but for Tom, Dubuque not only marked the end of the line, but the end of the world, about the only world he knew.

At the age of sixteen, Tom, restless to be on his own, left the farm his parents had bought in Harper's Ferry, Iowa, after emigrating from County Cork, Ireland. He hoped to become a cowboy, his childhood dream, but unable to find work chasing cattle in the dust of a prairie paradise, he settled for the more stifling dust of a Colorado mine. Hardly had he come up for air, however, when he rushed off to Waterloo to work as a brakeman on the railroad. At least it would no longer be night in the middle of the day and he could see the stars.

A fellow railroader, George W. Abel, grew fond of him and introduced him to his daughter, Alleta, whom the young man married in 1914. A year later, Abel was killed when a train ran over him, and Tom took his mother-in-law, May, into the Sullivans' home. The household was typically Irish, harboring all the joys and sins that eternally blessed or plagued Irish life anywhere, though May's family was not of pure vintage. Some of her ancestors had been Scottish, and her grandfather, Jewish.

"I guess you could say the boys are typical Americans," she once remarked. "A good mixture makes good Americans."

The home was, on the whole, a happy one. Still, May, a motherly woman with dark hair and bright eyes, never fully recovered from her husband's untimely death, and even years later she was constantly evoking tender moments with him as if they had transpired yesterday. To keep her mind off the tragedy, she plunged into a housekeeping routine that consumed her from dawn to dinner—permitting her daughter, who had grown obese in the 1930s, to spend most of the day swaying in a rocking chair on the front porch.

Alleta had a pumpkinlike face with crescent eyes and a thin, curved smile. But her expression was stern as she sat fanning herself with a folded copy of the *Waterloo Courier* and imperiously presided over the street activities of her children and others, making sure they did not slam baseballs through glass windows or engage in brawls. Still, her eyes mirrored a glint of pride when her sons, who usually did not look for a fight, turned like tigers on anyone who dared attack or insult one of them.

They became well-nigh invincible after their father bought them boxing gloves and they trained among themselves. In fact, George would earn the nickname "John L.," after the heavyweight boxing champion, and Frank would one day be the champion welterweight boxer of the USS *Hovey*, the destroyer on which the two brothers would serve. The boys threw their hardest punches when protecting the good name of sister Genevieve, whom they treated as a kind of revered mascot. More than once, Alleta ponderously rose from her squeaky throne and waddled to the cinder-paved street to intervene personally in a battle royal, especially if danger loomed for her brood. Other mothers on the block resented her. Always blaming their kids for starting a fight!

Meanwhile, after a night of railroading, Tom usually spent most of the day sleeping. He found his job as freight conductor tolerable and he loved his family, but he nonetheless felt cheated by fate. Why was he riding a train instead of a horse, working in moonlight instead of in sunlight—though moonlight, of course, was better than the gaslight of the mine. Whatever the cause of his underlying discontent, Tom found relief in drink. On awakening, he would often tiptoe to the garage to indulge a snort of whiskey or wine he had produced himself, unknown to his wife, who banned the "evil liquid" from the house.

Tom sometimes filled a thermos with the alcohol and took it to work. If he became intoxicated on the train, the understanding engineer would stop it before it reached the station so Tom could jump off without his not-so-understanding boss seeing him stagger into the morning.

Alleta, who ruled the family roost—except when her mother squealed out orders in her shrill, toothless voice—was incensed when she suspected her husband had been drinking. And she could usually tell not simply by his breath, but by the quality of his voice. Normally, Tom was silent. While others talked, he chewed tobacco and simply listened, his long Irish face with close-set, merry eyes and thin, easily smiling lips reflecting interest but little inclination to contribute even the most fleeting sound. When he did speak, he mumbled. Only when he drank did the words flow in a voice that was reasonably audible. This giveaway would trigger a verbal tempest that would last until Tom—immaculately dressed in a suit and vest becoming a man in his prestigious position—put on his hat, grabbed his lunch pail, and sheepishly shrank away to the railroad.

Despite these occasional domestic storms, life at 98 Adams Street was generally serene. This was perhaps surprising, since the parents were not strict disciplinarians and pretty much gave the children a free hand—as long as they didn't use it to pound a neighboring boy into mincemeat. Tom, of course, was seldom awake during the day or around at night, though occasionally his Irish temper would flare when the boisterous antics of the boys disturbed his sleep. "Keep those sons of bitches quiet!" he would yell to Alleta through the window, forgetting for a moment that they were *his* sons.

On the other hand, Alleta, fairly anchored to the rocking chair by her obesity, had neither the strength nor the mobility to chase after them, aside from her occasional forays into the street. It was simply easier to leave them alone, though she tried to confine them to the backyard or the street in front of the house to keep them out of trouble. Anyway, George and Frank, the two elder boys, could usually be trusted to keep their brothers in line. Underscoring the family hierarchical psychology, the boys generally traveled in a pack, with the younger ones dragging a few yards behind the elder ones. As for Grandma May, she was a hopeless libertarian who constantly spoiled the children, and not a jar of sweets in the kitchen was off-limits to them.

Fortunately, the brothers needed little discipline, though they got into their share of mischief. Tom was furious when he discovered one day that his sons, who in their teens developed a taste for alcohol, had drunk all his wine in the garage. But what could he do—raise hell and let his wife know that he had hidden it for himself? The youngsters also occasionally stole watermelons out of railroad cars, and on Halloween they might push over an outhouse or break streetlights. After school they would often gather in a friend's garage and smoke until they got sick.

Still, the Sullivan sons, though high-spirited, were probably as well-behaved as any youngsters in Waterloo and spent much of their time basking in a wholesome outdoor life that would have appealed to Huckleberry Finn. They rode wild ponies bareback in the pastures and went hunting for squirrels, rabbits, and pheasants (sometimes out of season) in the hills. Cedar River, though, was their favorite haunt. They bagged ducks and geese on the slow-flowing water and went fishing for bluegills, catfish, bullheads, and carp while lying on the crusty bank, perhaps picnicking and singing, as they loved to do, Irish ballads such as "Danny Boy" or "When Irish Eyes Are Smiling." They went swimming there, too, and rafting or boating when the water was high enough, though they became somewhat wary of this sport after one terrifying incident.

The four older brothers patched up an old rowboat with dried mud and launched it, but the mud soon washed away and the boat began to sink. The boys, with three-year-old Albert in tow, were thrust into the water and carried downstream as they frantically tried to keep the baby's head above the surface. When it looked as if they would all drown, the current, by some miracle, delivered them to shore just in time. This incident helped convince them that only by staying together would they all be saved in any future disaster. It also gave the older ones a greater sense of God's presence and helped to induce them to attend Sunday mass more regularly, even though their parents, while devout Catholics and rock-solid members of St. Mary's parish, did not strongly press them to do so.

Alleta was too immobilized to go to church herself and often had the priest come to her instead. And Tom, as he got older, only attended sporadically, for after returning from the railroad on Saturday night, he needed sleep more than prayer. But his sons usually showed up, if sometimes with a hangover. God, they felt, would probably pull them out of the river next time whether they went to church or not, but why take the chance? The church was a kind of insurance policy.

Tom and Alleta also did not insist that their sons finish high school, though hoping they would. After all, with the Depression, many students were dropping out to seek work. Tom clung to his job of freight conductor, dealing with bills of lading and other documents, and was able to support his family with his salary of about eight dollars a day. But the bad times had nevertheless hit the Sullivan household. There was less food on the table, while Tom no longer could afford to dress elegantly so that people would know he was of some importance. He thus went to work now in shabby old shirts and trousers. Let everyone know that for all the prestige of his job, he was a simple railroad man with hands callused by hard work from days past, hands that the clothes of a dandy could never really hide.

And so there was little objection when the boys said they would look for work. They had never relished school anyway—especially St. Mary's, where they constantly sought distractions from the nuns' religious teachings. One time, Frank was soundly slapped by the presiding sister after he chased another pupil around the classroom and knocked over a statue of the Virgin Mary. Soon, by mutual agreement, the boys left St. Mary's to attend a public school, but stayed only for two years. Genevieve was the sole Sullivan to graduate.

Since it was traditional for at least one son of a railroadman to follow in his father's profession, George, in 1932, got a job on the railroad, still clinging to the dream that he would one day be an engineer with the privilege of blowing the whistle. George was perhaps the most moody of the brothers. In photos, he was often the only unsmiling one, and his eyes, set in a square, rugged face, had a kind of brooding look, which his large, clenched jaw accentuated—a look perhaps reflecting the heavy burden of caring for his younger siblings.

Like his father, George did not talk much—until he imbibed a beer or two. He would then loosen up, and his sense of humor would bubble forth, as if from the bottle itself. A few more drinks and he would almost be transformed into the life of the party. And he sometimes was, especially at the dances he loved to attend with his family and Bill Ball. Surely if his partner happened to be Ruth Leet, who, with the beer, brought out the "devil" in him. The couple also roller-skated together, held hands at the Saturday matinee movie, and occasionally raided watermelon-loaded boxcars, feeling the momentary thrill of a Bonnie-and-Clyde relationship.

Though the brothers were not usually jealous of one another, Ruth remembers that George and Red got into a hassle because George felt his younger brother was trying to steal his girl. "George was my first date," Ruth reminisces. "We loved each other and he would do anything for me. He was so warm and tender."

But when George began working on the railroad, he had little time to show tenderness to any of his several girlfriends. He started by shoveling coal, then worked the signal switches. He didn't mind the job, but he did the hours. He was on call day and night and could be fired if he missed a few calls. Normally, "call boys" bicycled to the worker's home, or more often to the saloons, to inform the unlucky victim that he must rush to the station. But since the Sullivans had a telephone, George sat night after night waiting for a call to duty—while his brothers and friends were drinking, dancing, raising hell. When his yearnings grew irresistible, however, he would sometimes leave the phone to pursue his fancies.

With his first paycheck as a signalman, he bought a case of liquor—each one-fifth of whiskey cost a whopping one dollar and fifty cents—and threw a party at his uncle's farm that, even today, his friends describe with joyous nostalgia. George walked in with a tall, willowy teenager, Irene, who, after consuming her first drinks ever, threw off her clothes and danced around stark naked in the swirling haze of a wild, unforgettable night that ended with George and the others tossing the screaming young woman into a water tank.

George's boss was among those who apparently couldn't forget. The trains may not have stopped running that night because George Sullivan, the signalman, was beyond the reach of even the most relentlessly pursuing "call boy," but he soon found himself out of a job.

This put Frank, who had also been working for the railroad, in an awkward position. Since he was shy and reserved, even when drinking, and cared more about boxing and baseball than girls, he didn't feel the job impinged that much on his social life and was glad to have it. It was perhaps his less flamboyant tastes and willingness to follow the rules that had given him the stamina and perseverance to become a boxing champion. Even his infrequent, rather toothy smile, which lit up a long, narrow face compressed between large ears, seemed to suggest he would rather be taking a punch than a picture. And he was serious about his job as he was about everything he did. But if the younger boys looked up to Frank, in part because of his resoluteness, Frank looked up to George. And when George left the railroad, apparently fired, his brother proved his loyalty by leaving it, too.

As the Depression deepened, reaching a nadir in 1936, when Iowans suffered from a severe drought in the summer and a record cold in the winter, a job in Waterloo became almost as rare as rain. So, in 1937, George and Frank, hungry for adventure anyway, joined the Navy.

Times gradually improved, however, and the other three brothers, Red, Matt, and Al, as well as Genevieve, managed to land jobs at Rath's, joining about 5,600 other workers there. Rath was the largest independent meatpacking house in the United States and the main industry in Waterloo before John Deere Tractors expanded. And the pay started at sixty-five cents an hour—more than the railroad offered.

Even so, Red, in particular, was unhappy. He hated the dull routine: chop up the frozen meat; thaw it out; run it through a grinder; dump it in a mixer; cool it; cure it; stuff it into a celluloid casing; tie it up; hang it in the smokehouse; cool it again; dry it; hang it on rails—all this work so some slob could gnaw on a lousy sausage! Red couldn't wait until the bell rang and he could punch the clock and, in his fantasy, the foreman who goaded him to work faster.

Actually, speed was Red's specialty. He had saved up enough money to buy a motorcycle with an earlier part-time job carrying ice to the boxcars, and no one in town could beat him in the cross-country race and the motorcycle hill climb. The climb, especially, was dangerous, and his parents urged him to conquer his competitive urge. But Red wouldn't hear of it. His daring had made him one of the most popular figures in Waterloo— except with the police. Just to defy them, on Sunday mornings before church he would thunderously barrel through the city streets, waking the whole neighborhood and stirring the killer instincts of the cops. They could never catch him. Wherever Red parked his motorcycle, people would gather around to admire their hero and his magic vehicle. It was not surprising, therefore, that he asked himself: Should a hero be lugging meat around all day?

It was Red himself and not only his motorcycle exploits that appealed to people. The best-looking of the five brothers, he had wavy red hair, a warm, slightly tilted smile, and blue, whimsical eyes. He had an engaging personality and a sensitivity that charmed the ladies, though sometimes it led him to the brink of battle with anyone who might malign him, his family, or his motorcycle. In the telling words of a friend, he "wouldn't take shit from nobody."

If Red often left women swooning in his wake, he was looking for a special kind of girl he could cherish as much as he did his motorcycle, one he would recognize at first glance. Meanwhile, his motorcycle remained the prime object of his affection. He was, in any case, happy just to form new friendships with both men and women, and he needed friends more than his brothers did. The two eldest, George and Frank, were especially close, as were the two youngest, Matt and Al, and each of these twosomes had friends their own age. But Red was the lonely one in the middle—a little too young for one group, a little too old for the other. So he found it hard to leave, even temporarily, the world his motorcycle had opened up and enter one that smelled of salted beef and sausage and gave frustrated bacon bureaucrats power over men of spirit like him.

Matt, too, was tired of the meatpacking world, but apparently not for the same reasons. Understandably, since the two brothers had contrasting personalities. Matt resembled George in many ways and even looked like him. He was reserved, sometimes withdrawn. Still, his eyes usually reflected good cheer, seldom the melancholy often mirrored in George's eyes. Women found him "gentle" and "sweet," and many were captivated by his smile.

But Matt didn't often smile at work. He had no image to preserve as the gregarious Red did, and he found his job easy. That was the trouble; it lacked challenge. Probably the most ambitious of the Sullivan brothers, Matt told friends that after saving some money, he hoped to finish high school and then look for a higher-paid administrative job. He didn't want to lug meat around the rest of his life any more than Red did.

Although younger than Red, Matt felt, as his older brother did, that he had enjoyed the single life long enough and was eager to settle down. But unlike Red, he was too shy to pursue the ladies aggressively. He perhaps envied his younger brother, Albert, who was engaged to be married.

Actually, all of Albert's brothers seemed a bit disturbed that the baby of the family, only seventeen, planned to marry first and would present their parents with their first grandchild. What's more, the girl was from the west side, where people were of a different breed—largely white-collar workers, who never used their hands except to write reports, and the business-men they worked for, who had nice homes and cars and viewed the poor workers on the east side with a certain contempt. Gangs from both sides frequently attacked each other, and school teams from both played each other with the ferocity of medieval gladiators fighting to the death.

Even so, the family liked Katherine Rooff, or Kena, Al's fian-cée. She was gentle, pretty, thoughtful. But she was still west side. Her father, though beginning life in Waterloo as a Bulgar-ian immigrant, had owned a popular beer garden before he died, and the uncle who raised her was a contractor in the construc-tion business. A cousin was in the plumbing business, a second one in hardware, and a third in real estate. People who may have started poor, but who now had money, prestige, and power. And Katherine had finished high school, while Al had completed only two years.

It was a mistake marrying into a family that might look down on his own. Westsiders! . . . And besides, Al was so young. Why couldn't he wait—like his brothers?

But Al wouldn't listen. He seldom did—yet usually got his way. Though the youngest brother, Al, in a sense, led the pack, shrewdly using his comparative youth to demand attention, knowing when to whine, when to pout. The family could sel-dom resist his entreaties.

Al, who was shorter and thinner than his brothers, was perhaps the most affable of the brood. Like Matt, he smiled often, though he was far more outgoing, and looked somewhat like a young Irish Frank Sinatra, with a bony face and flashing eyes. He was usually satisfied with whatever fate had in store for him, and even liked his job at Rath's, humming Irish tunes as he ground rounds of beef or hauled racks of lamb. In fact, according to his foreman, Al was "tickled to death" with his job.

Especially after he met Katherine, who, seeking an independent life, worked in the sliced-bacon department. Six months later, in May 1940, they were married. The wedding took place in St. Mary's Church in a ceremony that brought the east and west sides together in a rare display of civic unity. At the reception that followed, raucous railroaders, potbellied politicians, brazen businessmen, and muscular meat carriers sat side by side popping dumplings and beef patties into their mouths and sipping homemade wine and prized whiskey drawn in part from the precious stocks that Tom Sullivan had hidden in his garage. The best man was Katherine's cousin, Leo Rooff, who would one day become mayor of Waterloo and the symbol of a city struggling for harmony. Less than a year later, a son, James, screamed his way into the world, the product of a municipal as well as a marital union.

Shortly, George and Frank returned home after their four-year stint in the Navy and joined their three siblings as employees of Rath. Now there were two more disgruntled brothers. After four years at sea, imbibing the excitement of new places, drinking in exotic bars, learning how to use new weapons, it wasn't easy exchanging a cannon for a meat cleaver. But with the cataclysm at Pearl Harbor, the time had come to put down the cleaver and return to the cannon.

"That means Frank and I are going back," George said when the news of war echoed through the static in the Sullivan living room.

Frank agreed. "Yes, and the sooner the better."

Red and Matt then said they would go, too.

Albert suddenly rushed in. "Have you heard the news?" he cried. "I wonder if Bill was in it."

With trepidation, they pondered the worst. Surely the *Arizona* must have been hit. But they braced themselves with brave words. Bill Ball could take care of those "Japs."

When Al learned of his brothers' plan to join the Navy, he said he would enlist, too. But he had a family, the others pointed out. He couldn't just leave Katherine and the baby.

"Don't worry," Al replied. "She'll understand." She would want him to do his part.

His brothers surrendered.

"Well, I guess our minds are made up, aren't they, fellows?" George said. "And when we go in, we want to go in together. And if worse comes to worst, we'll all go down together."

When the boys saw their mother come in from the kitchen in tears and knew she had overheard them, one of them reassured her, "Don't worry, Mom, we'll be back."

Alleta didn't try to persuade them to wait. She knew her sons; they would not change their minds.

"The boys were fatalists about it," she would later say. "They felt that when your number was up, there was nothing you could do about it but die fighting. They would take their chances together."

She consoled herself with the thought that George and Frank were, after all, seasoned sailors. They would know how to protect the younger ones. Anyway, they would have to serve their country sooner or later. So Alleta dried her eyes and stoically accepted their decision. And Tom, waiting as usual for a cue from his wife, remained as silent as ever.

But the Navy was not so pliant. It had a policy of splitting families in wartime so that if a ship was hit, no more than one family member could be counted among the casualties. The Sullivans, however, were resolute. They marched into the Navy recruiting center and made their request to an officer. Would he promise to let them stay together? they asked. Otherwise they would not enlist voluntarily.

The officer was astounded. Never before in the history of the Navy had five brothers served on the same warship. He was sorry, but he couldn't make any promises. Their request was contrary to Navy policy.

The brothers rushed home and whisked off a letter of protest to the Navy Department in Washington, and shortly they received a reply. After careful consideration, the letter said, the Navy agreed to waive its rule on family enlistments and let the four unmarried boys stay together. But, according to Navy rules, Al was exempt from military service because he was a family man and would not be accepted.

Al was livid. He would not be left behind, he cried, and Katherine remained silent. She needed her husband and the baby needed his father, but, understanding the relationship of the five brothers, she felt she could not oppose his enlistment. If the Navy, however, refused to take him . . .

After much angry letter-writing and table-pounding, the Navy decided to break yet another rule. It did need men desperately— and five brothers aboard the same ship would make bigger headlines than four. Could it ask for a better recruiting angle? The Sullivans could all fight together. And presumably die together, too.

The Sullivan boys were elated, experiencing the sensation they felt as kids when, to save the family honor, they clobbered any neighborhood gang that dared to insult one of them. And this time Mama wouldn't be shouting commands from her rocking chair to stop the fight before someone got hurt. Elation, however, soon melted into grief when news came that Bill Ball had been killed aboard the *Arizona*, and his brother wounded, during the Pearl Harbor attack. The Sullivans boiled with a new motivation. They would be fighting not simply for their country, but for Bill; they would wreak vengeance on his killers.

The family spent the Christmas holidays together, exchanging gifts and leafing through an album filled with snapshots of George and Frank as sailors, posing on their ship and in remote corners of the globe. Days of fun and romance that for a few hours made the brothers forget their grim vow and dream of their coming adventure as if they were planning a pleasure cruise.

But reality soon burst the bubble of fantasy. And on January 2, 1942, the day before the boys were to depart for boot camp, they visited St. Mary's Church together with Katherine to witness the baptism of Al's baby. Al wanted Jimmy baptized before he left—just in case he wouldn't be back for the event.

The next morning, before embarking on their journey, the brothers attended mass and received a blessing from their priest, Father Clarence Piontkowski, whom they had liked ever since they were students at St. Mary's School, though they thought less of the nuns he picked to teach them. Crabby old women who slapped them with rulers for alleged misbehavior and lack of interest in Bible study. Yet now the brothers wished they had a more intimate knowledge of the Book. It would be easier to die if they had to.

The next day, the Sullivans and other Waterloo youths exulted in a tumultuous send-off at the railroad station, where relatives, friends, and others who had touched their lives gathered to wish them well—schoolteachers, priests, neighbors, politicians, fellow workers, and members of Red's motorcycle club, who shouted, "Good luck, Nine Lives," a nickname Red had earned because he had so frequently emerged intact after motorcycle accidents. No one could kill Red!

As the train was about to pull out, Matt embraced his mother, who was trying to suppress tears, and said, "Don't worry, Mom. How could anything happen to us if we stick together and protect each other?"

And amid a forest of waving arms, the train groaned out of the station, gathered speed, and hurtled toward the unknown, its whistle blowing furiously, reminding the Sullivans of a childhood aglow with this call to adventure, glory, and a utopian destiny.

Shortly the Sullivans were simulating battle at the Great Lakes Training Center, then, in early February 1942, marking time at the Brooklyn Navy Yard, where they were assigned, on their request, to a new light cruiser that had just been commissioned there—the USS *Juneau*. In the receiving station at Pier 92, George began talking with a fellow volunteer over coffee in the canteen.

"Did you ask to be on this ship?" the man asked.

"Sure did," George replied. "We heard it's the fastest fighting ship there is."

"We asked also," the stranger said. "We even wrote the President."

"We?"

"Yeah, the four of us—the Rogers brothers. I'm Joey. We want to fight, but we also want to live through this war. So why not get on the best damn ship in the Navy?"

CHAPTER

· 3 ·

The Four Rogers Brothers

IT WAS NOT SURPRISING THAT JOSEPH ROGERS AND HIS THREE younger brothers, Patrick, Louis, and James, wanted to fight. They had been fighting all their lives. Joey was, in fact, a professional boxer, and the others, semipros, all of them potential champions. Nor was their battle simply against other boxers. They had been fighting adversity, and themselves, since childhood. For they were the children of a mobster, whom they loved dearly even as they sought to hide his shady triumphs behind conquests of their own.

The boys' father was Thomas Rogers, a second-generation Italian American who, while growing up on the streets of New York in the early 1920s, earned a living as an enforcer for the notorious bootlegger, Ownie Madden. In this era of Prohibition, either speakeasies would buy beer and whiskey from Madden, or the burly Rogers, once an amateur boxer himself, would lay waste the establishment.

Rogers lived a good life, until one day federal agents chased him into the subway, where he climbed on the roof of a moving train, fell off, and lost part of his foot under the wheels. A watchman took him to the hospital, and the agents never found him. But he began to wonder if gangland life offered him much of a future. And his doubts grew when he married a young, deeply religious Irish girl, Winifred, who, ironically, believed he worked for the subway. When she finally suspected the truth, she pleaded with her husband to leave the gang and New York. He knew such a move could invite death, but he agreed.

And so, at three A.M. one morning, the couple, with their children and only a suitcase of clothes, fled to Darien, Connecticut, where they moved into a five-room house. Rogers then changed his profession from mob enforcer to paperhanger and housepainter.

But Winifred soon died of tuberculosis during her sixth pregnancy, and her husband, overcome with grief, blamed himself for making her suffer. He blamed God, too, and refused to set foot in church ever again. And as if in deliberate defiance of God, he returned to his old ways—but not to his old gang, which was avidly searching for him. Why plaster walls when he could peddle booze? Besides, didn't he have a large family to support?

Rogers shortly remarried and bought four acres of land in nearby Ridgefield, moved there, and built a gas station and a refreshment stand—as a cover for a bootlegging business. In his house, he constructed a secret room that could be entered only by standing on the toilet and crawling through a medicine cabinet. Here, he turned out whiskey by the gallon, with the help of his eldest son, Joey, who knew nothing about his father's past.

Then, one day when he was twelve, Joey found out. A large car pulled up, and four men stepped out. "Where's Tommy?" they asked.

"Back there somewhere," Joey replied, pointing to the garden.

About twenty minutes later, he saw his father, pale and frightened, being led back by the strangers. Apparently Tommy Rogers had made a deal with Ownie Madden's men, promising them a cut of his bootlegging profits. When the men had driven off, Joey asked his father:

"Jesus, Pop, who are those guys?"

"I might as well tell you," the father replied, and he spilled out the details of his sordid past to the astonished boy.

Joey was tormented by a moral ambivalence. He revered his

father, who, in his eyes, could do no wrong. Yet Pop had been a mobster, and if the youth could forgive a little bootlegging, a rather "technical" violation of the law, he could hardly overlook his father's violent role of enforcer. And when his three younger brothers learned the truth, they, too, suffered. But however painful the sons' dilemma, it was unthinkable that they disobey Pop, even if they had to help him dodge the law. It was about this time that Joey, like his father, lost faith in God and turned atheist. How could he love both God and Pop?

Eventually the police raided the house and found the liquor, but a good lawyer got Rogers off with a stiff fine. With the end of Prohibition, he opened a nightclub, but had to close it when he lost his liquor license for selling whiskey after hours. He then bought a farm and when it, too, began to fail, simply set fire to the farmhouse and collected the insurance money. The family then moved to Bridgeport, where, in the late 1930s, Rogers prospered in real estate.

Meanwhile, he turned his attention to his children—four boys and a girl from his first wife, and five from his second, Arlene. He was especially devoted to his four elder sons, since he felt a special obligation to their mother, and was ready to meet their every need. But one thing they didn't need, he felt, was education beyond grammar school. What they needed was money, not math. When they started to make money, they would soon learn how to count. And this logic hardened in his mind when he stumbled on an opportunity that could eventually make them rich.

The opportunity was born, actually, when Joey was twelve, out of Rogers's concern for the boy's frail health. To help him build up his body, the father added a gymnasium to his gas station and bought him boxing gloves. Soon Joey, as he gained strength, became a talented boxer, and would have his first amateur bout when he was sixteen. His brothers, who sparred with him, showed great promise as well. Having excelled in amateur fights, they all entered semipro tournaments and continued to win—Joey and Louie as welterweights, Jimmy as a lightweight, and Pat as a bantamweight. After eighty matches, Joey would turn professional.

The father was convinced that his sons could be champions

someday, but they had to devote every minute to boxing. And they did, sometimes fighting three times a week, earning seven dollars a fight for winning, six dollars for drawing, and five dollars for losing. They trained so intensively that once Joey knocked Jimmy out to prove that he was wide open.

Joey, in fact, seemed headed for the top after having scored 130 knockouts in 154 fights, and winning almost all the rest by decision. But then, one night in 1941, as he sat in his dressing room winding tape around his hands in preparation for his possible eighteenth straight victory, the boxing promoter approached him and wasted no words.

"Joey, listen to me," he rasped. "You're gonna take a dive in the third round!"

In shock, Joey gasped, "What do ya mean, take a dive? And if I don't?"

"Then both your legs will be broken and you'll never fight again."

Joey rushed to his father at ringside and asked him for advice. The elder Rogers, turning pale, knew only too well what an enforcer was capable of doing.

"You have no choice, Joey," he said. "Dive!"

Joey was devastated. His father had nurtured his career from the start, step by step. Now the old man was asking him to take a dive, to ruin his career, to commit a crime. The terrible ambivalence of his relationship with his father now struck home with brutal force. Yes, he had a choice. He could go to the police. And yet, he knew his father was right. The promoter could see to it that his legs were broken. And even if he didn't, the man was powerful enough to have him blackballed from the fight game.

With tears in his eyes, Joey climbed into the ring to the roar of the crowd and was "knocked out" in the third round.

Filled with shame and anger at himself and the world, Joey felt humiliated, corrupted—and he didn't even have a God to turn to. Thus, he was almost relieved when, on the morning of December 7, 1941, he heard the news blaring over his car radio that Pearl Harbor had been bombed and the United States was at war. With his crushing defeat in the ring, he might find it hard getting another fight, but here was a fight he didn't have to beg for. Perhaps by defending his country he might even be able to cleanse himself, in some measure, of the moral grime that soiled his soul. After the war, Joey vowed, he would make a comeback and punch his way to the world championship—though, in fact, he suspected his dream had died with that knockout blow.

Joey and Pat had already served in the Army one year and were now in the State Guard, since they expected a war to break out and wanted to be ready for it. But with Pearl Harbor, Joey decided to join the Navy because it seemed the quickest way to strike at the Japanese. He ran into the house, crying, "We're at war with Japan. I'm going to join the Navy!"

His father, who wanted his sons to fight, but only in the ring, banged his fist on a table and shouted, "You're in the State Guard. It's a good racket. You stay home and fight here!"

Though Joey was a rather gentle person outside the ring, he looked tough, with his broken nose and cold stare, which always appeared to be sizing one up for an uppercut. But now, with his eyes lowered and his head drooping, this twenty-four-year-old pugilist seemed like a little boy who had been denied a coveted toy for his birthday. How could he defy Pop?

But then Pat came to his aid. The best looking of the brothers, with dreamy brown eyes and a warm smile, Pat was mild-mannered and caring, hardly the prototype image of an aggressive prize-fighter. As the second eldest, at twenty-one, he followed Joey's advice almost religiously, even if it conflicted with his own instincts. He was engaged to a young girl, Rosalie, but she didn't object when he joined the Army, so he wasn't worried about her. Now, he said, knowing his father would explode:

"Joey, if you join the Navy, so will I."

Tommy exploded—but Pat wouldn't back down. Though he had never disobeyed his father before, somehow it was harder now to displease Joey than Pop.

But the two younger brothers, Jimmy and Louie, were silent. Jimmy, the youngest at seventeen, had a thin face and a slight physique that belied his pugilistic talent. But his taut expression mirrored an iron will that would compensate for his unimpressive build. His father was, in large measure, responsible for giving him grit. In one unforgettable bout, after he was knocked down twice, his manager, seeing that he was badly hurt, motioned for him to stay down. But Pop, who was at ringside, did not agree.

"Jimmy," he urged, "go get 'im! You can do it!"

Jimmy dizzily rose and tore across the ring. With a single punch, he knocked his foe cold. Yes, he could do it.

Could he now disobey Pop? Anyway, he had just started working at General Electric and was making good money. And he, too, had a girlfriend, Marion, whom he planned to wed, though he so hungered for a champion's crown that he felt he should delay marriage until he won it. Now, he was reluctant to let even a world war stand in his way, and Joey knew it. But bolstered by Pat's brave stand, Joey snapped:

"Well, Jimmy?"

The question was like an order.

"Count me in," Jimmy replied.

"No, you're too young," his father hollered. "You're only seventeen. You don't have to join nothin'."

But the father knew that his sons had for once overruled him.

Only twenty-year-old Louie held out. He had an excellent sixty-five-dollar-a-week job at the Bridgeport Brass Company. And he was engaged to a girl, Irene, whom he wanted to marry immediately. Louie, though also slender, had the face of a fighter. His piercing eyes and slightly parted lips suggested a cat poised to pounce on a bird. But he was insecure. He might never get back his job—or his girl.

After the other three had signed up with the Navy, Louie came to them. Irene would wait for him, he said, smiling. And so he made it a foursome.

The father decided he might as well capitalize on his defeat. A little publicity wouldn't hurt. Might even help their boxing careers after the war. He visited the local newspapers, and headlines blared the next day that the "Four fighting Rogers are joining the Navy for the fight of their careers."

When the brothers read that the new cruiser *Juneau*, one of the fastest ships in the Navy, was preparing for combat, they knew it was for them—as long as they would not be separated. Joey, who could read but not write, asked his father to write

President Roosevelt requesting permission for his sons to serve on the *Juneau* together.

"Gee, Joey," the father replied, "I don't know if what you're asking is possible, but I'll try."

He soon received a reply: the President would do his best to meet the request. And he met it. How could the rule be waived for the Sullivans and not for the Rogerses?

And so, in early February 1942, the four boys, amid great local fanfare, boarded the train for boot camp in Rhode Island. As soon as the train had pulled out, their father met with the press. He was sending his sons into the Navy, he said, because he thought it was his patriotic duty.

Three weeks later, the brothers were back for a short leave before heading for Brooklyn and the *Juneau*. Their father greeted them with four engagement rings.

"Boys," he said, "give these rings to your girls before you leave."

Only Joey balked, though Jimmy was still not sure if he would marry before he became champ. "I only know Nancy four or five months, Pop," Joey said. "I'm not sure how I feel about her."

"Never mind, give it to her," said the father. "It'll make her feel good."

The brothers were to go out that night with their girls, so Joey, not wishing to spoil this farewell spree for Nancy and the others, reluctantly agreed; he took the ring. And that night, the four couples danced and drank till dawn, each girl flashing a sparkling diamond on her finger, each brother trying his boisterous best to forget that this good-bye could be forever.

Later, on the train going home, while his brothers still reveled tipsily in their commitments, Joey was solemn. A feeling of guilt intensified his war anxieties. He had been weighed down with shame for his dive in the boxing ring, and now he felt burdened by a diamond ring he had placed on the finger of a girl he did not really love.

"Pat," he said to the brother he felt was most understanding, "I'm going to tell Nancy I don't want to be engaged."

"Don't do that," Pat urged. "She'll die!"

"I don't love her," replied Joey. "Anyway, I might not even come back. It'll be a long war, and I don't want anyone waiting for me."

Joey would tell Nancy on his next leave. It would be easier fighting, knowing he was honest with her. But no use telling Pop. He wouldn't understand.

In a few days, the family was at the train station again, once more the heroes of the moment.

"Joey," said his father before his sons boarded the train, "you're the oldest. Look after the boys, especially Jimmy. I'm counting on you."

"I promise, Pop," Joey replied.

Then, as the two embraced, the father slipped his son a piece of paper. "Here's a code," he whispered. "Each name on the list represents a different place. Mention the appropriate name in your letters and I'll know where you are. Don't let anyone see this or they'll throw me into Alcatraz."

And soon, the four Rogers boys were happily ensconced aboard the USS *Juneau*. They would shortly be at war, but somehow, at this moment of departure, they weren't afraid. Perhaps the boxing ring had hardened them to danger, even mortal danger. Or maybe, as Joey would suggest, it was "because we expected to die."

CHAPTER

· 4 ·

The Captain and His Sons

ABOUT SEVEN HUNDRED MEN LINED UP AT ATTENTION ON THE MAIN deck of the *Juneau* as Captain Swenson boarded the ship. Most of them, having just joined the crew, had never seen Swenson before and nervously saluted as he slowly walked by, stopping here and there to chat with someone.

"Never mind saluting," he would say, smiling. "Where're you from, sailor?"

The men were soon at ease. This was no scowling, cold-eyed skipper who didn't really care where they came from or what kind of people they were as long as they obeyed orders. This captain clearly cared. He treated the sailors as if they were his newly found sons. He even gave orders with a paternalistic touch, gently yet with a voice that carried the quiet authority of a whip. Choosing four orderlies at random, he took one aside and asked him to do an errand for him. "And take the day off," he added, to the new orderly's delight. With such a skipper, the men felt lucky indeed to be on the *Juneau*.

Besides, a more beautiful ship had never sailed the seas. The *Juneau*, a light antiaircraft cruiser, was brand-new, having been launched on October 25, 1941, less than a year and a half after its keel was laid. Weighing six thousand tons, the ship was made for quick sailing and maneuvering and not for heavy bombardment. Its decks were dotted with sixteen 5-inch .38-caliber guns, four quadruple 1.1-inch gun mounts, and eight 21-inch surface torpedo tubes. But the steel armor encasing the vessel was only three and three-quarter inches thick, not very heavy and hardly an effective shield against torpedoes.

The *Juneau*'s thin skin, however, didn't worry the men. After all, their supership had many fast-firing guns and a new type of radar. And it was designed for a phenomenal speed of thirty-two knots, fast enough to lose any enemy submarine. Of course, it was mainly meant to protect aircraft carriers from bombers swooping down on them, but that was fine with the men. It would be more fun shooting down enemy planes than blasting away at other ships.

On March 22, 1942, while Captain Swenson gazed at the sea from the bridge, his face an ambivalent blend of pride and concern, the *Juneau* weighed anchor and headed out for its first shakedown cruise. Swenson perhaps reflected on the words he had written to friends only several months earlier:

"When I say my prayers at night, I ask for a new six-thousand-ton-cruiser. They are very scarce and I have been kept a long way from the place where such prayers are heard, so my faith is very weak."

But now he commanded a six-thousand-ton cruiser and his prayers were for those aboard, who could not know that this was a ship of death. And adding to his apprehension was his limited experience in operating this kind of vessel. He had been given command just shortly before the *Juneau* was commissioned and had almost no prototype data to study since his ship was only the second of a new class of cruisers. He often had to rely for instructions on the captain of the USS *Atlanta*, the first of the class.

Swenson had been so busy learning the details of operation that his men had to find out about their combat assignments, the ship's condition of readiness, and other vital matters more often through his commanders and orderlies than through the battle bill. He even neglected to remove the commander's insignia from one of his coats and replace it with a captain's.

Yet, Swenson ran a disciplined—and happy—ship. His men

didn't need the captain standing over them with a whip to obey him. They did so because they wanted to please him. The crew was in good spirits despite having to sleep on the floor of the mess hall because bunks hadn't yet been installed. The glory of going out to sea on this magnificent ship for the first time under the command of a captain who symbolized their good fortune rendered all discomforts trivial, even unworthy of the traditional gripe.

In the next few days, the men carried out training operations in Chesapeake Bay, then patrolled the Martinique-Guadeloupe area to prevent the escape of Vichy French men-of-war moored at Fort-de-France and Pointe-à-Pitre. So far, being at sea for the *Juneau* crew seemed almost like going on a pleasure cruise, with occasional stops at exotic places such as St. Thomas in the U.S. Virgin Islands and San Juan, Puerto Rico, where the men filled the bars, dancing and drinking with tawny-skinned girls eager to do their share in lifting the morale of the Navy.

Somewhere milling in these crowded honky-tonks were the Sullivan brothers, but they apparently showed remarkable restraint in the face of such temptation. George displayed considerable skill in absorbing alcohol without ever letting revelry, or the girls, get out of hand. Frank was always subdued anyway. Al was too concerned about his wife and child to let himself go. And Red and Matt somehow felt a strange loyalty to a couple of young women they had, it seemed, met in their dreams.

In January, when the brothers first signed up for the Navy, photos of them were flashed to newspapers around the country. Soon, letters of congratulations and admiration poured in, including some with flirtatious overtones. Red particularly liked a letter from a seventeen-year-old girl who lived near Pittsburgh. Margaret Jaros, intrigued by Red's smile, had taken up a dare from her girlfriends to write him. Since she had two brothers in the service and often wrote to their buddies, why shouldn't she write to Red, even though he was famous? If he was single and didn't have a girlfriend, she thus wrote him, would he correspond with her? She felt a special bond with sailors.

To Margaret's astonishment, Red replied immediately. He had been moved by her frank, open, almost elegant manner of writing. Yes, he would like to correspond, he wrote. She then sent him a photo of herself, and this forged the friendship. For Margaret was a pretty brunette with large dark eyes and a shy smile—the kind of girl Red imagined he would one day meet and know instantly that she was meant for him.

Red wrote Margaret about the wonders of daily life in Waterloo, about his motorcycle exploits, about familial love and the brothers' wish to stay together, even unto death. He said his one aim now was to help get the war over with as soon as possible. Red poured out his heart to his pen pal, feeling that he had finally found a soul that could understand the music in his own. He was impatient to meet Margaret in person; in late May, the ship would be returning to Brooklyn for several days overhauling, and he would head straight for Pittsburgh.

About the same time that Red started corresponding with Margaret, Matt, too, was drawn to one particular letter. It was from another seventeen-year-old admirer, Beatrice Imperato, who had also seen a news photo of the Sullivans and was fascinated by Matt's "playful expression." He looked like a "fun person." In her letter, she wrote that he was "somebody I would be interested in." Would he write back?

Matt did, and again the photo of an attractive brunette won a Sullivan's heart. He, too, was determined to see his pen pal when he returned to the United States. And Beatrice, who at first wondered if a girl who was "hip New York" could find much in common with a boy from the cornfields of Iowa, soon realized from his letters that he was no "hick," but an intelligent and sensitive young man. She, like the others in the foursome, could hardly wait for the encounter she sensed could change her life.

For both Red and Matt, the wait was nerve-tingling. What if the girls in person proved a disappointment? How could they so easily withdraw from the relationships, which, though spun from afar, were nevertheless tightly woven, if with the fragile threads of romantic imagery that might serve simply to ease the loneliness of battle and death.

The two brothers needed someone to accompany them to their respective rendezvous, feeling that a third person would help depersonalize the meetings and make withdrawal, if necessary, easier. Both turned to a third brother, Frank. Not reputed as a ladies' man with a glib tongue, he wasn't likely to dilute their own appeal. He would serve as a kind of chaperon, helping to keep the conversation going and whisking them away if disillusion should render talk painful.

The *Juneau* pulled into Brooklyn harbor on May 21, and that same day Red phoned Margaret; within an hour he and Frank jumped on the train to Pittsburgh. There, in front of the Seventh Avenue Hotel, Red and Margaret met. They knew each other at first sight from their photos, which, it seemed to both, had suddenly come to life. They smiled and were silent, until Red, who somehow could not regain the sophisticated air he had developed with the ladies in his glorious motorcycle days, began to speak of the rather simple things he had written about—his family, his hometown, his hobbies.

The three continued chatting in a restaurant over hamburgers and malted milks, though Red did most of the talking. Margaret was shy, and Frank, a bit embarrassed to be there. Then they went to see a movie at the Stanley Theater and munched on popcorn, though Red and Margaret were barely aware of the picture that was playing. That evening, the couple went to a party thrown by a shipmate of the Sullivans who lived in Pittsburgh, and the next two days they talked incessantly about their lives, their dreams, their future.

"Probably by the time the war is over," Red said, "you'll be married."

"I think," Margaret answered, "it'll be a long time till I marry."

Then the moment came to part, and while driving to the train station, with his brother and his other shipmate locked in conversation, Red whispered to Margaret, "Will you wait for me?"

But too bashful—and shocked—to reply, she merely gazed straight ahead. When they arrived at the station and the boys were about to board the train, Red, with flushed uncertainty, drew her to him and kissed her—the most intimate moment of their meeting. Frank wondered why the hell he had ever come along.

Even so, Frank almost immediately embarked on his second

mission of romantic exploration—with Matt. This time the meeting took place at the Crossroads Cafe on the corner of Broadway and Times Square, the heart of "hip" New York. Beatrice was "overwhelmed" at the sight of her correspondent.

"I thought he was the handsomest man in the world," she would say.

Again malted milks were ordered and words were excitedly exchanged about Iowa, the Sullivan family, and other topics only too familiar to Frank, who gave signs of wanting to get up and rush to the nearest bar for a beer—or maybe a double whiskey.

Matt saw Beatrice several more times during the leave, and once he met her father, a tailor.

"Matt," the father said, fearful that a multitragedy was in the making, "take my advice and tell your brothers to separate."

Beatrice also urged Matt to do so. But he was adamant.

"No," he said, "this is the way we want it."

But she shouldn't worry, for all of them would be back. Nobody could hurt the Sullivans. And Matt gave Beatrice a silver and jade bracelet.

"I love you," he said. "Please wait for me."

She would.

With a mixed feeling of joy and sadness, Matt then said goodbye for the last time, and on June 1, he rejoined his brothers aboard the *Juneau*. It was the way they wanted it.

After sailing to Argentia, Newfoundland, on another training mission, this time with a six-ship task force, the *Juneau* dropped anchor in Boston Navy Yard on June 24 to be fitted out with the much awaited new radar system. Red and Matt were delighted with this stopover. They didn't need radar to tell them where they were headed. Red was especially happy to find a letter from Margaret waiting for him. He quickly tore it open to read her answer to a question he had asked the last time he wrote her: Would she accept a ring for her birthday? (He didn't dare call it an engagement ring.) Now, her enthusiastic yes seemed to light up the page.

Once ashore, Red rushed to a jewelry store to buy a ring, hoping to give it to Margaret personally. And he asked her on the phone to meet him in New York. She went—and waited in vain. Red did not show up. Margaret was in despair until, about two weeks later, a letter and a package arrived from him. The ship, Red explained, had received sealed orders sending it out to sea shortly after he had spoken to her, and he was no longer allowed to communicate with anyone ashore. But when he was given leave again, would she marry him? Until the war was over, she could live with his parents. And then he offered what was perhaps the ultimate proof of his love: if Margaret thought that his motorcycle activities were too dangerous, he would give them up—and, in fact, he would soon ask his father to sell the motorcycle, the symbol of so precious a period in his life.

In the package, Margaret found the "birthday" ring—a pearl set between two small diamonds. In joy, she wore it to work that day to show it to her friends. Everyone marveled at its beauty, but one young woman remarked that, nevertheless, "pearls bring tears."

Margaret's joy suddenly dissolved into fear, which she tried desperately to suppress. She didn't wear the ring to work again, but wrapped it in a Kleenex tissue and placed it in a cupboard. Then, one day, she looked for it and it was missing. She confronted her aunt, with whom she was staying:

"Did you see a ring in this cupboard? It was wrapped in a Kleenex tissue."

"I saw some Kleenex there," the aunt said, "but I was cleaning the cupboard and threw it out."

Margaret was crushed. Was this a sign? With a shudder, she recalled the words of her friend at work: "Pearls bring tears."

Meanwhile, a ring figured in the tears of another young woman. Joey Rogers, after having given his girlfriend, Nancy, a diamond ring, was determined to call off the engagement, as he had told his brother Pat. Just before the *Juneau* was to pull out of Boston, Joey, who had not felt so despondent since he took a dive in the ring, went to see his fiancée and, over drinks, painfully uttered the truth.

"Nancy, I don't want you waiting for me."

The girl burst into tears. "Take me home!" she sobbed.

When they arrived at the door, her mother, dismayed by her daughter's anguish, demanded, "What did you do to her?"

Joey tried to calm the maternal fury with assurances that he was only acting in Nancy's best interest, but without success. Yes, he asked himself, what had he done to her? Yet he felt a certain relief in his misery. There was something purifying about telling the truth, however bitter. And didn't he need a lot of purifying?

Joey was glad to get back to the ship. Now he could concentrate on fighting the greatest battle of his life—and making sure his brothers were not among its victims. He had promised Pop.

CHAPTER

· 5 ·

Messages from Heaven and Earth

WYATT BUTTERFIELD, A WIRY AMATEUR BOXER IN TRENTON, NEW Jersey, dreamed of being a hero. And he felt like one whenever he entered the ring. To Butterfield, boxing was pleasure, not just a workaday job, a profession or semiprofession as with the Rogers brothers. After flattening his opponent, he would stand there triumphant, arms in the air, wallowing in his victory. It was almost like a narcotic. He needed to hear the roar of the crowd—the cheers, the whistles, the shouts of approval. He pummeled enough foes to reach the welterweight final of the Golden Gloves before losing a close decision.

But when the war broke out, Butterfield packed his boxing gloves, quit his job at a rubber plant, dropped out of business night school, and rushed to the Navy recruiting office to enlist. Wyatt was sent to the *Juneau*. Now he could be a hero in the war as well as in the ring. He looked forward to joining the *Juneau* boxing team and sparring with fighters of the caliber of the Rogers brothers.

The presence of the Rogerses, and the Sullivans, aboard the

Juneau made Butterfield think of his own five brothers, but he was not sorry that they were on different ships—all except one, who had "treacherously" joined the Army. He loved his brothers, but each wanted to carve his own path in the world as their father had done, rising from a low-paying job as laborer during the Depression to a supervisory position with an oil company in just a few short years.

To prove himself in the war, Wyatt was determined to return home a hero, to be lionized by family and friends. And as a member of a gun club who loved "shootin'," he saw his chance. He would now simply aim at "Japs" instead of deer or pheasant. Just give him a gun and he'd win the war almost single-handedly. And the thought of riddling the enemy brought a smile to his thin lips and a glow to his piercing eyes. He could do it because he had the will. He still couldn't believe he had lost the decision in the Golden Gloves final.

Nurturing Butterfield's will was his self-discipline, which he considered a by-product of his mother's martinet treatment. When one of the children disobeyed his father, a rather easygoing man, he would give the child two warnings before spanking him. But Mother mercilessly wielded the strap, with no probation period, for virtually every act of misbehavior. Her rigidity strengthened not only his character, Butterfield would later feel, but his resolve to show the same merciless enthusiasm in punishing the Japs—though his strap would be a gun.

So when Butterfield joined the *Juneau* crew in February 1942, he asked to be a gunner's mate and was put in a gun mount as a trainer. He was exhilarated, especially since this time he would be killing not for fun but for a cause. He was now a member of the world's greatest gun club.

But if Butterfield thought he had the best job on the ship, he soon found himself with a second one that was even better. When Captain Swenson had gone around the ship meeting his men for the first time, he chose Butterfield as one of his four orderlies. And to Butterfield, serving Swenson was like serving his father—though the captain may have been a bit tougher on the boys when they misbehaved.

And they often did, for there wasn't much fun and games aboard ship. Aside from an occasional movie, boxing was about the only entertainment on the *Juneau* in those early days of the war. Even liberties were few. They were especially rare during several weeks at sea after the ship left Boston on July 1 and churned to Trinidad for exercises with aircraft, then to Recife, Brazil, on convoy duty. The men, however, did have a few hours to chase girls on the beach and stock up on bottles of Chanel No. 5 for the women back home before heading for a sweep of the central Atlantic to drop depth charges on suspected enemy submarines.

Nobody—but the captain—was too unhappy when, on August 12, one depth charge exploded prematurely and apparently cracked some seams in the *Juneau*'s fantail. This would mean a few days' liberty in Balboa in the Panama Canal Zone, where the ship would stop for repair—and everybody knew about the bars of Balboa.

That same day, the men on Japanese submarine *I-26*, having just returned to their base in Truk, southeast of Guam, after a long sojourn in the Pacific, were going on a spree of their own. And they didn't wait to hit the bars on this headquarters island. Officers and men guzzled down beer by the crateful right on the upper deck of their submarine while joyfully breathing in the fresh air they had inhaled little of during the many weeks at sea.

The men had good reason to celebrate. In those weeks they had sunk four merchant ships off the Australian coast—one at Sidney, and three at Melbourne—and had seriously disrupted communications between Australia and New Zealand. Congratulations from headquarters in Tokyo, Truk, and elsewhere were pouring in almost as fast as the beer was pouring down parched throats.

The crew had always considered their submarine a lucky craft, especially because of the number 6 in its designation, for this number traditionally brought good fortune. And so far in the war, their luck had held. But not only superstition gave them supreme confidence; so did their skipper, Minoru Yokota. Yokota, thirty-nine, was, in fact, viewed by his superiors as one of the best submarine commanders in the Japanese fleet. He had to be in order to achieve his status, for he did not fit into the mold of a typical Japanese officer.

For one thing, Yokota did not give the impression of someone who could successfully wield authority. If his men were, like most Japanese, short by Western standards, he was shorter than most of his men and of slighter build. And his placid, rather gentle countenance, embellished by a neat black beard, made him look like a benign schoolmaster rather than a tough task-master. More important, he was one of the few military men who did not share the almost universal view that the Emperor was godly, the Son of Heaven. For he embraced not Shintoism but Christianity and thus did not believe that to die for the Emperor was to gain eternal salvation. His men had to trust that he was willing to die simply as a patriot, without any divine compensation, an assumption not easily made in a land aflame with religious zealotry.

And yet Yokota, a native of Hiroshima, managed to convince even his most fanatical Shintoist superiors and subordinates that his patriotism alone would inspire him to perform even the most suicidal acts if necessary in a war against an enemy that largely shared his Christian faith. The Navy leaders knew that he had firmly opposed going to war, feeling that the Allies were potentially too powerful to tangle with. But they did not attrib-ute this view to the influence of Western religion. After all, many of the top naval commanders shared his skepticism and were only pushed into war by the Army leaders.

Yokota's doubts apparently persisted even after war broke out, for he suspected the early Japanese victories were delusional, a suspicion that seemed to harden after the Americans emerged victorious in the Battle of Midway in June 1942. He was not handicapped rationally, as were most Japanese, by a false cer-tainty that heaven guaranteed them victory. In fact, the Navy, ironically enough, viewed his rationality as a great military asset. So, whatever his ideological or religious commitment, his superiors were ready to gamble on him. And up to now he had turned out to be worthy of the number 6.

Yokota's eighty-two officers and men not only respected their skipper because he was an exceptional leader, but loved him because he, like Captain Swenson on the *Juneau*, cared about his crew in a personal sense—a rare quality among Japanese commanders. Ashore, he would visit them in their tents and give them cigarettes. And after some grueling mission, he would let them rest as long as possible. They would never forget the moment he informed them of the planned attack on Pearl Harbor. He stood before them and spoke of his intense feelings of responsibility toward them.

"We are going to war," he said, his eyes moist with tears, "and I am responsible for your lives. I'd like to let you speak with your families, but I'm sorry that I cannot."

Still, while all the men were moved by Yokota's thoughtfulness, some felt he was a little too thoughtful at times. Especially on the first day of the war when, en route to Pearl Harbor to take part in the attack there, he sighted an American merchant ship and hesitated to give orders to sink it immediately.

"Why, sir, can't we attack right now?" the weapons officer asked Yokota.

"No," the skipper replied, "we must warn them first. You can see through the periscope that this ship is unarmed."

The weapons officer could hardly believe what he heard. But according to Tsukuo Nakano, a petty officer second class who was a torpedo man subordinate to the weapons officer, Yokota was adamant. He would not issue the order to sink the ship until warning shots were fired over the vessel to give the men aboard a chance to escape. It simply didn't seem fair to the skipper that he kill the men on an unarmed ship.

Fair? Was this not war? many of Yokota's men exclaimed. It was his religion, they quietly charged. This was not the way of the samurai; sentimentality had no place in battle. Nevertheless, since he always emerged victorious in battle, they did not lose trust in him despite the troubling Western strains in his character.

Now, as *I-26* docked at Truk, this faith had solidified into near worship, and there was much gaiety as crew members raised a glass to the health of the commander, while scores of sailors on shore cheered them. Yes, under Yokota, the men were sure they would register even greater victories.

And little more than a week later, on August 21, they would be given the chance. *I-26*, together with other submarines in port, was ordered by Sixth Fleet headquarters to sally out to patrol enemy positions and strike at every American ship in sight. The craft headed for the eastern waters off San Cristóbal Island, southeast of Guadalcanal, sound-patrolling by day and gliding on the surface by night.

Posted at the lookout on the port bridge was Petty Officer Nakano, the torpedo man, who stood there every night but saw only a boundless expanse of water, without even a seabird specking the sky. How could that be? Reconnaissance had informed headquarters that the enemy was mobilizing a large fleet in this area. But the sea was as smooth as oil, reflecting only the bright sprinkle of stars—and then, on the morning of August 31, something else. He saw through his binoculars a vision in the waves. Nakano's boyish face, with rather chubby cheeks and narrow, humorless eyes, suggested a soul with little emotion. But now his shock seemed to make every muscle in his taut face quiver.

"Mother!" he gasped.

Nakano had not seen his mother since he was on leave months earlier. A widow, she had, as usual, been working hard on the family farm near Tokyo. His poor dear mother, who was now living alone in constant dread that she would never see her two sons again. Her elder son was serving in the Army in China, and Nakano himself had joined the Navy at eighteen, ready to die for the Emperor. Scouring the Pacific now, he remembered how she would get up before dawn, while everyone in the village was sleeping, in order to visit the local shrine, where she would pray for the safety of her two boys. Rain or shine, snow or sleet, she would go, even during his leave.

Now Nakano saw her again, her beautiful, weather-beaten face gently mobile in the glassy, undulating sea. What did this vision mean? Had she passed away and come in spirit to see him? Was she praying so intensely that her prayer was being answered through this means? Or was this simply a manifestation of the tight bond of love between them? He loved his mother so deeply, perhaps too deeply for a man whose life and eternal fate might depend on hating—hating enough to kill other men. Was that not the one reservation he had about Commander Yokota? The skipper's religion wouldn't let him hate. Conversely, if Nakano seemed afraid to love too much, his own religion ensured he would not hate less. Anyone who threatened the Emperor, the core of this religion, automatically deserved punishment and death.

Suddenly, Nakano was back in the real world as the chief signalman shouted, "A blackish object in sight ten degrees left on the horizon!" Nakano leaned forward and gazed through his binoculars in the direction of the port bow. Yes, there was an object and it looked like a ship.

The alarm bell rang, and Commander Yokota rushed to the bridge and popped his head out of the hatch. Simultaneously, Petty Officer Shoji called out, "An airplane at forty degrees on the right!" The navigation officer reacted with, "Stop both sides! Submerge quickly!"

The bridge crew leaped into the hatch, and a few minutes later the I-26 was underwater.

Nakano was excited. At last enemies to punish and kill.

On the torrid morning of August 22, the *Juneau* was about to sail off and trade the tranquil waters of the Panama Canal Zone for the troubled waters of the South Pacific war zone. But what had happened to a good part of the crew? Captain Swenson, standing on the bridge, soon found out. He silently fumed as he watched his men stagger up the gangplank—laughing, babbling, bubbling, falling over each other—after spending three intoxicating days in the bars of Balboa. The lucky ones made it; the others stumbled right into the sea.

On Swenson's orders, the more sober men rushed to extract their more adventuresome shipmates from the drink; then, when the last sailor had tottered aboard, the gangplank was raised and the ship pulled out. Among the 698 men safely aboard were the five Sullivans, who walked a relatively straight line, and the four Rogerses, who, as disciplined boxers, had learned to restrain their thirst for alcohol.

Swenson, the men found, acted as their fathers would have. He punished them. In fact, there were mass court-martials and dozens were thrown into the brig—but the door remained unlocked.

"I don't want anyone locked up in case we get hit and they're forgotten," he ordered Butterfield, who passed on the order to his superiors.

And Swenson had good reason to worry about what might happen to his "sons." American ships in the Pacific were beginning to crowd the ocean floor. About two weeks earlier, on August 7, the U.S. First Marine Division had battered its way ashore at Guadalcanal and Tulagi in a desperate effort to keep the Japanese from gobbling up New Caledonia, Fiji, and Samoa, the stepping-stones to Australia and New Zealand. Until then, the Japanese, despite setbacks at Port Moresby and Midway, had been scoring one victory after another.

And it now seemed they might even wipe out the American force that had invaded Guadalcanal. For on August 8, the second day of the U.S. offensive there, the three fleet aircraft carriers that had supported the landing were suddenly pulled out of the area for fear they would be sunk. The Japanese were quick to note the power vacuum left by the departing carriers and that night launched a surprise attack against the American surface fleet anchored off Guadalcanal at Savo Island as U.S. ships were discharging cargos of ammunition, food, and vehicles. Without losing a ship of their own, the Japanese sent four first-line Allied heavy cruisers to their graves and damaged several other U.S. vessels in one of the most devastating Allied naval defeats so far in the war.

Then, day after day, Japanese bombers sent tons of dynamite screaming down on the sparsely defended Marine strongholds at Tulagi and the site of a partially built Japanese airfield on Guadalcanal that the Americans had captured.

The two islands might have fallen to the Japanese by now but for an incredible engineering feat performed by the Marines. They finished building the airfield, now called Henderson Field, in two weeks, permitting two squadrons of fighters and bombers to land on August 19—the day the *Juneau* arrived in Balboa. Thus, the following day, an American infantry battalion, with U.S. planes zooming overhead in deadly support, smashed a land attack on the airfield, the first U.S. infantry victory of the war.

But the American commander in the area, Vice Adm. Robert

Ghormley, was overcautious and would not risk more ships or ground forces to clear the way for the landing of reinforcements—or even to stop the Japanese from landing their own. A "Tokyo Express" of destroyers brimming with troops and provisions snaked nightly through the "Slot," the narrow passage that stretched from Bougainville southeast to Guadalcanal, past the island chain of Santa Isabel and Choiseul on one side and New Georgia on the other. Meanwhile, night after night, the U.S. forces were the target of merciless bombing.

Like creeping rot, demoralization contaminated the American fleet throughout the Pacific. And Captain Swenson was well aware of it as he headed toward the epicenter of disaster. But he would not allow it to dampen his spirit. He could not let himself dwell on the fragility of his own ship, and the more reports he read of the defenseless defenders, of the sinking of vessels infinitely more durable than the *Juneau*, the more he forced reality from his mind. Yet he could not completely eradicate it. What if his men knew? . . . And somehow, the "scandal" at Balboa no longer seemed important to him.

Swenson, the men noted, had mellowed considerably and often seemed introspective and remote, as if his thoughts were far from the war and the "sons" who might die with him. He was perhaps thinking of his own son—and daughter. At any rate, before he left on this journey, they had been more on his mind, it seemed, than had his first venture into combat as the commander of a cruiser.

Swenson had written numerous letters to his son, advising him on everything from the importance of choosing the right roommate at the Naval Academy to the need to abstain from drinking even a drop of alcohol. He even sent friends on visits to the Academy to look after his son. Thus, he wrote the wife of one of them:

"I would appreciate having you entice [Bill] down to Annapolis and giving Robert the 'fish eye.' I can't believe that he can go very long without needing his ears pinned back by somebody. . . . I believe he chose his roommate on account of him having twin sisters on the stage. This does not appear to me as being a very weighty reason. I am just as interested in getting your impression of his roommate as I am in having you put him on the right track."

Swenson was especially concerned with Bob's study habits and athletic progress. "If you once get your French to the point where you get familiar with constructions," he wrote his son, "it rides along much easier from that point."

And then: "Let me know how the fencing is going on and whether you feel that your poise is improving. . . . I would like to see you improve your tennis." And he was delighted that his son had run the "quarter mile in the phenomenal time of sixty-seven."

As for Bob's health: "It pleases me very much to know that you are taking care of your health and not smoking or drinking anything stronger than tomato juice. . . . You are now equipped with a good body, a good mind, a good disposition, a good character. . . . The most important is good character. I hope you will take a sensitive pride in being a man of your word."

And when Bob found a girl: "Love is a grand thing but don't let it get you down on the first play. Spend a little time looking around and giving yourself an opportunity to recover from the first shock. . . . Give height, weight, age and coloring of girl. Remember, women age quicker than men."

All in all, Swenson was proud of his son. "I heard almost universal praise of your conduct among my friends you have met," he wrote him. "Nothing could give me more satisfaction."

Swenson wrote his most poignant letters to his daughter, Cecilia. Though they were still not reconciled, he offered her the most intimate fatherly advice.

"I wish," he wrote her, "that you were at college or in school rather than tutoring at home. There is so much that a girl your age misses by not making contact on her own with people her own age. In a few years it will be very difficult for you to do so with spinsterhood the inevitable result."

Shortly before Swenson was to leave for overseas, he pleaded with his daughter to attend a family gathering at Annapolis, writing: "The biggest happiness I could possibly have right now is to know that you would be there with us."

When Cecilia declined, he wrote back: "Knowing me as a stranger whom you have met in a more or less formal manner when family problems were under discussion and with me always on the other side, I can understand why your personal feelings toward me should be quite different than mine toward you. . . . I still remember you as the little blue-eyed, golden-haired light of my life who was my first child. . . . This all happened when you were too young to remember me. Any recollections you might have came after your mother and I separated.

"In the four years since I found you again I [have] had the feeling that someday I would have the opportunity to get acquainted with the grown-up little girl I remember with such affection. This war and my prospective assignment has brought me up to a point where I can't feel entirely certain of that future opportunity. . . . I have therefore asked you to join me for a few days before I leave so that I can get to know you and you me, just as Robert and I have done to our mutual happiness."

And Swenson concluded with an almost pathetic intensity: "I want you to come to visit me so very much that everything else including my new ship seems secondary."

But Cecilia was unyielding.

Though shattered, Swenson continued to send her messages of endearment—and console himself with Bob's devotion and that of his other "sons" who depended on him to bring them home safely.

Captain Swenson called in Wyatt Butterfield, who was standing outside his door, and ordered, "Tell the men in the brig that we're going into battle and that everyone is forgiven."

When told, the men filed out of the brig pardoned or on probation, ready to fight with even greater zeal than before for the American way of life, including the right to get dead drunk—except, of course, during a battle, or perhaps even before one, in deference to their beloved skipper.

Butterfield was nostalgically reminded of his real father, who always gave him another chance to repent after he had misbehaved. But he thought his mother's stricter attitude should apply here. Most of these men were young and inexperienced at war. Maybe they needed a good strapping to give them the discipline needed to survive. They had to know when to exercise restraint and when to yield to impulse, when to protect themselves in the midst of death and when to play the hero at the risk of death. He would survive, he was sure, and even cover himself with glory, because he knew how to discipline himself—and to calculate risks.

Tsukuo Nakano grasped at his own moment of glory as *I-26* dove into the sea and prepared to attack the "blackish object" on the horizon, while attempting to escape observation by the plane that had also come into view. He rushed inside the submarine to his post.

When *I-26* had plunged steeply into the sea, the sound room reported to Commander Yokota, "Group sound source at twenty degrees on the left front!"

The skipper responded, "Depth eighteen! Up with periscope!"

Patrolling at periscope depth, the officers could detect a large enemy force headed by an aircraft carrier. And soon the ships were identified: the carrier *Saratoga,* three cruisers, and seven destroyers.

The Shinto priest aboard the submarine muttered, "Come on, our brilliant enemy. You are worthy of our metal. We will bury a couple of your ships under the seabed!"

Itching for battle, the zealous priest poured sake over the launching tubes to bring the submarine luck.

Finally, Yokota gave the order: "Prepare for a torpedo attack!"

The conning tower then reported the enemy's azimuth, speed, and distance every minute. The first target: the *Saratoga.*

At four-thirty P.M. the commander ordered, now in a tense voice, "Azimuth seventy degrees on the left, enemy's speed twelve [knots], distance eighteen hundred [meters]. Ready! Fire!"

Four torpedoes sped away at three-second intervals, each with a loud boom. Ten seconds passed, then another ten. Quiet reigned, punctured only by a report from the sound room: "The propelling sounds are all advancing in a straight line."

Then, an explosion—and a shout of joy. But only one hit? Before the commander could find out, his binoculars captured an enemy destroyer bearing down on his submarine.

"Depth seventy! Quick!" Yokota cried.

And from the sound room, the scream, "Two sound sources! Very close!"

I-26 started to submerge at an angle of twenty degrees, with the commander yelling from the conning tower, "Hurry up with depth!"

The submarine went down at high speed—"Thirty, forty . . ." As Nakano read the revolution indicator of the depth gauge aloud, the enemy destroyer passed overhead with an ominous screwing sound. The next moment, about a dozen depth bombs rained on *I-26* at close range, shaking it with the force of an earthquake. Amid hysterical cries, the lights went out and rust and paint from the bulkheads showered the interior as the craft listed sharply to starboard and seemed about to turn over.

In the command office, codebooks that had been piled on the gyrocompass were scattered over the deck, and the heat grew unbearable. Nakano, who was in the room, turned on an emergency light and peered at the depth gauge. The craft was already below the safety limit of one hundred meters! Soon the severe water pressure, Nakano realized, would crush the ship. Without waiting for an order, he shouted, "Negative blow!" And after some draining, the vessel stopped sinking and started rising.

But the depth bombs exploded without end as the surgeon captain ran up and down the corridors treating the wounded with flashlight in hand.

Finally, Yokota, hoping to avoid the bombs, ordered, "Depth seventy! Course, two hundred and thirty degrees!"

The submarine crept directly under the enemy ship at a speed of three knots, then stopped as the engines were turned off. In silence, *I-26* lay underwater like a dead whale, while the temperature inside the craft rose to 40 degrees centigrade (104 degrees Fahrenheit) and the air pressure rose as well. Everyone removed his shirt and breathed hard from the lack of oxygen. Nakano's eyes grew dim, and his head buzzed. As he was losing consciousness, he pulled out a drawer of the tool chest and put his head on it, fantasizing that he would find some fresh air there.

The oxygen level, he realized, was very close to the minimum necessary for survival. Oxygen could be generated by putting the compressor pump in motion, but the noise would betray the submarine's location.

"We must wait," said Yokota, "until the very last moment."

Nakano prayed to his gods. And he thought of his mother's vision on the water. Had she been sent to warn him of this mortal moment?

CHAPTER

· 6 ·

Baptism of Fire

AFTER MONTHS OF SIMULATED BATTLE, THE *JUNEAU*, ON SEPTEMBER 11, set out to confront the real war, joining a twenty-one-ship task force in the New Hebrides that was bound for Guadalcanal so that fresh units of the First Marine Division could wade ashore under an umbrella of deadly steel.

No one was more eager for combat than Cox. Joey Rogers, and he didn't have to wait long. While other ships rained death on Japanese forces dug into the damp earth of the island, the men on the *Juneau* blazed away at planes overhead, watching in white-faced horror, between bursts of fire, as Marines streamed out of their transports and lurched toward the beach, falling like saplings in a storm. Joey suddenly lost his taste for battle and wept even as he furiously helped to fire a 5-inch gun. Though he had experienced the brutality of the ring, he was not prepared for this.

Nor for what would happen a few days later, on September 15. As the aircraft carrier *Wasp* clumsily splashed along, surrounded by smaller, sleeker ships, a great explosion from an apparent torpedo hit ripped through that massive vessel, and before Joey's startled eyes, the steel rolled back at the waterline and a huge gap opened up in the hull, coughing clouds of black smoke.

"All hands man battle stations!" the loudspeaker blared. But when Joey started to run toward his station, he tripped over the anchor chain and slid along the deck for about thirty feet. Though his head was deeply gashed, he scrambled to his feet and limped to his 20mm gun on the flight deck, where he saw men from the *Wasp*, silhouetted against a wall of flame, jump from the decks into the water. Ignoring his pain, he fired frantically at planes overhead. He had been wounded in the ring many times, but he had never quit, at least, voluntarily. And he wasn't going to quit now—except for a few minutes to snap pictures of the burning hulk.

Tommy Rogers had given Joey a little camera, which the son carried with him, though it was forbidden to take photos in combat. Joey had never been able to fathom his father's criminal tendencies, but he could understand the pernicious thrill of playing Adam, of defying and matching wits with authority, especially if the risk was high—for example, a trip to Alcatraz, the punishment most cited by his father as one to avoid, and thus one to risk. He himself could be court-martialed and thrown into the brig. Joey felt as if he were once more climbing through the medicine cabinet into his father's booze-reeking secret room. Besides, he wanted something to show his grandchildren—if he lived through the war to have any.

Captain Swenson, who was tormented by doubt that any of the men on his fragile ship would live to have grandchildren, feared that the responsible submarine, and perhaps others, would strike again. And he knew what a torpedo could do to his craft. Yet so many men were riding the waves that he couldn't fire depth charges, since they would not distinguish between a man and a submarine. He felt compelled, however, to pick up as many survivors as possible. Wouldn't he want someone to pick up his son?

"Get those men up here!" Swenson ordered as his ship slid by the flaming giant, appalled by the sight of men, injured and burned, jumping off the flight deck to be sucked under the dying vessel or washed under his own. Bodies were strewn over the placid sea, many floating on backs broken from the leap.

Juneau sailors pulled dozens of survivors aboard, wounded, screaming men. Finally, as other American ships arrived to help, Swenson gave the order to move on. And when all the men had been rescued, Allied torpedoes put the blazing monster out of its misery. Swenson clearly had mixed emotions. He was elated that he had helped to save so many lives and was relieved that his ship had not been torpedoed, but he was despondent over the implications of the battle. A huge aircraft carrier had gone up in flames. What would happen to his light cruiser if a torpedo hit it?

The *Wasp* lost 193 dead, but over 1,900 were rescued—and one of them was the brother of Russell Coombs, a sailor on the *Juneau*. Russell was doleful when his brother was not pulled aboard the *Juneau*, and as soon as the ship anchored in Nouméa he rushed into Allied headquarters to inquire about him.

"I know he was on the *Wasp*," he said.

Yes, he was, Russell was told. He had been rescued by another ship. In fact, his brother was right there in Nouméa!

In joy, the two brothers were soon reunited.

"Why don't you come on our ship?" Russell suggested.

And his brother agreed.

So did Captain Swenson. It apparently didn't seem fair to him that the five Sullivans and the four Rogerses should be on his ship and the second Coombs brother should be rejected. So another brother climbed aboard the *Juneau*. But Swenson might have wondered if his sense of fairness would cheat still another family out of more than one son. With no alternative, he simply resigned himself to the possibility of catastrophe.

Who would live and who would die would be decided by a Higher Authority.

Meanwhile, the crew of the *I-26* was suffocating as it waited at deadly depth for the enemy bombs to stop exploding. Suddenly, the sound room reported: "Enemy's sound sources have receded. Sensitivity zero."

Commander Yokota and his men silently rejoiced. The enemy must have either given up or run out of bombs. Anyway, why stay there and die? Better to die in action, Yokota now agreed. If the enemy was still there, the crew of *I-26* would hit and then go to heaven. Not so terrible a fate, even for a Christian. The men readied themselves for death.

"Prepare for a torpedo battle!" Yokota ordered from the conning tower. And the torpedo crew assembled in the command room.

"Depth eighteen!" And the ship rose. Then: "Up with periscope!"

The periscope poked into the air. No enemy there. The commander ordered, his voice now hoarse, "Main tank blow! Surface!"

With a cry of jubilation, the men opened the high-pressure air valve fully, and the *I-26*, for the first time in seventeen hours, leaped to the surface like a trained dolphin.

Tsukuo Nakano was soon at his post on the port bridge again, greedily breathing in the salty air, tasting the joy of life with each breath, stuffing his chest and belly with it. He would later learn with disappointment that the *Saratoga* had been damaged but not sunk.

Next time, Nakano was sure, his gods—and the spirit of his mother—would help *I-26* sink a ship. And they would not settle for even the gravest wound.

Nakano's gods would be facing a man who was like a god himself to many U.S. sailors in the Pacific area. He was Vice Adm. William F. (Bull) Halsey, who, on October 18, descended from heaven in a four-engine Consolidated patrol bomber and landed in Nouméa Bay to learn the momentous news. An officer who had pulled up to the plane in a whaleboat gave him two envelopes, one from Adm. Chester W. Nimitz, Commander in Chief, Pacific (CINCPAC). Halsey tore it open and could hardly believe what he read:

"You will take command of the South Pacific area and South Pacific forces immediately."

"Jesus Christ and General Jackson!" Halsey exclaimed as he broke into a startled grin. "This is the hottest potato they ever handed me!"

He then opened the second envelope and found a congratulatory letter from the man he was replacing, Bob Ghormley, an old football teammate at the Naval Academy. Bull Halsey sympathized with his friend, but knew it was time for someone with his own aggressiveness, tenacity, and gambling instinct to take over. And so did the top naval brass in Washington and Pearl Harbor. Ghormley had simply been too cautious, fearing to use the full force of the U.S. Navy to land reinforcements in Guadalcanal and block the Tokyo Express. He had begun to act more aggressively, and a flotilla of his warships had completely smashed a superior enemy force, including many troop transports, at Cape Esperance on October 10 in a great morale-lifting battle. Even so, within forty-eight hours, spirits plummeted again when two Japanese battleships steamed toward shore and raked Henderson Field almost at will, killing more than forty defenders.

Halsey, on the other hand, had demonstrated as a commander of destroyers and aircraft carriers that he was as tough and forceful as he looked. His jowly, bushy-browed face, while featuring wide lips that formed a kind of perpetual smile, was intimidating even when he wasn't spouting orders in his booming voice. And one of his first orders was to consolidate his Pacific units into dynamic fighting flotillas that would finally crush the Japanese effort to retake Guadalcanal.

Thus, the *Juneau*, which had been sent to the New Hebrides area with Task Force 17 to help protect the aircraft carrier *Hornet*, soon became part of Task Force 61, together with Task Force 16. The aircraft carrier *Enterprise*, the centerpiece of Task Force 16, would join the *Hornet* under the protective umbrella of the antiaircraft ships of both forces.

So the *Juneau* would be kept busy, which was what the men wanted. Pretty dull plowing day in and day out through an infinite sea looking for action that seldom came. And for no one was the work duller than the man whose job it was to look, to keep his eyes on the endless stretch of watery emptiness until he found himself counting sea gulls to stay awake, if there were any.

One of the lookouts was SM1c. Lester Zook, who had joined the old Navy in 1938 and was delighted to be serving now on one of the first ships in the "new" Navy, learning how to use the latest radar and other miracle devices. The *Juneau* was to him a huge laboratory, and he had gleefully tested the virgin equipment as a member of the precommissioning team preparing the ship for combat.

Zook viewed the war in part as a clash of technologies, and he wanted to know how everything worked. He was also a careful observer of how other men worked, a perfectionist who criticized anyone who did not perform his job with maximum efficiency. Once when the bridge ordered Zook to summon the chief signalman, he reported back that the man was too drunk to obey. Soon the fellow was clambering down the gangplank, never to be seen again. Zook shed no tears.

Even Captain Swenson, beloved by almost everybody, was not immune from Zook's critical barbs. Why was he so dependent for operational information on the captain of the *Atlanta*, the *Juneau*'s sister ship? And was it really good for morale to court-martial all those men for getting drunk in Balboa? One had to be selective in imposing punishment.

If Zook was hard on others, however, he was also hard on himself. Whatever his duty, he would perform as well as he could. And while he was often reluctant to bestow praise on others, he was less reluctant to receive praise. When he served as a tailor on an earlier ship, he sewed hash marks on uniforms with the care one might reserve for the President's tails. He still fondly remembers how an officer complimented him for doing "the best job ever" in pressing his sleeves without creasing them.

Zook sometimes reveled in praise even if he did not deserve it. On one occasion, when the *Juneau* was moored at Norfolk, Virginia, he uncharacteristically neglected his duty as lookout and indulged in a game of cribbage with a comrade. Suddenly, someone came running to him. A ship was on fire! the man cried. Zook immediately shouted, "Fire!" and the burning vessel was saved in time. The officer in charge of the fire-fighting operation congratulated him, saying admiringly, "Alert watch."

Zook saluted in his snappiest manner and replied in a humble voice, "Thank you, sir."

Afterward, Zook less humbly cautioned the man who had informed him of the fire, "Don't tell him what really happened."

Zook's enigmatic smile, which stretched an already expansive jaw, and his quizzical eyes, which seemed to be constantly ferreting out and analyzing the inner thoughts and intentions of people, gave the impression of a man with ambition who knew what he wanted but wasn't quite sure how to get it.

Perhaps this was because he identified so closely with his father, who had been a brilliant medical student at the University of Nebraska, but was drafted into the Army in World War I and never had the opportunity to resume his studies. During that war, he met the woman he would marry, and soon there were three children, including Lester, the firstborn. After the war, he lacked the funds to return to medical school and, to feed his family, went to work as a mailman in Lexington, Nebraska.

The Zooks survived in a "strata above the poor," though Lester's grandfather, a carpenter, built a spacious house for them. The father was strict with the children and did not hesitate to wield the strap at the drop of a lie—or even a jar of cookies. He was driven by a desire to see each of his children be somebody, the somebody fate had never let him be.

Still, if Lester's father was to be a letter carrier, he would be the best and most important one in town. He became president of the local letter-carriers' association. And even when he was ill, he stoically delivered the mail, finally dying in 1937 with a mail sack on his back, as Lester would proudly boast.

Lester was studying at Kearney State Teachers College in Kearney, Nebraska, when his father died, and since he'd lost his mother a year earlier, he suddenly found himself an orphan. Shattered, young Zook dropped out of college. He had been a mediocre student anyway and spent more time playing center on the football team than studying. Although extremely intelligent, Zook was skeptical about the benefits of formal schooling. What good had it done his father? He preferred on-the-job training. And he needed to get some now, since his parents had left the children little money and he was already eighteen. Besides, he hoped to marry as soon as he found the right girl, and he had to earn at least a minimal living first.

The Depression, however, was in full swing, and a living eluded him—until hunger drove him to the Navy recruiting office. He surely wouldn't get rich, but twenty-one dollars a month plus all the food he could eat wasn't a bad deal. By counting every cent, he was even able to support his younger brother and sister for a while.

Zook soon found that the Navy offered him a greater technical challenge than school had. After serving as a signalman aboard the USS *New Mexico* for four years, he joined the *Juneau* crew, and now, with the war, he would give his best even if he died on the job as his father had. And he knew the odds were pretty good that he might.

Nevertheless, peace at times could be pretty nerve-racking, especially when he was searching the sea hour after hour for enemy craft and seeing nothing but a calm, untroubled world of water and sky he knew was deceptively transient.

At about this time, Tsukuo Nakano and his comrades were celebrating the fate their gods had ordained for them. If not for their divine grace, the crew would surely have died from the blast of depth bombs or the lack of oxygen when *I-26* dived into dangerously deep waters to escape detection by the enemy. What a joy to surface at their base in Truk, to see Commander Yokota smiling as he stood on the gun battery and peered through his binoculars toward shore.

"Get ready for entry to the harbor!" he cried. "Forward both sides at the original speed! Open front and rear hatches!"

The men, draped in oil-stained fatigues, climbed to the deck one by one and breathed in the fresh air in ecstatic cadence, shielding their eyes from the glaring equatorial sun. They smiled, laughed, joked, inhaled cigarette smoke as if it were almost as important as air.

"The joy of returning alive under the storm of depth bombs," Nakano would say, "defies all description."

The crew basked in the glory of a hero's welcome, even warmer than the one they had received after their triumphant return from Australian waters. A light plane circled over the *I-26* waving its wings. Motor launches sent from Sixth Fleet headquarters sped toward the submarine, its occupants cheering wildly. Other submarines flag-signaled congratulations. Welcome home! And now the exhausted crew could finally rest.

But not for long. On the third day in port, the men were eating at tables set on the deck of the submarine when Commander Yokota stepped aboard from a motor launch. He had just come from headquarters carrying a large envelope under his arm. Usually Yokota smiled in the presence of his men, but not this time. Looking downcast, he vanished into the interior of the craft.

Nakano and the others suspected trouble, and their suspicions grew when the senior officer emerged and said the commander would soon appear on deck to inform them of coming operations. Only once before had Yokota gathered his men to personally issue instructions—as they were about to head for Pearl Harbor. The commander now stepped on deck, and he looked just as concerned as he had then. He would tell his anxious audience why.

The Americans, he said, were seeking to turn Guadalcanal into an unsinkable aircraft carrier as a springboard for an attack upon Japan itself. Indeed, the island was a strategically priceless base for them.

"Therefore, we must recapture it as soon as possible," Yokota warned.

The Imperial Army had sent thirty thousand infantrymen and three thousand Marines into Guadalcanal, and in suicide attacks they had set fire to American-controlled Henderson Field and supply dumps under cover of darkness. But the enemy responded not by fighting the brave Japanese soldiers, but by trying to starve them into submission. They were cutting off the Japanese supply route to the island by bombing the supply ships.

"Thus, our casualties keep on growing, ammunition and food have almost run out, and overall strength has diminished considerably."

The Japanese fleet had launched *marutsuu*, special transport operations. Destroyers loaded with troops and supplies would be sent to the Runga base on Guadalcanal at night. But, unfortunately, enemy aircraft and ships, aided by radar, were sinking the destroyers one after another with concentrated fire. Now the Japanese supply route to Guadalcanal was virtually severed.

And so, Yokota said, his slim shoulders sagging, the large submarines assembled at Truk, including the *I-26*, had been assigned to the supply mission and would supplement the work of the destroyers.

"We must supply our officers and men on Guadalcanal at any cost," the commander concluded firmly.

Nakano and the others were shocked. A submarine used for *marutsuu* work? It wasn't a supply ship, they grumbled; it was an attack craft. Let the surface forces do it. What a blow to their prestige! And they knew the commander agreed, but he was helpless.

Shortly, the men were piling drum cans and waterproof rubber bags stuffed with rice and other provisions on the deck of the *I-26*, and loading twenty tons of munitions inside the submarine's barrel-shaped magazine. Actually, the *I-26* had a double mission—unlike most of the other submarines. It was to carry not only provisions and arms, but also a full load of aviation fuel in its airplane hangar on the deck in order to perform sea-to-air fueling. Afterward it was to patrol enemy sea routes— an important concession to Yokota, who insisted that he have some time to strike at enemy vessels.

When, that evening, the *I-26* and the other submarines were bulging with their vital cargos, they floated out to sea one by one. Members of Yokota's crew, refreshed by a cool sea breeze, were now in a lively mood, for they would get their chance to sink American ships after all, even if they had to humble themselves first. And they would surely be lucky again, since the number 6 was continuing to bless them. They were departing at six P.M. in the afternoon of October 6 and were on the sixth submarine to leave the port. Now all they had to do was send at least six enemy ships to the bottom of the sea.

As the *I-26* plowed through the glistening waves toward Guadalcanal, cruising on the surface by night and below by day, the crew scrupulously heeded the commander's order to watch carefully for enemy planes and ships, but not to attack at this stage. They remembered the skipper's admonition: "The supplies and munitions must be unloaded at Guadalcanal at any cost."

Finally, on the night of the fourth day, as *I-26* reached the base at Runga and, at periscope depth, edged cautiously toward shore to unload its precious cargo, the sound detectors indicated that two high-velocity craft were patrolling the area every two hours.

Alert to this danger, Yokota drew up a plan of operations for the following night. He called in Petty Officer Miyashita and with his forefinger traced on a chart the route that the man would take in his midget submarine to carry the cargo to shore. Launching time would be nine P.M., the launching point, a thousand meters from the coast. Meanwhile, Miyashita should pack his personal items to be sent to his family in the event of his death, which seemed likely.

The next night, October 11, as the submarine moved toward the launching point, the commander ordered, "Up with periscope!"

He then gazed through the mechanism and Guadalcanal came into view in the shape of a dark cloud. All clear. At eight-thirty P.M., a flash signal was sent to the base through the night periscope, and soon blue lights could be seen waving up and down—the friendly identification signal. The commander then gave the order to get ready for launching, and the submarine surfaced into the calm, black night.

Miyashita climbed into the cockpit of the midget submarine, which was fixed to the stern of the *I-26*, and examined the driving apparatus by feel. All was in order. Yokota apparently failed to see a shadowy object, a shade darker than the sky, moving northward on the horizon, one of several warships that were about to strike at a Japanese flotilla in the Battle of Cape Esperance. They would catch the Japanese by surprise and yield America a major victory. In any case, Yokota would not have jeopardized his supply and fueling mission by attacking the ship.

"We go underwater now," the commander told Miyashita. "You go straight in the direction you are facing now, and you will reach the coast of Guadalcanal. Go!"

And as Yokota entered the conning tower, the mother craft slowly submerged, leaving the baby on the surface to head for land.

Suddenly the sound room reported, "Two sound sources of screw at thirty degrees on the right. Sensitivity two."

The commander groaned, "The same guests at the same hour as yesterday." And he ordered, "Depth seventy. Submerge quickly!"

As the patrol boats passed harmlessly over the submarine, the sound room reported it had caught the propelling noise of the midget submarine—it was safely advancing toward the base.

Yokota sighed. He had outwitted the enemy. Yes, Japan, he was sure, would hold Guadalcanal. As he thanked God, his face, though alight with emotion, seemed to reflect a familiar loneliness. Everyone else was thanking other gods.

As Lester Zook stood at his post on the bridge of the *Juneau* peering through his binoculars on the morning of October 26, he saw off the coast of the Santa Cruz Islands the vague outlines of several ships approaching—enemy ships! Hardly had he given the signal when Japanese aircraft in lethal formation thundered overhead, dropping bombs like huge hailstones in the sunshine. Their main targets were the two aircraft carriers, *Hornet* and *Enterprise*, and they were striking home even as planes abruptly took off from the wobbly decks to meet this sudden scourge.

The crew of the *Juneau* would now see its first real action of the war. With bombs and shells showering the task force, the gunners aimed their weapons at the sky and fired at the enemy planes without pause.

Helping to direct the fire of the 20mm and 1.1-inch guns was Lt. Charles Wang, who, with two other officers, presided over Gun Control 2, adjacent to Battle Station 2, which was perched just behind the after stack on a high platform surrounded by a splinter shield. If the main control battle section forward on the bridge—Captain Swenson's command post—was knocked out, this station would assume control of the ship.

Though Wang, twenty-seven, was subordinate to several other officers, he clung to the memory of that glorious moment when he "commanded" the *Juneau*. He happened to report for duty on the day the ship was launched, and since he was the first officer to arrive, he was in command.

"Just sign here," he was told, "and go down to see your ship launch."

And he thrilled to the sight of "that slick, thin beauty hitting the water." Later, he would fondly recall, "I was the first, so to speak, commanding officer of the *Juneau*."

LEFT TO DIE

Exuberant, energetic, daring, Chuck Wang had been in command all his life. In his hometown of Philadelphia, he had been a Boy Scout leader, a camp counselor, captain and quarterback of his high school football team, president of his senior class, an honor student, and chairman of the Golden Jubilee Ball. At the University of Kansas, where he studied premed for two years, he scored top grades while flitting from one campus activity to another, even winning a prize as a member of the college glee club.

Endowed with an athletic physique, striking blue eyes, and a stubborn chin, Wang was a popular figure, especially with the girls, and his receding hairline seemed to add to his macho aura. But if he was something of a social lion, his roar was subdued by a streak of hermitism perhaps rooted in a deeply religious psyche nourished by Catholic teachings.

Wang spent some of his most satisfying moments at Sunday services in church exploring the human spirit, and in the school laboratory examining the human cell. At the age of sixteen, he decided he wanted to be a doctor like his father, who worked as a gastroenterologist for the Veterans Administration and examined patients privately after hours in an upstairs room of the Wang house.

Chuck had a mild, gentle temperament, like that of both his parents, who were of aristocratic German heritage. And though he savored the joys of life, he was preoccupied by the agents of death. He would be a pathologist—a doctor who dealt with diseased human cells so that he could better understand how healthy ones worked. Wang always liked to get to the root of things, to delve into both the minds and bodies of fellow humans. Thus, he was seldom bored, whether gregariously mixing with people or aloofly studying their composition under a microscope.

When the war broke out, Wang quit college, went to a Navy officers' training school and then to a torpedo school, before being sent to the *Juneau*. Now, as he directed the fire of his men, his confidence bolstered by the Miraculous Medal he wore around his neck, he would profit from the opportunity to study their behavior and capacity for punishment, as well as his own, in a crucible heated to the deadly temperature of war.

* * *

One of Wang's men, George Sullivan, stood ready to release depth charges at the slightest hint that a submarine was prowling in the area. A torpedo fired by a submarine was usually well aimed and more likely to damage and sink a ship than a land or air missile, and George knew that he might hold in his hand the key to the crew's survival.

A few feet away, George's seventeen-year-old buddy, Allen Heyn, in his zeal to prove his grit to skeptical elders, was helping to fire a 1.1-inch gun with such intensity that, after a while, the barrel became too hot to handle and had to be put in a water tank to cool. George and Allen had become good friends despite the gap in their ages. George, at twenty-eight, was the "old man," while Allen was the youngest crew member on the ship. As a mere "kid," he was generally regarded as the least likely candidate for survival.

But George, apparently, could sense that this "kid" had the makings of a first-class sailor. George didn't speak much, but whenever he offered advice to Heyn and other young seamen, Heyn had his ears tuned and was the most willing to learn. And he had an even warmer relationship with Albert Sullivan, also a member of Heyn's division, since they were closer in age. They would often exchange stories about their lives back home, and Heyn sympathized with the younger Sullivan. Poor Al—all he ever thought about was his wife and baby.

Heyn was far less homesick, for there wasn't much at home to go back to. In fact, he had always been a bit lonely there— perhaps because he subconsciously mourned for his twin brother, who died when he was an infant of six months. Now, one elder brother was serving on the battleship *New York*; another, an engineer, was building airfields in Saudi Arabia; and his father, also an engineer, was working at a gun factory in Washington, D.C.

It would be lonely indeed at the family farm in Callicoon, New York, or at the summer home in Staten Island. Actually, Heyn had lived a happy, comfortable middle-class childhood— no regrets. But he was embarrassed to think that his parents had had to sign for him so he could join the Navy at sixteen, soon after Pearl Harbor. They had pleaded with him to wait, arguing that he hadn't even finished his junior year in high school. But he wouldn't listen. Weren't his brothers doing their part? And every time he heard "The Star Spangled Banner," he wept. He thanked heaven that the Navy was in such urgent need of men that it had bent the rules for him. Anyway, he would soon be seventeen, and then his enlistment would be "legal."

And Heyn thanked heaven, too, that his name started with H. At training camp in Newport, Rhode Island, all the H's were shipped off to the *Juneau* to complete its roster. Thirty-five men were lucky enough to draw this new wonder ship.

Yet life had not been all joy aboard this vessel. Heyn was prime bait for some of the older sailors, who had little respect for youngsters, especially "know-it-alls" like Heyn, who dared to claim that he knew something about how to run a ship. Adding to his problem was his appearance. Heyn looked like a juvenile, with his smooth-skinned baby face lit by a full-lipped smile and innocent, doelike eyes and set off by a shock of dark, wavy hair that fell over his forehead. Nor did he help matters when he tried to grow a beard to make himself look older, for the fuzz only drew guffaws and more ridicule. Why, Heyn mused, couldn't all the men be like George and Al Sullivan?

But they weren't, and their needling was the least of his troubles. Two men on board harassed him physically. Once they tried to sexually attack him in the shower, and when he resisted, they beat him up and threatened to throw him overboard.

"If you say anything, we'll kill you!" one of them warned.

Heyn remained silent, but if he boiled within, he would not let this incident or other humiliations distract him from his duties. After all, things could be worse. Had he not seen those bodies floating in the water, half blown apart? He could hardly consider himself unlucky. Besides, he found comfort in the comradeship of a few friends like George and Al—and Frank Holmgren.

Holmgren, a lean, handsome youth with playful eyes and a pixieish smile, knew Heyn from boot camp and was one of the H's sent to the *Juneau*. Now he was in the same division with Heyn and George and Albert Sullivan.

The son of a mechanic in Eatontown, New Jersey, Holmgren joined the Navy at nineteen after graduating from high school.

Whenever he would see the sleek ships floating out to sea in the newsreels, he would have an urge to rush down to the Navy recruiting office and enlist. But Holmgren was doubtful that the Navy would welcome him, and he didn't accept rejection with grace. He was tough enough; he had even played football in high school. But he had a nail-biting habit, and he had heard this was enough to disqualify him. What was worse, he couldn't swim. Would the Navy take someone who was almost sure to drown if his ship went down?

So Holmgren gave up his dream of a naval career and concentrated instead on another dream; her name was Joyce Heidt. Joyce's father, a policeman who guarded the Eatontown borough hall, would usually let Holmgren replace him when he had to be absent, and Joyce would keep her sweetheart company. A great job, and he was being paid for it!

Holmgren had almost decided to marry Joyce when the war broke out. Four of his buddies pleaded with him to enlist in the Navy with them. After all, they argued, he owed his country a lot. Holmgren was in a quandary. What should he do, he asked himself—pop the question or pay his debt? As he agonized over his decision, those newsreels reeled through his mind. . . . Yes, he would join the Navy—if it would have him. All five boys thus went for physicals and, ironically, only Holmgren passed. However, the Navy would make him wear white gloves at all times until his fingernails grew back to normal length. Men who bit their nails were nervous and might not be able to survive in stressful situations. Nobody asked him if he could swim.

Holmgren thus signed up alone—though his closest friend, Charles Hayes, who was rejected because he was overweight, would starve himself and later join him on the *Juneau*. No more evenings in borough hall sitting by the fire with his beloved. He kissed his parents and Joyce good-bye, and Joyce gave him a wishbone for luck.

"Always keep it with you," she said, "and you will be safe."

The wishbone apparently gave Holmgren a sense of security, for he was soon able to discard the white gloves as his fingernails grew long enough to satisfy the Navy. And what if he couldn't swim? He would never need to.

Nor did the wishbone fail him when he clambered aboard the

Juneau. Captain Swenson picked him as an orderly, a job he shared, when he wasn't loading 1.1-inch guns, with only a few other privileged men, including Wyatt Butterfield. But how long could his luck last?

As the missiles sprinkled around the *Juneau* that morning of October 26, a strange thing happened. About a thousand yards away, the *Hornet*, severely wounded, began to list, with smoke spiraling ominously into the sky. Suddenly, signalmen on the *Juneau* who shared the job with Lester Zook saw a signal being flashed from the carrier, with the blinker light aimed directly at his ship.

"Go to *Enterprise*," the signal ordered.

The signalmen were puzzled. The *Hornet* was in deep trouble. Why should the *Juneau* be sent elsewhere? Was the *Enterprise* in even deeper trouble? One man instantly relayed the order to Captain Swenson, who was equally puzzled. But orders were orders, and so the *Juneau* steamed toward the *Enterprise* some distance away, leaving the *Hornet* to the protection of other ships.

As the *Juneau* approached the *Enterprise*, all the cruiser's guns were blasting away at enemy planes swooping down on the aircraft carrier, which, although hit, didn't seem as badly damaged as the *Hornet*. The *Juneau* guns scored hits as well on nearby Japanese ships and helped to disable two enemy carriers.

When the two fleets finally disengaged later in the day, the *Enterprise* was still afloat, though badly crippled. Zook, proud of his ship's performance in defending two carriers, flashed a query to one of the other cruisers in the American task force: What had happened to the *Hornet*? As Zook watched for an answer through his binoculars, he saw his counterpart on the other cruiser thumbing his nose at him.

Zook was shocked. That was the sign deriding a renegade ship that had displayed cowardice under fire.

When Captain Swenson learned of this, he was crushed. Cowardice? He was a coward? In desperation, he contacted headquarters.

Why had he run away? he was asked.

He didn't run away, Swenson replied in bewilderment. He

was ordered to leave the *Hornet* and rush to the aid of the *Enterprise*—and his men had done one hell of a job defending both carriers. And while the *Hornet*, he now learned, had been mortally wounded and put out of its misery with American torpedoes, his ship, with all its firepower, could never have saved it. The punishment that carrier had taken, the captain argued, was simply too great.

Headquarters then explained that the message "Go to *Enterprise*" had been directed at planes that were heading for the *Hornet* but could never have landed on it because it was sinking. In fact, some of these planes, on the way to the *Enterprise*, ran out of fuel and had to pancake in the water. And the *Juneau* had picked up several of the crews at great risk to itself.

Now the pieces of the puzzle fell into place. The signalmen had erred in thinking the message was intended for the *Juneau*. Even so, Swenson felt, his men had done a superb job and helped save the *Enterprise*, though they hadn't been asked to. Without the support of the *Juneau*, that carrier might have joined the *Hornet* at the bottom of the sea.

Nevertheless, the captain remained despondent. Many of his colleagues would still think of him as a coward, an officer who fled and left the *Hornet* to die. Would the Navy, he must have wondered, now remember the man who was once accused of abusing his own daughter, the man whose character it once questioned—and might now question again? Would his ship have to perish in battle to finally prove he was a good captain?

"Well done!" Swenson told his crew, which had shot down eighteen planes during the battle. It had performed admirably.

So had the whole American flotilla, but in fact the Japanese had won the Battle of Santa Cruz, at least tactically. They had sunk an aircraft carrier and seriously damaged another, leaving the Allies with only one immediately usable carrier in the area. And they had sunk as well three other warships, while shooting down seventy-four planes. The Americans, on the other hand, had failed to sink any ships, while damaging four vessels and shooting down sixty-six planes. But these statistics did not tell the whole story.

Indeed, jubilance among the top Japanese commanders

quickly dissipated, and Vice Admiral Chuichi Nagumo, who commanded the victorious fleet, was soon the gloomiest of all. With good reason! Admiral Isoroku Yamamoto, Commander in Chief of the Japanese Combined Fleet, was giving him a shore job for not scoring a more decisive victory. Nagumo's colleagues greeted the news with mixed feelings. They liked him, but felt he was too exhausted for combat duty.

One fellow officer who went to see him in his Truk headquarters, unsure whether to offer congratulations or sympathy, was Commander Tameichi Hara, skipper of the destroyer *Ametsukaze*, which had taken part in the battle. Hara found Nagumo a haggard old man, though he glowed as he told his visitor:

"Glad to see you, Hara. You have done a terrific job. I am proud of you."

Hara reddened and, after a clumsy silence, said: "You don't look well, Admiral Nagumo. Are you ill?"

"Oh, just a touch of flu," Nagumo replied. "Once back home. I'll be in good shape, and will return soon to join you in the fight."

"You deserve a rest," said Hara. "You have been in combat continuously for a year. Compared with your duty, I've been on a pleasure cruise."

"Well, you'll have a tougher time from now on. All the carriers except [one] are going home for repairs. And we have lost some of our best fliers. It will be some time before new fliers can be properly trained. . . . Just between us, Hara, this battle was a tactical win, but a shattering strategic loss for Japan. As you know, I made a special study of America's war potential during my stay in the States. Considering the great superiority of our enemy's industrial capacity, we must win every battle overwhelmingly. This last one, unfortunately, was not an overwhelming victory."

Nagumo might have added that his men had failed to achieve their primary objective—to land troops and supplies on Guadalcanal.

Hara suspected that Nagumo was right. And he blamed, in part, Admiral Yamamoto, despite his reputation as Japan's greatest naval strategist. Yamamoto had built this reputation on his skill as a gambler. He had gambled the most when he attacked

Pearl Harbor and won, at least temporarily. But then, somehow, he lost his gambling instinct. He split his forces between Midway and the Aleutians in the hope of limiting his losses, and, at Midway, as he sat helpless aboard the *Yamata*, the world's biggest battleship, he learned that he had lost his four great aircraft carriers—and the battle.

Chastened by Midway, Yamamoto was reluctant to call for reinforcements and expose his battleships to enemy shelling at Guadalcanal. The admiral, in short, had become overcautious in Hara's view, and as a result the fighting at Guadalcanal had hardened into a stalemate. Nor was Hara impressed by the admiral's argument that the Army was reluctant to furnish him with enough troops to warrant large gambles by the Navy. Yamamoto, he thought, should make his considerable weight felt more effectively and prevail on the Army to confront the Americans with overwhelming force.

This was the right time to act. Though Japan had won only a Pyrrhic victory at Santa Cruz, this victory had sent morale soaring among those military men less perceptive than Admiral Nagumo and he. Conversely, American morale, he was sure, must have plummeted. And as Sun-tze, the military sage of ancient China, wrote in the seventh chapter of his *Analects*, Hara's military bible: "One should avoid a force while its morale is keen, and one should hit when its morale ebbs."

Yes, victory from now on would have to be overwhelming.

Once again, Commander Yokota's exhilaration quickly dissolved into anxiety. After successfully penetrating the steel ring around Guadalcanal with food and munitions for the men isolated there, *I-26* had gone to the designated spot where it was to refuel seaplanes. But was this the right spot? The navigation officer had tried his best to find it, observing the stars, computing to the last inch. But with some skepticism, Yokota asked him:

"Are you sure this is the place?"

Friendly planes were expected to fly to the location the following day, and Yokota had to confirm the submarine's arrival there before the night was out. The commander glanced at the water and, before the officer could reply, snapped:

"It looks pretty shallow to me!"

But according to his calculations, the officer nervously replied, this was the right place.

Despite his assurances, however, Yokota sensed danger and ordered a reduction in speed, then went to the chart room to check the location himself. Suddenly the chief signalman shouted:

"A reef ahead!"

"Stop the submarine!" Yokota ordered over the loudspeaker.

But before the echo of his voice had faded into the engine's drone, the I-26 struck the reef with a tremendous crash. The commander looked toward the bow and, ignoring the navigation officer, cried:

"Motor sternward full!"

Tsukuo Nakano, at his battle station on the port side, was surprised to hear the order. Normally, to dislodge a craft from a reef a submarine had to be lightened as much as possible before moving sternward. Yokota, Nakano guessed, was apparently overwrought. This seemed quite human to him, since the skipper was burdened with the responsibility of saving eighty-two lives in the midst of the enemy. And he tried to calm the commander down with an optimistic report over the phone:

"All is normal on the port side!"

Whatever the possible calming effect of this news, Yokota would not order the craft lightened even after his order failed to free the submarine. Instead, he cried, "Negative blow! Counterbalance! Shift water sternward."

But despite the full backward motion propelled by motor, all that moved was the seawater, which streamed sternward in a torrent. The submarine remained rooted to the reef.

In desperation, Yokota now ordered, "Blow front fuel tank!"

Since this move could damage and possibly doom the submarine, the chief engineer and the senior officer rushed to the bridge to stop the commander.

Before trying a fuel blow, they urged in near-panic, they should try to go astern with the diesel engine.

The commander agreed and ordered the chief engineer to attempt a backward motion with the main engine. As this engine revved up, a flood tide of water gushed forward under the submarine and shook it so violently that the telescope platform fixed on the bridge seemed about to fall apart, while dark clouds of smoke curling from the exhaust port threatened to suffocate the crew.

This looked like the end to Nakano. The luck of the *I-26* had run out. He would never see his mother again—except in heaven.

CHAPTER
· 7 ·

Rings of Fate

AFTER ITS STAR-CROSSED EFFORT TO SAVE TWO AIRCRAFT CARRIERS, the *Juneau* sailed back to Nouméa and anchored alongside several other cruisers. Crew members, unaware of the mistake that had sent the ship from the *Hornet* to the *Enterprise*, were in high spirits, especially after the lavish praise of their captain. They wanted to celebrate, but after the Balboa scandal they showed remarkable control in the bars. Besides, men couldn't live on booze and bar girls alone, though some were ready to try. There was boxing, too.

Everyone knew of the pugilistic prowess of the Rogers brothers and watched them defeat all other boxers of their weight aboard—though Joey did not himself box, but coached his brothers. While he still hoped to return to the ring one day, he had not yet recovered fully from the blow to the head he had sustained in the war, or from the blow to the psyche he had received in the ring. He still didn't feel clean enough to return to the game, even on an amateur level. Besides, as a seasoned professional, he could demolish any boxer on the ship if he wanted to—but would this be playing fair?

Aside from the Rogers brothers, the *Juneau* boxing team had some talented fighters, including Wyatt Butterfield and a heavy-

weight named Eddie Heinzinger, who some said had the makings of a world champion. Frank Sullivan was another excellent
boxer, but he had broken his hand while training before the war
erupted, and all he could do now was sit at ringside and remember how he had licked everyone on the block in those rousing
brawls in Waterloo—when his mother wasn't looking.

But why waste energy fighting one another when they could
show the other ships which vessel had the toughest crew? The
Juneau team looked around for a "sucker" ship to challenge
and found just the one—the USS *Northhampton*, which was
anchored nearby and had a good boxing team. The challenge
was accepted, and within hours every available penny on both
ships was bet on the respective teams.

Coaching the *Juneau* fighters was an old fight fan, Lt. Roger
W. O'Neil, a physician and preacher who amazed even a professional like Joey Rogers with his knowledge of boxing. Joey himself was too busy coaching his brothers to help perfect the
talents of others. Besides, O'Neil, as a healer of their wounds,
was universally loved by the men. Though an officer, he was
just one of the guys, "shooting the bull" with them, guiding
them on family problems, and appearing almost hurt when anyone had the audacity to salute him. All this, and lessons on
how to slug a guy out, too. If Captain Swenson was like a father
to the men, O'Neil was like a brother.

And he was apparently a good coach, for the *Juneau* boxers
won every bout decisively. The three fighting Rogers brothers,
Heinzinger, and Butterfield all knocked out their foes, with Butterfield savoring his victory, as usual, with the special passion
of a man intoxicated by the narcotic of popular acclaim. And
now, suddenly, the men of the *Juneau* were "rich," and morale
soared to a new high. Captain Swenson shared their joy. He
needed a lift. But was this an omen of future good luck, as the
crew thought, or simply the sunshine before a storm that would
sweep away wishful dreams as illusory as leaves drifting in a
treeless land?

Swenson had no illusions. He knew that ship after Allied ship
was being sunk, and that the chances of a vessel emerging from
a battle unscathed or even afloat, especially one as fragile as his

own, were diminishing rapidly as fiery sea battles raged across the South Pacific.

Finally, the Navy, in its *Information Bulletin*, advised all brothers and other close relatives aboard the same ship to apply for duty on separate vessels in order to minimize family casualties. Clearly, the Navy had second thoughts about its decision to let the Sullivan and the Rogers brothers serve on the same ship, though it did not force them to separate, for that would bring public attention to its original "error," to all the ballyhoo it had circulated about the "families that stayed together . . ."

The Sullivans ignored the advice, but Joey Rogers, as his brothers' keeper, began to wonder if his family should not take it. He had already seen the ghastly visage of death and was consumed by the image of men turned into inanimate wax dolls. Men who might have been his brothers, gone all at once, forever. Could he really keep his promise to Pop and protect all his sons?

Destiny would now intervene in an odd way—all because Joey was a lousy tailor. When he had come aboard the *Juneau*, the crew needed a tailor and Joey volunteered, though he had never even threaded a needle in his life. Sounded like an easy job, and he could learn as he sewed. At the same time, Pat became a barber, and Louie a laundryman. (Jimmy was appointed a captain's orderly like Wyatt Butterfield and Frank Holmgren.) Why not learn a trade—just in case?

But Joey operated his sewing machine as if he were in the ring jabbing an opponent mercilessly. If he broke no bones now, he broke needles by the score. So, while in Nouméa, Joey took time out from training his brothers and asked the supply officer if he could go ashore and replenish his needle supply. The officer pointed to a ship anchored nearby and said:

"That's a supply ship there. Take a launch and get what you need."

When Joey climbed aboard the ship, he wandered into the mess hall where he heard whoops and cheers. A boxing match! There were even training facilities available. The Navy wanted to separate brothers. Well, he had found the ideal ship. The four Rogerses could split up, and Jimmy and he could switch to it. Jimmy held the most promise as a boxer and would benefit most from this training. As for himself, he had given his word to Pop that he would take special care of his little brother.

Joey approached a group of men and said, "I've got three brothers over there on the *Juneau,* and we're all boxers. Could two of us swap with two of your guys?"

"You mean that beautiful cruiser there?" said one man, pointing to the *Juneau.* "Sure, I'll go."

Others now clamored to go, too. And shortly, the executive officer of the ship chose two and approved the switch.

Joey quickly returned to the *Juneau*—without his needles—and called his brothers to a meeting in Pat's barbershop.

"They got boxing matches over there all the time," Joey told them. "The Navy wants us to split up, and that's a good ship to be on."

Pat and Louie wanted to stay aboard the *Juneau.* Pat was earning extra money from tips, and Louie from extra duty, and both were sending the money to their fiancées so they would have a nest egg when they got married.

"We'll stay," Pat said. "You and Jimmy go."

That's just what Joey wanted. He turned to Jimmy and said, "Jim, come with me. You're the youngest, and Pop said I should keep an eye on you."

"Yeah," Pat agreed, adding, "Jimmy, you're unbeaten. I guarantee you that after the war you'll be the world champion."

Jimmy then said, looking at Joey, "I don't give a shit. Where you go, Joey, I go."

Joey rushed to tell his executive officer, who immediately got Captain Swenson's approval.

"Good idea," the skipper said. "Let them do it. The Sullivans shouldn't be together either." Now if only they would follow suit, he could sleep a little better at night.

And, in fact, the Sullivans began to consider dividing up after the Rogerses informed them of their plans.

"It's using your head to split up," Joey told George Sullivan. "If the ship is hit, you might all get killed."

Maybe Joey was right, George conceded. He'd talk to his brothers about it and they'd probably agree now. There were an awful lot of ships going down.

"Well," said Joey, nodding toward the supply ship, "what about that one over there? Come with us."

No, George replied, he and Frank were in the Navy before the war and had a lot of friends who were now at sea. When they came across some of those friends, he and Frank could switch to their ship.

At the same time, Jimmy, as he packed his gear bag in the locker room, told Albert Sullivan about the swap.

"Maybe you're doing the right thing," Al said. "I'll talk to my brothers. Yeah, we might split up, too. Lots of luck."

"Good-bye, pal," Jimmy said. "Don't wait too long."

There were more good-byes at the gangway as Joey and Jimmy were about to jump aboard the motor launch that would take them to their new home. The four brothers hugged and kissed.

"Take care of yourselves," Pat said to his two departing siblings. "We'll see you as soon as this mess is over."

"Yeah," replied Joey, "write once in a while and let us know how everything's going. We'll keep in touch."

There was silence for a moment, and Joey and Jimmy felt like throwing down their gear bags and staying aboard. But a launch from the other ship was already on the way to the *Juneau* with their replacements.

Destiny had spoken.

"We've made it!" Tsukuo Nakano screamed as the *I-26*, swirling in smoke, freed itself from the reef with a slight creak. Saved by the gods once more! And once more Commander Yokota smiled in relief after a narrow escape. He had by now determined exactly where he was to meet the planes to be refueled, and he immediately ordered the crew to head for the spot, about ten miles away. When the submarine finally reached it, he decided to float during the night and dive underwater at dawn, October 18, to wait for the planes.

While waiting, he ordered his senior officer to send one of his men on a dangerous mission to investigate whether the reef had damaged any of his six torpedo launching tubes. The man would have to swim beneath the craft to check them.

"Does anyone swim well?" the senior officer asked his men

at breakfast. Petty Officer Shoji replied, "I do," and he volunteered for the mission.

Shortly the *I-26* surfaced under a glittering morning sun, and Shoji, wearing fatigues and a new pair of Army gloves, prepared to dive into the rolling waves.

"In case the enemy attacks," Yokota told him, "we'll immediately go underwater. You just swim in place and wait for us."

A lifeline was then tied around Shoji, and he leaped off the deck of the starboard bow into the sea. The commander waited anxiously on the bridge. As the minutes passed, they seemed like hours. Why didn't Shoji return? Perhaps a shark . . . ?

Finally Shoji popped his head out of the water. "Get up here quickly!" Yokota cried. The young man climbed up a rope to the deck and rushed to the bridge.

Four of the six launching tubes were completely crushed, Shoji sadly reported.

Yokota, too, felt crushed. That meant he would be able to fire only two torpedoes at a time when *I-26* went searching for prey. What terrible luck. This time, the number 6 did not work in the submarine's favor.

But there was little time for fretting. Two seaplanes soon flew over low and banked their wings, a friendly identification signal. The commander ordered, "All prepare for refueling!"

The planes landed on the water and, one by one, skimmed alongside the submarine to be refueled. One crewman aboard the first plane leaned out of a window munching a rice ball and washing it down with a bottle of pop. Nakano pondered the incongruity of the scene. It was a beautiful sunny day, and the sea was calm. The kind of day, joyous and peaceful, he would spend picnicking on the farm—munching on rice balls and sipping pop. . . .

Suddenly there was a shout: "Enemy plane!"

Then the order: "Stop fueling! Submerge at once!"

The first seaplane, already fueled, zoomed up toward the enemy aircraft, and the second followed as soon as the rope connecting it to the submarine had been cut. But the American plane made a wide swing to the left and vanished in the distance.

I-26, which had made a quick dive, now resurfaced. "We bet-

ter not stay here any longer," Commander Yokota mumbled.
And the submarine dove again and headed southeast on its third
mission—to seek out an enemy ship. Two torpedoes, one ship.
The reef had robbed him of additional prey. And who could
depend on a mere two torpedoes to hit one ship?

Aboard the *Juneau*, the Sullivans maintained a collective link
with home even as they considered splitting up. Red, the most
exuberant of the brothers, did most of the writing. In one letter
to his mother, he wrote:

"Our mail took quite a while to catch up with us, but when
it did, oh, boy, what a treat! Fifty-three letters came at once.
But we haven't time now to read them all. We're going out
looking for jaybirds (enemy planes). . . . Don't worry about us.
Keep your chin up. We'll be all right. We're looking after each
other."

And to his beloved Margaret, who begged him to take care of
himself, Red wrote: "If the motorcycle racing didn't kill me,
how in the hell can the Japs get me and keep me away from
you?"

Red did not know that his family was almost as crazy about
"Marge" when she visited them as he was. As his sister, Genevieve, would write to him on October 28:

Dear "Pal" Red,
    Had to write and tell you I think Marge is a peach. . . . I
stayed off work three days, so I could entertain her and
show her Waterloo. . . .
    Marge is coming back this summer for a week and wants
me to go back to Pittsburgh with her for a week. Again Red,
I'll say she's grand; mom and dad think so, too. . . .
    Tell the boys to write me. I miss you all, though I try to
keep my chin up. . . .
                                    Your pal and sis with Love,
                                                    Gen
P.S. Marge's ring is very nice. She sure thinks the world of
you, Red.

Red would never receive the letter—or know that the ring had been inadvertently thrown away. Nor, even in the midst of battle, would he, or his brothers, doubt that they would survive— together or apart. Red would even remind his mother of the childhood incident that had helped to reinforce their confidence that they lived charmed lives:

"Do you remember the time we boys went out on the Cedar in the old rowboat? . . . Keep your chin up."

CHAPTER

· 8 ·

The Last Gamble

SHORTLY AFTER THE NAVAL BATTLE OF OCTOBER 26, COMMANDER Hara strode into Admiral Yamamoto's headquarters at Truk on naval business and found a grim and tense man, almost devoid of fight. His brushlike hair had grown noticeably grayer in the past few months and his thoughts seemed distant from the turmoil of battle.

This was not the same Yamamoto who had staged the spectacular strike at Pearl Harbor. His delicately structured face and five-foot-three-inch form belied his toughness and tenacity, although the Russo-Japanese War of 1905 had left him with numerous scars. He was known in Tokyo's geisha district of Shimbashi as "Eight Sen," since the geisha manicurists charged one sen per finger and two were missing from his left hand.

The attack at Pearl Harbor was Yamamoto's supreme gamble, and it had not paid off, at least strategically. He had bitterly opposed the Army's proposal to launch a war against the United States, fearing that America's potential military power could lead to disaster. He thus warned the cabinet with remarkable frankness, courage, and foresight:

"If I am told to fight regardless of consequences, I shall run wild for the first six months or year, but for the second and third years I have utterly no confidence. . . . We would have to march into Washington and sign the treaty in the White House. I wonder if our politicians have confidence as to the outcome and are prepared to make the necessary sacrifices."

When the cabinet refused to listen to him, Yamamoto, bowing to the inevitable, calculated that Japan's only chance for victory lay in forcing America to accept a negotiated peace. And to do this, he would have to knock out the U.S. fleet in a single, devastating, surprise blow. He thus proposed and vigorously lobbied for one of history's greatest military gambles. The irony was painful. As he would confide to an old classmate a day before his forces reached Pearl Harbor:

"What a strange position I find myself in now—having to make a decision diametrically opposed to my personal opinion, with no choice but to push full speed in pursuance of that decision."

Now, less than a year later, his warning to the cabinet about possible defeat seemed to be materializing. Since that single mighty blow demolished neither America's war machine nor its will to fight, Japan would have no partner at the negotiating table. And while the enemy was growing stronger each day, Japan was growing weaker.

Yes, his fears had been justified. He was especially tormented by a kind of mystical belief that he had not much longer to live and therefore might never have the chance to finish what he had begun at Pearl Harbor, even if Japan's fortunes took a turn for the better.

"I fear," he wrote to a friend in late August 1942, "that I have perhaps one hundred days left to me, and that I must complete my life in their passage."

On October 2, Yamamoto vented his frustration to another friend: "Things here are proving hard going. I felt from the start that America was not likely to relinquish lightly positions established at the cost of such sacrifices, and I pressed the view that a high degree of preparation and willingness to make sacrifices would be necessary on our side, but everybody here always persists in facile optimism until the very worst actually happens. I envy them."

Even so, Yamamoto appeared to be conquering his own pessimism, which Hara so abhorred by the end of October. For the Army, it seemed, had finally begun to realize that Japan was losing its hold on Guadalcanal and almost any hope of winning the war. Perhaps, it apparently concluded, Yamamoto was right after all. In past weeks, not only had many Navy craft been lost, but many Army units had been licked—driven into the jungle from the perimeters of Henderson Field.

And so, with the Army's approval, Yamamoto planned another huge gamble. Some sixty thousand men would land in Guadalcanal with supplies for twenty days and attack the airfield, while naval guns turned its planes and facilities into twisted steel and rubble. At the same time, he would lure into a night battle what he felt was a dwindling American force in the Pacific. If he won the gamble, Japan would probably be able to raise its victory flag on Guadalcanal in December, and from there his forces could perhaps hop all the way to Australia and New Zealand. With those lands stuffed in its bulging pocket, Japan could offer a peace it would dominate. If he lost the gamble, his country would almost surely lose the war.

Hara was pleased to learn that he would play a role in this plan. His destroyer, *Amatsukaze*, would be one of seventeen warships, including the battleships *Hiei* and *Kirishima*, that would churn through the Slot escorting transports to Guadalcanal as destroyers did on a smaller scale every night. Then they would rain shells on the airfield, finally clearing the way for Japanese troops waiting in the surrounding fetid forests to storm the field. This would be the decisive attack, the key to glorious victory. According to Yamamoto's information, the Americans had nothing in the area that could challenge such an armada.

Bull Halsey could not have agreed more heartily. In the first days of November, evidence mounted that Japan was preparing a giant offensive that could cancel out the recent American land victories. On the night of November 2, the Tokyo Express landed fifteen hundred troops east of Henderson Field. And between the second and the tenth, destroyers and even cruisers shuttled between Truk and Guadalcanal sixty-five times loaded with reinforcements and tons of equipment for Japanese forces west of the airfield. Some of these vessels were sunk, but others managed to slip through the many gaps left by missing links in the Allied bracelet of steel ringing the island.

During this time, reconnaissance pilots flying over the serene waters of Truk, Rabaul, and the Shortland Islands of the Upper Solomons spotted swarms of Japanese ships meshing into chaotic formations like minnows in a fishbowl. Halsey knew a battle was brewing and wondered how he could enter it with his depleted ragtag fleet of largely old and undermanned vessels. He decided he had better hold on even to his damaged ships rather than send them back to Pearl Harbor for repairs. The flimsiest vessels would be thrown into the coming battle, the *Juneau* among them—though they might be pitted against battleships. Major enemy landings must be stopped, while American landings must be accelerated. And the airfield must remain open so that planes could help in this crucial effort.

Halsey would send four naval groups to Guadalcanal, including almost every ship he could get his hands on; if its engine worked, the craft was good enough to fight. Commanding the operation would be Rear Adm. Richmond K. Turner, who headed the Amphibious Forces in the South Pacific.

Two main task groups, one under Turner himself and the other under Rear Adm. Norman Scott, would escort transports crammed with supplies and about 5,500 troops.

A third group commanded by Rear Adm. Daniel Callaghan would support Turner's group, screen the unloading operation, and challenge the Japanese units that dared shell the airfield.

A fourth group formed around the carrier *Enterprise* was to help divert the bombardment, but since the *Enterprise* was still under repair at Nouméa, this group would not be available in time to take part in the operation.

Turner and Scott would depart at different times from their bases, joining near the point of landing adjacent to the airfield. The exact times hinged largely on Japanese plans. Since U.S. Navy cryptologists had broken the Japanese naval code in the first days of November, they knew from intercepted messages exactly what Admiral Yamamoto was scheming. Thus, on November 10, Admiral Nimitz cabled Halsey:

"There is every indication that a major operation, assisted by carrier striking forces, is slated to support movement of Army transports to Guadalcanal. While this looks like the big push, I am confident that you and your forces will take their measure."

Halsey smiled. He was throwing everything he had into the operation, but did Nimitz think that Bull Halsey was God?

"It's good to know that the old man has so much confidence in me," he said wryly to Capt. Miles Browning, his chief of staff, as he handed him Nimitz's message.

Halsey sensed that the decisive battle of the Pacific war was at hand, and that a miracle might be needed to win it. But wasn't that his job now—to do what only God could do?

As Captain Swenson read his orders assigning the *Juneau* to Admiral Callaghan's Task Group 67.4, he saw his worst fears coming true. Because the Navy was so desperately short of better-suited ships, the *Juneau*, which was built strictly to fire at aircraft, would now have to attack surface vessels and expose its thin skin to their fire, perhaps the fire of battleships with their powerful 14-inch guns. Since the flotilla would be arriving at Guadalcanal at night when it would be safer for the soldiers to dash ashore and the sailors to unload the supplies, there would probably be need only for suicidal ship-to-ship fighting, not for antiaircraft defense. As for the Sullivans, it was too late to split them up; they were now a family in grave peril.

Nor was Swenson alone in his mounting concern. His men, like those of Japanese submarine *I-26*, found a certain mystical message in numbers. While the *I-26* crew attributed its good luck to the submarine's constant association with the numeral 6, the men of the *Juneau*—and the other ships in Task Group 67.4—were confronted with the unlucky number 13.

Thirteen ships constituted this group, whose numerals (not counting the fraction) added up to thirteen. And they would reach their destination on Friday the thirteenth. Of course, the destroyer *Fletcher* seemed in the most trouble of all. Its bow number was 445, numerals that totaled thirteen, and it was armed with thirteen guns. How fortunate were those not aboard *that* ship!

Vice Adm. Hiroaki Abe didn't need an unlucky number to envision disaster. He had not wanted the job, yet he was now commanding one of the two naval bombardment forces that would clear the way for eleven heavily escorted Army transports scheduled to sail from Shortland Island to Cape Esperance, off Guadalcanal, in the early morning of November 12—just as the American forces were also heading for a showdown.

The transports would be carrying seven thousand soldiers, over thirty thousand artillery shells, and supplies for thirty thousand men starving in the jungles and dying at enemy hands without the means to fight back. Abe's escort, Battleship Division 11, which belonged to the Advanced Force of the Combined Fleet commanded by Adm. Nobutake Kondo, would shell Henderson Field. And the Eighth Fleet, under Adm. Gunichi Mikawa, would heavily bombard it the next day to further smooth the way for the landings. By this time, Admiral Yamamoto and his lieutenants calculated, the airfield with its planes and installations would be ground into dust and the American hold on Guadalcanal finally broken.

Abe, a destroyer specialist and combat veteran known for his extreme caution, was highly skeptical, however, that Admiral Yamamoto's battle plan would work. Abe was to lead a seventeen-ship squadron, including two battleships, one cruiser, and fourteen destroyers, in a shore bombardment with incendiary shells—just as another force had done about two weeks earlier. But while his predecessor succeeded, the Americans, he was convinced, were not stupid enough to be caught a second time with their guard down. Even his vastly superior firepower did little to bolster his confidence; while his two battleships carried sixteen 14-inch guns, the Americans, according to his information, had no battleships available and their cruisers could fire only 8-inch guns.

Abe's pessimism was apparently fueled in part by a severe depression triggered by the fate of his lifelong friend Rear Adm. Aritomo Goto, who was killed in the Battle of Savo Island at the moment of Japan's greatest sea triumph. Goto had died believing that he was a victim of Japanese fire. As he lay on the devastated bridge of his cruiser, he mumbled, "*Bakayaro! Bakayaro!*" meaning "Stupid bastard!"—an epithet apparently intended for the man who supposedly fired the missile, or possibly for himself.

Abe could not forget that terrible death scene, as described to him by survivors, and he didn't feel that virtual suicide would be a more satisfying way to die. Yes, many Japanese troops had landed on Guadalcanal without a single Yankee in sight, but this, he felt, was a deceptive lull. He sensed that this time the Americans would be waiting for him, and he wondered how many of his ships would be sailing back to headquarters.

Commander Hara was more optimistic as Admiral Abe's task force began its three-hundred-mile journey from Shortland Island to Guadalcanal. Yamamoto had finally embarked on a new gamble that could yield handsome dividends. Still, Hara kept in mind the warning of Admiral Nagumo after the battle of Santa Cruz: "You'll have a tougher time from now on." Nor could he ignore Abe's "defeatist" mood.

Hara had learned from his samurai grandfather, who had implanted in his mind numerous images of battle glory in hopeless situations, that a warrior must never give in to the evil of defeatism, even if death was inevitable. How brave and wise his grandfather had been. Hara could close his eyes and picture the old man, white-haired and erect as he sat reciting analects of Confucious before the family altar, which housed the tablets of his ancestors and his lord.

And Hara would remember even more vividly how this exalted figure lay on his deathbed surrounded by the family and called for his grandson. How he placed his treasured samurai sword in the child's tiny hand. Coughing as he struggled to speak, the old man murmured:

"Tamei, this is yours. Now listen carefully to your grandpa's last words. You are the son of samurai and you will remember that a samurai lives in such a way that he is always prepared to die. Don't misinterpret that teaching. Never seek an easy death, for that would be against the true spirit of Bushido."

And now, as he sailed into the unknown, Hara would recall these words. No, he would not seek an easy death, whatever lay ahead. But he was not afraid to die.

At about two P.M., November 8, Admiral Turner's task group, covered by Admiral Callaghan's support force, steamed out of Nouméa harbor to a rousing send-off by the ships anchored in the bay. As whistles blew in screeching cacophony, white-clad crews stood at attention and smartly saluted their departing comrades, whom they would later join for the all-out confrontation with the enemy.

"Their expression of Godspeed sent shivers of pride down our spines," Wyatt Butterfield would later say.

But Butterfield—and most other members of the *Juneau* crew—did not shiver with fear, for they were sure that the *Juneau* could never be sunk. It was too new, too fast, too well-commanded. And the Sullivans, though now willing to consider splitting up, were among the optimists. They talked more about Waterloo than about war and could hardly wait to get back to shore and hear their names shouted at mail call. What was happening at home? They would spend almost their entire leave reading the dozens of letters that would be waiting for them.

On November 10, the third day at sea, shivers of fear did shake the crew as the flotilla splashed its way northward. For it sighted a large Japanese patrol plane, which followed the ships at a cautious distance, circling frustratingly out of the range of their fire. Though the pilot, it seemed, had no intention of attacking, the shivers did not cease, for he was evidently sizing up the strength of the force in preparation for a full-scale attack, perhaps within hours.

Admiral Turner saw this as an ominous sign. He immediately ordered all ships to go into an "Alert 2," and later into an "Alert 1," requiring the crews to man their battle stations. An eerie feeling enveloped the men, but they were relieved when that evening their group rendezvoused with the force of Admiral Scott, who was aboard the *Atlanta*. Together the two forces, preceded by Callaghan's support group, slithered through the twenty-mile-wide Lunga Channel between the lush coastlines of Guadalcanal and the neighboring island of Tulagi just before midnight and entered Ironbottom Sound.

At dawn, November 12, the armada arrived at a point off Guadalcanal adjacent to the airfield and dropped anchor. As the transports began to spew their troops and supplies, the *Juneau* and other warships maneuvered in a protective semicircle. Enemy artillery rained shells on the beach sporadically but was soon silenced by the guns of the Marines ashore and the ships

• 94 •

offshore. These ships moved up and down the beachfront, mowing down not only enemy soldiers but the coconut trees that hid them, while drilling deep holes in the jungle that would serve as graves for hundreds. Meanwhile, men unloaded the transports in feverish haste. When would an air attack start?

At about two P.M. the siren wailed aboard the *Juneau* and the boatswain's cry echoed through the ship: "All hands, general quarters! Man your battle stations! Prepare to resist air attack!"

Within minutes, the transports weighed anchor and the barges raced for shelter. Then the planes came—about twenty-five torpedo bombers and six Zero fighters—swooping down almost to water level.

One of the men waiting on the *Juneau* behind a 50-caliber machine gun at Battle Station 2 was SM2c. Joseph P. Hartney. His dark eyes, shadowed by heavy brows, reflected the tension of anticipation, as did his tightly clamped lips, which stretched like a pencil line curved down at both ends.

Hartney, at twenty-one, had been in the Navy for four years, having joined for a double reason. He loved adventure, and he wished to help his family, which had been thrust into poverty when his father lost his business in the Depression. He especially wanted to earn enough money to marry a girl named Lucy, whom he had fallen in love with when he was sixteen. As a young boy, Hartney, a New York native, had gone to live with his aunt in Connecticut to reduce family expenses. But as soon as he turned seventeen, he dropped out of high school to become a sailor, even though he was a good student. However, he eventually earned a diploma as well as a pilot's license while serving in the Navy.

Hartney's enlistment period was to end in May 1942, and he couldn't wait to finally come home to Lucy and marry her. Pearl Harbor ended that dream, however, and so he had to settle for a ten-day leave before shipping out with the *Juneau*. Still, those were a memorable ten days. Marriage? Not until the war was over, Hartney argued. He didn't want to leave her a war widow. But Lucy was determined. She wanted to get pregnant, she said, so that if anything did happen to him, she would at least have his child.

And so they were married and tried their best to produce a

living memory. Some weeks later, at sea, Hartney received the good news from his wife: she was pregnant. The father-to-be, in his joy, vowed to fight all the harder to help get the damn war over with. He had to survive now. Besides, he loved the Navy, and now he had the opportunity to repay it for opening the way to a bright future. But then, as he squatted behind his machine gun aiming at an enemy who was intent on killing him, it occurred to him that he might not have a future. He might never see his child. That was his greatest fear.

Hartney and the other gunners, including Allen Heyn and Wyatt Butterfield, let the planes roar toward them in an aerial banzai charge, holding their fire as Captain Swenson had ordered, and waiting for the command of Lieutenant Wang. The planes grew larger, larger, until the men could discern their khaki tint, the splash of red on the fuselage, and the gleam of their spinning props. Fingers trembled against the trigger. Finally . . .

"Commence firing!"

As Hartney would later describe the action: "A solid sheet of flame leaped out of the column. Every gun on the *Juneau* opened up, shaking the little ship with the tremendous force of the recoil until she bucked and shivered in her course. The 5-inch guns were the bass to the music we played—not the resounding roll of a battlewagon's turret guns, but a shattering clap, like the first reverberations of close thunder.

"The 1.1 cracked in earsplitting baritone, a violent, rending staccato. And filling in every split-second lull, the comparative tenor of the 50-caliber blended the whole into one continuous, nerve-blasting cacophony. And above the roar, and weaving their sound through the lower pitch, the shells whispered away into the distance."

With the ships maneuvering in a way that made them elusive targets, every Japanese missile missed its mark. At the same time, every plane hit a "wall of lead" and, with fire streaming from its tail, plummeted into the sea, some even before they broke formation to attack. And over the watery graves, parachutes with their human loads descended like giant flowers sent from heaven for the funeral. Those planes that could still struggle along, their engines whining and wheezing, fell victim to

Grumman Wildcat defenders that shot them down in streaking spasms of fury.

One Marine flier shot down a Zero, then dove and destroyed two torpedo bombers, knocking out the third plane before the first had splashed into the sea. The Japanese pilots, who fought fanatically, were dismayed by the fierce resistance. A particularly shaken airman who had been downed, shot his officer when the man tried to prevent him from being saved by an American rescue craft. Still, most of the Japanese refused to be rescued, shooting comrades who disagreed, then shooting themselves. It was better to rise to heaven than to fall into American hands.

Only one plane is known to have escaped the aerial slaughter. But the American fleet did not emerge from the attack unscathed. The sea devoured four American fighters, and missiles fired by friendly guns bit chunks out of several ships. The cruiser *San Francisco* sustained the worst casualties when a blazing enemy plane crashed into it, wiping out the crews of three 20mm machine guns that kept spitting bullets until the last second. The crash killed twenty-four men and wounded many others. Ironically, the executive officer, Comdr. Mark H. Crouter, though badly injured, refused to be evacuated and was killed that night when a shell exploded in his cabin as he lay bandaged in a bunk.

But the Americans had won the opening phase of the Battle of Guadalcanal, and the men in Admiral Turner's force rejoiced. Not for long, though, for everyone knew what was soon to come.

No one knew better, of course, than Admiral Turner. All through the day he had been perusing reports of a buildup of Japanese surface forces north of Guadalcanal. It seemed that there were forty-eight ships in the enemy armada, including at least two battleships, two to four heavy cruisers, two light cruisers, ten to twelve destroyers, and the rest troop transports.

Was his own small flotilla to face so formidable a force in what could be the decisive battle of the Pacific War? Admirals Turner, Callaghan, and Scott sat down on the sandy beach to reach a decision—how to meet the momentous threat, or at least survive it.

After listening to his two subordinates, Turner decided on his course. Callaghan, he said, would take over command of all thirteen healthy warships. He himself would lead the transports back to Nouméa with an escort of only three damaged or fuel-short destroyers and two old destroyer minesweepers.

But he would be placing himself and his men in great danger, the others pointed out.

Turner, however, was firm. There was no choice; every usable warship had to be employed in the coming battle. As it was, the Americans would be greatly outgunned.

Both Callaghan and Scott were unhappy. Callaghan had served as Admiral Ghormley's chief of staff but lost his job when Halsey took over as commander in the South Pacific. Halsey's problem was finding another prestigious slot for him. Callaghan had a chameleon career. In 1912, he had gone ashore with the force that landed in Nicaragua. In 1914, he had taken part in the Mexican campaign. And in 1916, he served as executive officer of the USS *New Orleans*. After many other naval assignments, he was appointed naval aide to President Roosevelt in 1938. He assumed command of the cruiser *San Francisco* in May 1941, and a year later became chief of staff to Ghormley.

White-haired, good-natured, but rather taciturn, Callaghan had no burning desire to play a blood-and-guts role amid smoking guns and smoldering decks. He preferred to sit and bellow orders in the quietude of the headquarters command room, where he perennially played the loyal subordinate.

But Halsey and Turner needed a combat commander urgently, and Callaghan needed a job. So he found himself head of Task Group 67.4, which had now become an attack force.

If Callaghan was unhappy because he would be commanding this force in the crucial battle, Admiral Scott was unhappy because he would not be commanding it. Scott was a combat veteran and war hero. In the Battle of Cape Esperance in October, he had brilliantly led the American force to one of the most decisive U.S. victories to date. He was a man who could never be comfortable behind a desk, but now he would be deputy to the ultimate desk man, Admiral Callaghan—and only because Callaghan had fifteen days seniority over him!

Still, Callaghan, with his good-humored, easygoing manner, was popular among the men—especially with the crew of the

San Francisco, which he had commanded before the war and would command now. And "Uncle Dan," as his sailors affectionately called him, loved them and their ship. Moreover, he felt a special loyalty to this cruiser because he was a native San Franciscan. Sentimentality thus helped to persuade him to make the vessel his flagship—even though it lacked the advance radar equipment that was installed on several other ships in his flotilla. He was, in a sense, returning home, and who wouldn't prefer to fight for his own home if it was in danger?

Nevertheless, just before setting out on his mission, Callaghan was seen pacing the flag bridge of his beloved ship, muttering that the venture was flawed and that if only he had enough time, he would try to convince Halsey of this. He did little to assuage the anxiety of his officers and men. They would be in for a rough night, he growled to those on the bridge with him.

At about five P.M., after the transports had begun unloading again, Admiral Callaghan's voice calmly boomed the expected yet shocking news over the IMC, the intership radio: the main Japanese force was bearing down on them. This was not the Tokyo Express, but a force of "forty-eight" ships, including battleships, heavy cruisers, light cruisers, destroyers, and transports. And he stated succinctly:

"We are going out to meet them!"

On the *Juneau*, the men looked at each other in silence. Forty-eight ships! They did not realize that although the Japanese had that many at their disposal, only seventeen were sighted heading toward the beach near the airfield—just four more than Callaghan had, but including two battleships against none for the Americans. No matter how lopsided the odds, this was it! Now the Marines, who had been fighting savagely in the jungle all these weeks against constantly replenished enemy forces, would no longer be wailing, "Where the hell is the fleet?"

As the transports finished coughing up men and supplies that evening, the *Juneau* sailors forced down their chow, showered, and put on clean clothes—it seemed the right thing to do before meeting one's Maker. Then they went out on the deck into the silky darkness of night, breathing in the still tropical air that smelled of gardenias, a sweet, sickening odor emanating from the steamy thickets of Guadalcanal. The smell of death.

Battle stations sounded, and soon the men were fondling the weapons they had to depend on to get them home safely to their loved ones. Hartney took out his wife's picture and "looked at it for one long moment." She must now be buying the rattles and the crib for the baby that would soon come. He slipped her picture into his pocket and felt his way along in the darkness to Battle Station 2. Already there was his best friend, John Rudolph, a signalman and former Army sergeant from Pittsburgh, who was usually brimming with good humor but was now grim. They stood silently by their gun, trying to ignore the unrelenting funereal scent of the gardenias.

Allen Heyn sat behind his gun at the same battle station and munched on a sandwich, grumpy because he had been kept on duty all day and now at night without any time off even to eat a hot meal with his shipmates or take a hot shower. But George Sullivan was, as usual, around to prop up his morale with stories of home and words of encouragement. George didn't seem to be afraid, so why should he be?

Though the custodian of about six hundred depth charges, George wondered whether he would have an opportunity to fire any of them. Submarines didn't usually get involved in major battles, especially in the straits, where it was hard to maneuver. He had heard Admiral Callaghan's announcement over the talker phone, and he couldn't imagine himself being left out of what could be the biggest sea battle of the war.

"I don't think I'll be doing much with the depth charges," George told Heyn.

"Well," Heyn replied, "we gunners can use help. How about passing us ammo through the hatch?"

The hatch led to the chiefs' quarters and lockers nearby, which were crammed with ammunition.

"I'll be glad to," George responded. "This is going to be a big one."

If Heyn drew strength from George's calm eagerness for battle, he detected a thinly masked concern in his friend's eyes. After all, there were five of them, five brothers—and this rather delicate ship was about to engage a greatly superior force. Was George now sorry that the five had not split up in time? Heyn did not know, but he could imagine his own feeling if his twin brother had lived and been on this ship. With death creeping closer, it was surely easier to face battle knowing that your loved ones remained behind than worrying that they might die with you.

Even so, George Sullivan was stalwart and could be a big help to the gunners. A good thing there was no real submarine threat to keep him busy.

At about this time, in submarine I-26, Commander Yokota muttered to himself as he peered through his binoculars at the dark, forbidding landscape of Guadalcanal, "They are good fighters. I expect a big game tomorrow."

Overhearing Yokota, Tsukuo Nakano grew impatient. Headquarters had informed the commander that the Japanese would launch a massive attack on the airfield the following day, and that American ships were lurking nearby. Now, Nakano felt, he might have the chance to sink at least one ship.

"As a torpedoman," he mused, "I cannot return home without having launched a single torpedo."

If only he could launch all six torpedoes at once! But only two launching tubes worked after that struggle on the reef, and so the chances of his hitting a target had been reduced by two-thirds.

As the submarine floated off the coast of the island of San Cristobal, southeast of Guadalcanal, Nakano noted how uneasy Yokota looked. He understood why. The I-26 was to meet submarine I-15 in this area and replace it, but the commander could not contact it. Suddenly, bombs could be heard exploding some distance away, and the I-26 trembled from the impact. American planes! Yokota knew now that American ships wouldn't be far behind. The planes were obviously seeking to clear the path for them.

He tried in vain to contact I-15 again and guessed that it had been hit by a depth bomb. Now it was payback time.

"Stop the engines!" Yokota ordered. And in the silence, the I-26, like a wily predator fish, waited for prey.

* * *

Admiral Turner expected the Japanese force to churn into this zone from the north at about midnight, so, close to ten P.M., he ordered his transports to stop unloading supplies even though about 10 percent still had not been carried ashore. Then Admiral Callaghan, who exuded the drama of an old sailing captain, ordered his ships into a single-line battle formation especially common to the era he seemed to represent. In the vanguard would be the destroyers *Cushing, Laffey, O'Bannon,* and *Sterett;* in the rear, the destroyers *Aaron Ward, Barton, Monssen,* and *Fletcher;* and in the center, the heavy cruisers *Portland* and *San Francisco,* and light cruisers *Helena, Atlanta,* and *Juneau.*

Callaghan felt that ships moving in a single column could better navigate through the channels and more easily communicate with one another. But for some reason, he failed to place in lead positions the three cruisers, including the *Juneau,* and the two destroyers that mounted the latest search radar. Instead, the *Atlanta,* with inferior radar, would lead the cruisers while he would continue to use the *San Francisco* as his flagship, though it also lacked the newest radar. He would thus have to rely on the vessels with superior radar in his task group to find out where the enemy was making its moves before he could give credible orders. He saw the disadvantages, but he would stick with the *San Francisco,* his baby, no matter what happened.

Nevertheless, what could happen worried Callaghan. His hodgepodge of ships had never operated as a team before that day. Nor was there time to give his commanders a battle plan or the intelligence data needed to keep them abreast of enemy movements from hour to hour, minute to minute.

Oh, how comfortable that swivel chair was back in headquarters, where he could shuffle papers instead of ships.

Shortly, with Callaghan's protective force leading the way, Turner directed his transports back through the Lunga Channel, as lightning flashed through the starlit sky, illuminating some cottonball clouds. After emerging at the southern exit, the two admirals bid each other good-bye, and while the transports headed toward Nouméa with a minimal escort, Callaghan, with grave misgivings, reversed course and once more his ships wended their way through the channel into Ironbottom Sound, this time to meet the enemy.

Admiral Abe, aboard the battleship *Hiei*, also drifted toward destiny with grave misgivings as he set out from the Shortland Islands on November 12. He headed south for Guadalcanal after the light cruiser *Nagara* and a group of eight destroyers arrived from Truk to join his two battleships, *Hiei* and *Kirishima*, and the three destroyers already under his command.

Hardly was Abe under way when, at about eight-thirty A.M., he sighted a B-17 silhouetted against the cloud-speckled sky. Like the Americans who had seen a Japanese plane scout the area while sailing to Guadalcanal from the opposite direction, Abe realized with a sense of dread that he would now lose even the advantage of surprise.

The admiral's primary mission, after all, was to bomb Henderson Field into cinders and pave the way for a landing of men and supplies, not to fight the American fleet. Thus, his battleships carried more incendiary shells to pound the airfield installations and aircraft than armor-piercing shells to fire at enemy vessels. He would therefore be able to inflict only limited damage, it seemed, on the American force. Even more frightening, if an enemy shell struck the incendiary missiles stored aboard one of his ships, it would turn the vessel into a torch. And, of course, he was aboard one of those ships.

Abe had hoped to slip into Ironbottom Sound and knock out the airfield before the Americans could strike. But now they would know exactly where the Japanese force was and how big it was and would no doubt be waiting for him. And this scenario hardened in his mind when he read reports of the Japanese air debacle while the Americans were landing reinforcements and supplies of their own.

Abe grew so anxious that he ordered a drastic change in his battle formation. He pulled his ships out of their single column and arranged them in a complex horseshoe formation made up of two separate arcs, with a third one, mostly transports and escorting destroyers, trailing behind them. In this formation, Abe believed, all his ships could fire at the enemy simultaneously and reduce the danger of a submarine or an aircraft launching a surprise attack.

To Tameichi Hara, aboard the destroyer *Amatsukaze*, this shift in formation was unwarranted and perilous. Such a "complex setup," he thought, was too unwieldy and could bring chaos in battle. Suddenly, thunderclouds gathered and a raging storm erupted, a driving downpour that almost turned day into night. Hara, barely able to see the nearest ship, waited expectantly for orders to slow down and move into a simpler, more manageable formation before the whole flotilla was thrown into disarray, with ships ramming into each other. But no order came.

In fact, Abe viewed the squall as a blessing. Who could attack him in such a blinding storm? When his staff officers advised him to slow down, he snapped:

"We must maintain this speed to reach the target area in time."

And his ships kept racing ahead at a speed of eighteen knots. Normally a squall on tropical seas hit a small area and lasted minutes, but now, hour after hour, torrents of rain swept the advancing fleet, drenching the men "like rats," Hara would say, and as the tension rose, sweat mingled with the raindrops.

The heavier the rain, the darker the day, the more buoyant was Abe. "This blessed squall," he told his officers, "is moving at the same speed and along the same course as we are." The ships were being carried by the storm.

When one of his scout planes reported that "more than a dozen enemy warships have been seen off Lunga," Abe was not greatly concerned.

"If heaven continues to side with us," he chortled, "we may not even have to do business with them."

Hara viewed the news differently and in his frustration saw heaven as turning against Abe's force.

And after several hours, at about ten P.M., Abe began to wonder if this might not, in fact, be true. The raindrops were like pearls, but pearls could be false and deceptive. His armada was safe as long as the storm lasted, but here he was approaching Guadalcanal and he couldn't even see his target. His men would be shooting like blind hunters. But he made the most of the situation. The storm did, after all, give him an excuse for turning back.

"All ships stand by for a simultaneous one-hundred-and-eighty-degree turn!" Abe ordered over the intership radio.

A 180-degree turn? Hara was stupefied. This wasn't what his samurai ancestors would have done. First, Abe recklessly raced through a storm, and now he was ordering a retreat. A large force could hardly make such a turn in good weather; in a storm, the maneuver could be disastrous. The ships might be separated in the wind and darkness or they might even collide. Coordination had to be almost perfect.

Then, to add to Hara's chagrin, the execution order was delayed, though timing was of vital importance. One minute passed, then a minute and a half. Still no order. "This can't be true!" he thought. Something had gone wrong! He cried into the radio-room tube:

"No execute order yet?"

"No, sir," a shaky voice replied. "Van destroyers *Yudachi* and *Harusame* have not yet acknowledged the standby orders."

Then, after three more minutes, the voice cried, "Commander, *Hiei* is talking to *Yudachi* and *Harusame* on medium-wave frequency."

"Oh, no!" Hara gasped. "Has *Hiei* lost its mind?"

The enemy could easily pick up medium-wave radio. Didn't Abe realize that now whatever advantage he had gained from concealment by the storm was squandered as a result of this stupidity?

Finally came the shout, "*Hiei* orders one-hundred-and-eighty-degree turn for all ships."

"Right!" Hara cried. "Turn one hundred and eighty degrees!"

And as his ship made the turn, he expected it to crash into another vessel at any moment. But it didn't. In fact, there were no ships anywhere to be seen through the murky air, since they were in a jumbled, uncontrollable order, each out of touch with the others.

Then, about thirty minutes after the ships had turned around, the squall finally ended. Glumly, Abe had no choice but to order another 180-degree turn. He would have to go back and shell that damn island after all.

Hara was gratified. Now maybe Abe would order a simpler formation. But the admiral called again for the same complex horseshoe, feeling safer with a broad front. And there was chaos again when the three destroyers on the right flank, while maneuvering, fell out of line and found themselves on the starboard quarter instead of on the port bow of the two battleships. Hara decided he would have to depend largely on the indomitable will of the samurai to prevail, or even to stay alive.

"Small island, sixty degrees to port!" a lookout shouted.

"High mountains dead ahead!" cried another.

Hara looked around and saw the shadowy form of Savo Island loom out of the darkness, and next to it the mountains of Guadalcanal outlined against the dark clouds. He "trembled in excitement" and inhaled the sweet-smelling tropical air.

"Prepare for gun and torpedo attack to starboard!" he ordered. "Gun range three thousand meters. Torpedo firing-angle fifteen degrees."

Hara's men ran silently to their battle stations, sensing they were about to engage in a savage battle.

But as Abe studied the reports piled on his desk, he was skeptical that enemy ships were any longer in the area, especially since observers on Guadalcanal now reported seeing no trace of American vessels off Lunga. He was reluctant to alert his ships for battle, even when he was only twelve miles offshore. Finally, he decided to gamble that the enemy ships reported earlier in the area had left. He hoped his men could now bombard the airfield without fear of naval guns responding. In a weary voice, he ordered his officers:

"Tell *Hiei* and *Kirishima* to ready main batteries for Type-3 shelling!"

On both ships, men carried the huge one-ton shells from their well-protected magazines to the turrets and stacked them up. Each of the vessels was loaded with hundreds of incendiary bombs. Abe was apprehensive. If he had guessed wrong, the Americans might blow up both battleships with two or three shells.

Then, at 11:42 P.M. the *Yudachi* reported starkly, "Enemy sighted!"

Abe froze. He had guessed wrong!

*　　*　　*

In the black velvet of a moonless night, the men on the *Juneau* could see nothing. Yet, Joe Hartney would write, "We had the feeling that we were being watched, that out there in the mantled sea, eyes peered at us, full of malevolence and hatred, waiting to pounce on us. Little pinpricks ran across our scalps."

The *Atlanta* was in the van, carrying the flag of Admiral Scott and now flanked by destroyers. And then came the other cruisers, with the *Juneau* bringing up the rear. The task group stopped between Guadalcanal and Florida Island, setting up a trap for the enemy armada.

Captain Swenson was tense as he paced the bridge. He told Frank Holmgren, who was on duty as his orderly:

"There's nothing for you to do here now, so you better go below and get some sleep; you won't get much tonight."

Holmgren, inferring that the long-awaited battle was about to break out, went down to his quarters and offered contrary advice to his shipmates:

"No sense hitting the sack. We're going to be up all night, anyway."

The men nervously sat around on their bunks waiting for further word when suddenly a voice boomed over the loudspeaker:

"Now hear this, now hear this . . ."

Muscles tightened, eyes met eyes. At last the moment . . .

"The captain has been advised that the workers at the Federal Shipbuilding Company, where the *Juneau* was built, have collected a fund for the crew of the *Juneau*. This fund is to be used for a ship's party or in any other way the crew wants to use it on its next liberty."

The crew listened in startled silence. This wasn't exactly the party it was expecting.

As tension mounted on the *Juneau*, one sailor with vision, Sea1c. Arthur Friend, went around with a knife slashing the ropes that tied the rubber rafts to the ship—just in case the crew had to abandon ship. Untied, the rafts would float when the vessel went down.

Friend had learned from childhood that having foresight was the way to survive. In Rigfield, Missouri, where he toiled in the fields helping his father, an impoverished sharecropper, he made sure they grew more than enough food so they could satisfy their hunger even if they lacked money to buy other necessities of life.

He dropped out of school at fourteen, after his family moved to southern California, and organized a country-western band in which he played the guitar. The band, however, broke up when the other musicians got too drunk to read their notes. With the Depression still on, jobs were scarce, but Friend was reluctant to go back to the farm to become a well-fed pauper again. He thought of joining the Army, but there might be a war and he'd have to sleep in the mud and "freeze my tail off." So he joined the Navy.

After serving in 1940–41 aboard the USS *Philadelphia*, which escorted ships loaded with supplies to Britain, Friend was, in the wake of Pearl Harbor, transferred to the *Juneau*. He immediately volunteered to cut hair in the ship's barbershop, together with Pat Rogers. Like Pat, he had never snipped a hair in his life, but it was easier wielding scissors than a machine gun or a mop. A way to make survival a little more enjoyable—and profitable, since his customers tipped him. Besides, he liked to talk, and in his sometimes unintelligible drawl he could talk to customers all day, though he didn't keep each too long or he would lose tips.

Square-jawed with mischievous, close-set eyes and a wide mouth appropriate to someone with so much to say, Friend was never lost for jokes or reminiscences of life on the farm. After the war, everyone learned, he would work on a ranch rounding up cattle and sit around a campfire at night plucking his guitar.

When Pat spoke of his fiancée, Friend talked of marriage, too. He had girlfriends but he didn't love anyone—except his mother. She was, he would muse with obvious pain, almost frantic with worry about him and his younger brother, Ralph, a Marine. His mother had more reason to worry about his brother than about him, Friend thought. Ralph, he regretted, was less cautious than he—joining the Marines! Storming a beach in a hail of bullets was not the surest way to stay alive and to keep Mama from dying of grief.

Anyway, Friend would try to marry before the war was over, whether he loved the woman or not, so a child would survive him in case he was killed. Then at least a little bit of him would continue to live even if he died. That was life, wasn't it? Surviving any way you could. . . .

And so Friend cut the ropes. Now let the damn ship sink! And he joined his fellow gunners, who, as Joe Hartney would write, could only stand by their guns and "wait and put their trust in the commanders."

One problem was that if the ship sank, help might not come immediately, for the task group was under orders to maintain radio silence. Any intership communication would have to be limited, and in the chaos of a night battle, a vessel could vanish into the depths unseen by friendly eyes. Nor would rescue ships necessarily be sent from outside the battle area, since radio silence meant no SOS.

So, understandably, some of the most frustrated sailors on the ship were the radio operators. The whole crew might die because they were forbidden to send messages. One of these frustrated radiomen was Sea2c. John Grycky, a twenty-two-year-old violinist from Caln, Pennsylvania, who tapped out code as zealously as he tickled the strings of his violin.

The son of a violin-playing shoemaker who had emigrated from the Ukraine in pursuit of the American dream, John was a dreamer, too. He dreamed of joining the Philadelphia Orchestra one day, an aspiration that seemed within reach when he was selected as a member of the all-state high school orchestra.

Young Grycky, tall and lanky with a strong cleft chin and a gentle expression, was already well-known locally as a member of the Grycky Trio, a teenage group that also embraced his younger sister, Lilyan, a pianist, and his younger brother, Robert, a trumpet player. The trio delighted audiences in almost every church, synagogue, and Grange meeting in the area, and often over the radio.

But Grycky was more than a talented musician. Thoughtful, generous, and idealistic, he touched people not only with his sensitive notes, but with his sensitive nature. His sometimes unruly little sister worshiped him as a second father, even though he constantly implored her to act like a lady. His fellow students, among them a pretty girl, Charlotte, whom he hoped to marry, blessed him for helping them with their studies. And when he taught music after graduating from college, his own students idolized him for pushing them to make the most of their talent.

If Grycky had many friends, there were none closer than four high school classmates who formed with him a club they whimsically called Knights of the Square Table. Its members were devoted to helping one another with their school and personal problems, playing outdoor games such as touch football, and simply enjoying each other's company.

With news of Pearl Harbor, Grycky put away his violin and, with his four friends, volunteered for military service (one failed to pass the physical). Grycky could have taken a job with the local Lukens Steel Company, which was doing defense work. But though he longed to remain home and marry Charlotte, he chose the military because it seemed the best way to thank his country for letting him dream a dream that could become reality—if only his hands, which were his life, escaped injury. Before the boys departed, they vowed that if any one of them did not return, the survivors would look after the victim's parents for as long as the parents lived.

Grycky joined the Navy and was overjoyed to be assigned to the *Juneau*. It was a safe ship, he wrote his doting mother, "I'm really lucky to be on it." He made good friends on the vessel, he said, but it was "too bad they are always under stress." Not him, though. Not as long as he could play an imaginary Mozart concerto.

Only one missive reflected despair. Grycky wrote his sister that he had received a Dear John letter from Charlotte. She had married someone else. His heart was broken, he wrote, and even Mozart, apparently, could not heal the wound.

But now, as the *Juneau* headed for a showdown with the enemy, could there be any thought of personal wounds? . . . How lucky to be on such a safe ship.

As Captain Swenson stood on the bridge searching the sea for a hint of enemy movement, he found solace, it seems, only in the fighting ability of his men, whose inexperience had once so worried him—and in the command ability of his colleagues on the other ships. He didn't know much about the leadership qualities of Admiral Callaghan, but he knew that Admiral Scott aboard the *Atlanta* was a brilliant commander, as was Capt. Cassin Young, the skipper of the *San Francisco*, Callaghan's flagship. And Swenson was intimately familiar with the command skills of Captain Hoover of the *Helena*, his classmate at the Naval Academy and good friend, whom he knew as a man of impeccable judgment and exemplary character.

Hoover's experience was rich and varied. He had been a naval aide to President Herbert Hoover and, as an expert in metallurgy, a member of President Roosevelt's Committee on Uranium, which dealt with the theory of nuclear fission. With the attack on Pearl Harbor, he became a destroyer division commander and played a heroic role in the battles of the Coral Sea and Midway, then, in October, after assuming command of the *Helena*, in the battle of Cape Esperance.

In this encounter, the *Helena* opened fire first when Hoover, in the best tradition of naval lore, deliberately misinterpreted an order. His signalman had requested permission from his superior to fire on the enemy and received a reply, "Roger." Actually, this signal was not intended as permission to open fire, but merely as an acknowledgment that the request had been received. But Hoover shrewdly interpreted it as meaning "permission granted" and ordered a barrage that netted one destroyer without help, and another destroyer and two cruisers with assistance. Little wonder that he was a three-time recipient of the Navy Cross.

Yes, with officers like Gil Hoover fighting alongside him, Swenson appears to have felt, the *Juneau* might survive after all. Armed with some hope, he went on deck and told his men:

"We'll see action tonight, but we'll get through it. We can either run or stay and fight. If we run, we lose Guadalcanal. So we're going to stay and fight!"

The men clapped and cheered, crying, "Yea!"

Still, as Swenson went back to the bridge, his expression reflected deep anxiety. He seemed distant again. Was he thinking of those lost years without his children? Of his daughter's estrangement? . . . Of the sons who would almost surely die before the sun came up?

Possibly within the hour. For the *Helena's* radar had picked up the enemy flotilla.

"Contacts bearing three one two and three one oh, distance twenty-seven thousand and thirty-two thousand," the *Helena* reported over the TBS (Talk Between Ships).

Admiral Callaghan then gave the order to all ship captains: attack the enemy head-on! And shortly, in the distance, Swenson made out the fuzzy profile of vessels approaching darkly in the distance.

On receiving word from the *Yudachi* that the enemy had been sighted, Admiral Abe frantically shouted, "What is the range and bearing? And where is *Yudachi?*"

Hardly had he spoken when *Hiei's* masthead lookout cried, "Four black objects ahead . . . look like warships. Five degrees to starboard. Eight thousand meters . . . unsure yet. Visibility bad."

Apparently to hide his dismay, Abe placed his hands over his face. Then he yelled:

"*Yudachi* ten thousand meters ahead [of *Hiei*] on our starboard bow. Ask him distance [from the enemy]."

Comdr. Masakane Suzuki, Abe's chief of staff, asked the lookout, "Is eight thousand correct? Confirm!"

"It may be nine thousand sir," came the reply.

In desperation, Abe cried, "Tell *Hiei* and *Kirishima* gunners to replace all the incendiaries with armor-piercing and set turrets for firing forward!"

They had to act before an enemy shell ignited their ships!

The admiral then slumped into his chair, his face mirroring the agony of indecision. Should he order his two battleships to turn around and move away from the enemy while they changed shells? No, he decided. At such short range, they would make perfect targets while turning.

Aboard the two ships, pandemonium reigned, with every crewman either hauling away the incendiary shells or rushing toward the magazines to grab armor-piercing shells. In their near-panic, *Hiei's* signal officers blared the news of imminent battle over every frequency, ignoring security precautions.

Hara watched from the bridge of the *Amatsukaze* as the *Hiei* sailors "scurried like scared rats." His own lookouts peered through their binoculars, seeking signs of the enemy. They saw nothing. But could one see a snake in the dark before it spit its venom?

"No sweat, boys," Hara said to his men. "We are well prepared to engage when the distance is down to three thousand meters."

But Hara sweated. Not even Abe could dull the edge of his samurai sword. But was it too late to kill the snake?

It was now about one-thirty A.M., Friday the thirteenth.

For both sides.

CHAPTER

· 9 ·

Friday the Thirteenth

WHAT HAPPENED TO ALL THE SHIPS? COMDR. KIYOSHI KIKKAWA was perplexed. As he stood on the bridge of the destroyer *Yudachi* peering into the black night, he could see behind him only one familiar shadow—the destroyer *Harusame*. He couldn't find the other three ships in the vanguard, for the two 180-degree turns had thrown the *Yudachi* out of the formation and now he couldn't even tell Admiral Abe where he was. Unknown to him, the three missing ships had blundered into the rear! It was like a game of naval musical chairs—no one ended up in his original position.

Kikkawa dreaded the night. Since the Japanese ships did not have radar, danger could suddenly spring from the blackness. And the *Harusame* was the only ship sailing with Kikkawa's; the main force trailed miles behind. Like Admiral Abe, Kikkawa was haunted by ghosts from past battles. In a sea clash off Bali the previous February, he was directing fire on a target when enemy ships on his opposite flank severely crippled his destroyer *Mitsushio*. Ever since then, Kikkawa had lost his daring. He was no longer the consummate samurai, like his close friend Tameichi Hara, and this pained him.

Suddenly, at 1:41 A.M., as the *Yudachi* cruised southeast from

· 114 ·

Guadalcanal, Kikkawa's binoculars framed a shadow about three thousand yards away moving due north. Kikkawa was aghast. A destroyer was bearing down on the *Yudachi* and was about to plow into it amidships! Visions of Bali flashed through his mind. Enemy ships were not supposed to be there! He wasn't ready to fight a battle!

Frantically, Kikkawa ordered his helmsman to veer sharply right in order to avoid the oncoming destroyer. He then radioed Abe, "Enemy sighted." But where was he? He still didn't know. Kikkawa had met the enemy, but was lost and cut off from the main Japanese force.

The *Yudachi*, followed by the *Harusame*, swerved in front of the enemy ship and barely avoided a clash. But as it raced away, Kikkawa expected to be blasted out of the water at any moment. Fear, tempered only by shame, overwhelmed him, and in his panic he ignored the angry look in the eyes of his officers and men, who wanted to fight whatever the odds. They just didn't understand what had happened at Bali. But strangely, not a single enemy shell whistled into his ship.

As the two Japanese vessels turned abruptly right, Lt. Comdr. Edward (Butch) Parker, skipper of the destroyer *Cushing*, was almost as startled by the sudden confrontation as his Japanese counterparts, even though the *Helena*'s radar had signaled a warning. With equal desperation, he turned his ship sharply left just in time to avoid a collision. After recovering from this close call, Parker realized he had a couple of perfect broadside targets, and within a minute his men were ready to fire four torpedoes at them. All he needed was permission from Admiral Callaghan.

At that moment, Comdr. Murray Stokes, who commanded the four destroyers in the American vanguard from the *Cushing*, was trying to get this permission. But the single TBS circuit had turned into a madman's symphony of garbled, almost unintelligible cries and queries. As word spread of the enemy sighting, men on every ship in the task group tried to use the TBS. Where was the main body of the enemy force? they asked. When should they open fire? Precious minutes passed before Stokes could verbally bull his way through to Callaghan—only to be told:

"Stop using the TBS!"

He would be informed when to open fire, Callaghan bellowed.

By this time, the two Japanese craft had already vanished into the darkness.

Admiral Callaghan's curtness reflected his shock at what seemed like the sudden breakup of his single-file formation. When the *Cushing* had turned radically left, the next few ships in line followed, almost crashing into each other. As the *Atlanta*, just in front of his flagship *San Francisco*, was turning, the admiral cried out in rage:

"What are you doing?"

"Avoiding our own destroyers!" the *Atlanta* replied.

"Get back into line and hold your fire!" Callaghan ordered.

At the same moment, Lt. Comdr. Bruce McCandless, navigator on the *San Francisco*, called down the voice tube to the flag bridge:

"The *Atlanta*'s turning left. Should I follow her?"

"No!" came the reply. "Hold your course!"

A few seconds later, however, the order was rescinded: "Follow the *Atlanta!*"

Clearly, there would be a collision if it moved back into line.

But not a word about opening fire.

Finally, some four minutes after the two forces had first sighted each other, Callaghan gave the order: "Stand by to open fire!"

And in the terrible silence, the men on the *Cushing* stood by—and continued to stand by even as radarscopes chillingly showed the ocean dotted with buglike figures ripe for oblivion. In fact, the men on every American and Japanese ship were puzzled by the tango of silence. The enemy was only yards away. Why not fire?

Abe's commanders were too busy hauling their armor-piercing shells out of their magazines? Well, they shouldn't have waited so long.

Callaghan had to rely on radar information from other ships

on the jammed TBS circuit? Well, he should have gotten on a ship with the new radar.

Lester Zook, as usual, was especially critical—and perceptive. As the order "Stand by! Stand by!" kept echoing from the *Juneau* bridge, he felt that Callaghan "didn't know what the hell he was doing."

Suddenly, as the *San Francisco* followed the *Atlanta* in a sharp turn left, enemy searchlights switched on and illuminated the *Atlanta* as if it were floating on a stage. The *Atlanta* then swung from left to right, crossing the *San Francisco*'s bow, and after eight minutes of silent confrontation between the two forces, belched a stream of starshells and other missiles at the source of light.

As night instantly turned into day, the whole Japanese armada suddenly lay exposed on the bed of water like a ghastly apparition in a nightmare. With a glint of terror in their eyes, men on every American ship gaped at the sight of two huge battleships heading directly toward them, splashing through a corridor formed by screening destroyers. Admiral Callaghan's task group, it seemed, had blundered into a trap between the two sides of Admiral Abe's rather twisted horseshoe, a trap, ironically, that Abe had never planned.

With the burst of shells from the *Atlanta*, every ship, arbitrarily zeroing in on an enemy vessel, let loose a continuous barrage, expanding the ocean stage into a world gone crazy, it seemed, with flashing guns, exploding stars, streaking tracers, raging fires, probing searchlights—all reflected, like a double dose of horror, in the glittering waters.

One enemy vessel set afire by the guns of the *San Francisco* charged down the line, illuminating the ships in its wake and providing a perfect target for every American craft along the gauntlet. Finally, as it wallowed in the water like a wounded whale, its searchlight caught the *Juneau* in its terrifying grasp.

Many of the *Juneau* crewmen were petrified. They felt, as one man would put it, "like I was naked on the stage at Radio City Music Hall, with a giant spotlight on me, and everyone in the audience had a gun." They dived behind bulkheads, gun mounts, or any other hiding place they could find, some weeping, others vomiting. A few lay flat on the deck, scratching with their fingers at the cold steel as if seeking to worm their way into the very structure of the ship.

But most of the crew remained behind their guns and opened fire on their blazing tormentor without waiting for Admiral Callaghan's belated command:

"Odd ships commence fire to starboard, even ships to port!"

When, minutes later, they learned of this order, they were contemptuous of it. They would fire at the immediate threat no matter where it came from. And among those who were desperately doing this were the men at Battle Station 2—Allen Heyn, George Sullivan, Joe Hartney, Lester Zook, and Wyatt Butterfield, among others.

Suddenly, Zook saw the burning ship's signal searchlight flash in naval language the words: "You are making a mistake."

Startled, Zook loosened his trigger finger. Was it saying that the *Juneau* was firing at a friendly ship? A trick! The vessel, he noted, was flashing a searchlight fourteen to sixteen inches in diameter; American searchlights were twelve inches in diameter. Also, the mystery ship's shutter worked differently from the American shutter. But Admiral Callaghan, on the *San Francisco*, apparently thought the ship was friendly, for his order rippled through the TBS:

"Cease firing own ships!"

Callaghan didn't realize it, of course, but his own flagship had been firing eight-inch projectiles into the *Atlanta*; either it mistook this ship for a Japanese vessel or tried to hit one on the other side of the *Atlanta* and struck the American craft instead. Perhaps when he did realize this he was inclined to believe the enemy message that Zook knew was a hoax. In any case, with the cease-fire order echoing over the TBS to all ships, the storm subsided. Gunners stared at each other in amazement. Couldn't they even fight before they died?

Moments later, the sky lit up again as the Japanese ships, profiting from the lull, loosed a river of shells from every direction, scoring blow after blow before the stunned Americans could answer again.

Callaghan's voice suddenly boomed once more over the TBS: "We want the big ones! Get the big ones first!"

But already, some of his ships were reeling before the fury of enemy guns. The *Atlanta,* pounded by both enemy and friendly shells, was a floating wreck. Its commander, Admiral Scott, and all but one of his top aides lay dead in the debris of the bridge, which had received a direct hit from the *San Francisco,* the flagship of the force he had wanted to command!

Still, the *Juneau* gunners, like those on the other American ships, ripped into the Japanese fleet with even greater intensity than before—though they were never quite sure whether they were hitting friend or foe. Joe Hartney, as he sprayed the spotlight of the blazing vessel, felt nothing now. He was just part of the 50-caliber gun that bounced in his hands as it ate up the ammunition John Rudolph, or Rudy, was feeding it.

The spotlight finally switched its glare to another ship up the column, but flames sprouting from other vessels brightly irradiated the *Juneau,* and shells kept exploding all around it. Utter chaos now reigned, with blazing ships crisscrossing the ocean, firing in all directions. The fighting was so close that it reminded Lieutenant Wang, as he directed the fire of 20mm and 1.1 guns from midship aft, of the days of John Paul Jones, seventy years earlier, when men actually boarded the enemy's ships.

Suddenly the *Juneau* was caught in another sweep of light from a ship that was charging directly toward it.

"Get those lights!" Rudy cried as they grew brighter by the second. "Get those lights! We don't stand a chance if you don't get those lights!"

And as Hartney's gun chattered, he saw "a great, boiling red flash." A shell from the enemy ship, believed to be the cruiser *Nagara,* roared red-hot over the *Juneau* and smashed into another enemy vessel, apparently the *Hiei,* on the other side of it. The *Juneau* was more fortunate. Its torpedoes slammed into the *Nagara,* almost lifting it out of the water, and Hartney saw the crew "running like ants" as flames ate up the decks.

Perhaps unaware that it had been wounded by friendly fire, the *Hiei* then turned on the *Juneau* and roared its anger with hardly a pause. But like the *Nagara,* the *Hiei* was too close on the *Juneau*'s beam to lower its guns enough to hit the

American craft and thus sent shells rocketing over it into the *Nagara* in unintended retribution. The shells miraculously missed the *Juneau*, both Japanese vessels, though having seriously damaged each other, raked the American ship with small-caliber cannon and machine-gun fire and caused many casualties.

As Hartney sprayed the attackers with his machine gun, moving in an arc around the firing pit, his foot struck something soft and yielding. He looked down and saw his best friend, Rudy, lying dead in a pool of blood. Nausea seized him. Was that Rudy—or himself? Could a vision of his own death be any more fanciful than this scene of men wildly blasting each other to bits?

Some distance away, Allen Heyn helped to fire a 1.1 gun while George Sullivan handed shells to the men loading the weapon.

"Let's give it to them!" George urged.

And his comrades complied, as shell after shell zipped through the smoky air that veiled the battle like a reddish gray gauze curtain. They hit in one direction, then another, as the ship drew fire from both sides. Suddenly, the barrel jammed.

"We'll have to fire another shell through the damn thing and clear it," Heyn said. "The gun might blow up, but we have no choice."

George agreed: "We can't just sit this out."

Tension grew as the clearing operation began. It seemed a lousy way to die—killed by your own gun.

But there was no explosion, and soon the weapon was smoking defiance again, as the two enemy ships continued to fire missiles over their beleaguered foe into each other's flaming hulk. The close-in fighting, it seemed, was saving, or at least prolonging, the lives of the *Juneau* sailors.

George Sullivan and his brothers, however, must surely have wondered if, in the midst of this murderous melee, God would pull them out of the river this time. Especially when a third Japanese ship joined in the frenzied assault on their cruiser.

* * *

To Commander Hara aboard the *Amatsukaze*, divine intervention had already saved the Japanese force, at least up to now. Why else "had the enemy allowed us to gain the precious eight minutes before the battle began?" he would ask. During those eight minutes, the pandemonium on the two powerfully armed battleships had ended, and all incendiaries had been removed and replaced with armor-piercing shells.

But disaster could still come, Hara felt, because of Admiral Abe's "foolish" decisions. "The seven hours of blind march and the two rapid 180-degree turns were too severe a test for any formation." Thus, the vanguard segments of the two arcs had been broken and the battleships within stripped of protection.

Still, Hara had watched with admiration from the bridge of his destroyer as the *Hiei*, along with several other Japanese ships, fired salvos at the *Atlanta* until it floated away dead in the water, its bridge destroyed. Abe, he thought, had avenged his friend Admiral Goto. What Hara didn't realize was that, like Goto, who may have been killed in the Battle of Savo Island by a friendly missile, Admiral Scott, ironically, had also been killed by one—as a postwar investigation of the damage to the *Atlanta* would determine.

Hara's joy, however, was short-lived. The *Hiei* had lit up the *Atlanta* with its powerful searchlight in order to zero in on it, but in doing so had become a prime target itself. The lead American ship, *Cushing*, cascaded shells and bullets into it, and many of these missiles crossed over the target and sprayed Hara's *Amatsukaze* just behind it.

"Gain speed!" Hara cried. "Let's get the hell out of here to starboard."

Suddenly, a couple of Japanese flares floodlit the scene, and five or six American ships in a column flashed to life in front of him like a painting in an art gallery. Hara "gulped," and his "heart bubbled with excitement." At last the chance to prove his torpedo theory, which the Imperial Navy adopted after he had developed it in the 1930s. By computing in a new way the timing of release, the curvature of course, and the degree of spread, Hara had become the highest-scoring torpedo officer in the Navy. Now he would test his theory in battle.

"Commander, let's fire the fish!" his torpedo officer yelled impatiently.

"Get ready, fishermen!" Hara barked. "The target, thirty degrees to starboard, is approaching. Adjusted firing angle, fifteen degrees. Navigators, turn right, close in, and follow a hyperbola."

When his ship had closed to within three thousand meters of one of the enemy vessels, Hara yelled, "Ready torpedoes, fire!"

As he watched prayerfully, he suddenly saw the *Yudachi*, guns blazing, cut in front of the American column. Commander Kikkawa, who had fled in panic when he first sighted the American armada, had, in his shame, suddenly decided to return to the scene and redeem himself even if this meant suicide. Now, like a raging rhino, he blasted into the American column, almost grazing the bow of the destroyer *Aaron Ward*, and forcing it to make a violent turn.

The second destroyer, *Barton*, then ground to a halt to avoid colliding with the *Aaron Ward*. And at that moment, the *Barton* exploded into a smoking fireworks display as two of Hara's torpedoes struck home. Hara watched in amazement as the ship, cut in two, disappeared into the depths with virtually the whole crew aboard.

"I heaved a deep sigh," he would say. "It was a spectacular kill and there was a roaring ovation from my crew, but I didn't hear it. It was all too easy. My own feeling was one of satisfaction rather than exultation. It was the first real war test of my theory, which was now a proved formula."

A few minutes later, there was another chance to prove Hara's theory as flashes from the fires roaring on the *Hiei* outlined a sleek craft with four masts.

"Definitely enemy," thought Hara. "Possibly a cruiser."

And he knew it was the enemy when he saw it exchanging fire with three Japanese ships, one of them the *Yudachi*, which was still charging into any American craft it could find with an almost fanatical zeal. But Kikkawa looked to be in trouble. And he was. The eight torpedoes he fired at the cruiser whizzed harmlessly past it. In return, he was treated to a powerful salvo that wreaked havoc on his own ship, and all he had left to counter it were guns, no torpedoes. A lost cause, he felt, for a destroyer could not outgun a cruiser.

"I felt I was pinned at last," Kikkawa would later say.

He had tried his best to repent for his early cowardice, and now he would go down with his ship so that he might honorably rise to heaven.

But just about then, Hara was shouting on his ship, only dozens of yards away:

"Torpedoes, ready! Target seventy degrees to port."

"Torpedoes ready, sir," his torpedo officer cried.

"All right, hold it, hold it . . . hold it, the target is moving ahead. Easy, easy . . . easier target than the last . . . steady, steady . . . fire!"

And four torpedoes sped into the night. Three minutes and forty seconds later, Hara saw a large, reddish flame rise from his target. As the men shouted with joy, the gunnery officer, Lieutenant Shimizu, asked for permission to shell the ship and finish it off. But Hara would not give it. By hitting and apparently disabling the cruiser, he may have saved the *Yudachi*. He thus felt magnanimous.

"No, Shimizu," he replied. "Let's leave the spoils for our friend *Yudachi*. Don't be impatient. We'll have plenty of targets. Shelling at this stage would only expose our position to the enemy."

And Hara, exhilarated by his success, went off looking for other prey. If only his dear grandfather could have witnessed this glorious moment and seen for himself that the child in whose hands he had placed his samurai sword as a deathbed gift was worthy of the honor.

The ship that Commander Kikkawa thought would send him to heaven was the *Juneau*, which was itself halfway there as it foundered in a crossfire between the *Nagara* and the *Hiei*, joined by Kikkawa's *Yudachi*, though these ships savagely pelted each other as often as they did the enemy trapped in the middle. One shell had wrecked the bridge of the *Juneau*, knocking out communications temporarily, but sparing Captain Swenson. All the missiles that had been whistling in the night, however, did less damage to the *Juneau* than did one of Commander Hara's torpedoes, which, eight minutes into the battle, crashed deeply into its hull with a muffled blast.

As Joe Hartney stood dazed by his machine gun, looking down at his dead friend Rudy, the *Juneau* seemed to leap about six feet out of the water, twisting and shaking, then sinking back down, dead in the water. Hartney was thrown to his knees. A torpedo had hit on the port side in the forward fire room, killing all nineteen men inside. In the plotting room next door, the men were thrust to the floor, but were saved from death by a double bulkhead, even though it had partially given way. The deck had also buckled and oil fumes were seeping through, while the keel had apparently snapped and the propellers had jammed, causing the ship to rise and settle in jerky cadence and list to the port side.

The *Juneau* thus spun out of control and swept in toward one of the burning ships that had been plaguing it, apparently the *Nagara*.

"We closed relentlessly on that island of fire," Hartney would later recount, "swept forward by our momentum and powerless to stop. I could see Japs leaping over the side into the water, men struggling in the inferno, a weird, unforgettable pageantry that Dante himself could not have dreamed up. I stared in shocked incredulity as the distance closed."

Through the turmoil, he heard the stark order: "All hands stand by for collision!"

Hartney felt the end was coming. Good-bye, little baby, whom he would never see or hold.

Minutes earlier, Allen Heyn, while firing at the enemy, saw the foamy wake of the torpedo in the water one hundred yards away, and apparently Captain Swenson saw it, too, for the ship started to turn with the engines running full astern. But it was too late. When the missile struck, Heyn was seated, training a 5-inch gun, and managed to hold on, but all the men around him were blown across the deck.

George Sullivan was thrown against a bulkhead and collapsed, his back severely injured. Where were his brothers? Were they okay? he wanted to know as he grimaced in agony.

Dr. O'Neil, the part-time preacher and boxing instructor, tried to ease George's pain as he lay on the deck.

Heyn, who suffered only bruises, would not leave his 5-inch gun. Since he had lost all firepower, he tried to work it manually. When that proved too difficult, he turned to the 1.1 and 20mm guns and aimed them toward the decks of the burning cruiser that the *Juneau* was about to crash into. He fired furiously, as did other crewmen, among them officers who even used their sidearms. Dying wouldn't be so bad, but Heyn worried about his mother. She might never know what happened to him. He would at least take with him some of those guys scurrying around the decks.

As the two ships were about to collide, the quartermaster operating the helm at Battle Station 2, which had taken over control after the bridge was hit, shoved the lever hard over. The *Juneau* cleared the enemy ship with just a few feet to spare.

But hardly had it escaped from this deadly threat when the *Yudachi*, smoking and smoldering from its own terrible wounds, closed in with murderous determination.

"It's coming right at us!" Heyn cried.

And the working guns on the *Juneau* blasted away at this destroyer until it faded into the night to be further ravaged by other ships.

Another massive sigh of relief. But then the third tormentor, the *Hiei*, found the *Juneau* a better target after having drifted farther away from it. Before, the battleship's guns could not be depressed enough to hit a target right under its huge nose, and so it had inadvertently poured missiles into a friendly ship. But now its shells screamed into the *Juneau*'s superstructure, piercing its light armor.

The *Juneau*, already settling ever more forward as water streamed through the gaping hole made by Hara's torpedo, staggered drunkenly under the impact of the new attack. Explosions reverberated below, generating a blizzard of steel fragments that virtually tore men's bodies to shreds, and fear spread that the ship, a powder keg of depth bombs, torpedoes, ammunition, and fuel, would simply blow up.

But not even the fury of the storm could stop the crew from repairing the power-dead gunnery system sufficiently to permit retaliation. Shells from Heyn's gun and others streamed into the battleship, chipping away at its own superstructure.

After the chilling encounter with the burning cruiser, Joe Hartney felt a renewed strength simply because he was still alive. And every time he glanced at Rudy's corpse, the fuel of vengeance propelled scores of bullets toward the enemy.

Suddenly a searchlight from the battleship tipped forward and the beam of light on the water revealed a scene that somehow seemed to symbolize the dehumanizing nature of war. Packed within the circle of light, like tiny pearls in a brooch, were hundreds of heads, with faces turned up and eyes glowing in the firelight. Men from some sinking Japanese ship fighting to stay afloat in their life jackets, seemingly disembodied men, with skulls carved out of plastic or wood.

Still more surreal, not one man found the courage to show human weakness in front of his comrades and cry out—even as the *Juneau* ground over them, tossing them aside with lethal abandon. Unnervingly, the eyes continued to stare like shiny buttons, but no longer with hate. The stares were now as placidly empty as that of Rudy lying crumpled at Hartney's feet. There were no enemies in heaven. And those on earth, Hartney now seemed to feel, were men like him, after all. Men who would try to kill him as he would them—before they all met later in a place where guns were banned.

Captain Swenson must surely have wondered why he wasn't already there. The bridge of the *Juneau* now leaned precariously to one side. And the ship itself was eleven feet down by the bow with a two-degree list, while only one screw worked, the main feed pump barely worked, communications didn't work at all, except for sound-power phones, and the steering wheel wouldn't steer, though the helm at Battle Station 2 functioned, if with difficulty.

Thus, about ten minutes after the battle started, the *Juneau* had become useless as a fighting unit. Still, Swenson could only have felt pride in the struggle that he and his sons had waged. And no one could ever again question his courage, as some unjustly did after the sinking of the *Hornet*. Though the most vulnerable of combat ships, the *Juneau*, caught in cross fire, had absorbed the best shots of a battleship, a cruiser, and heaven knew how many destroyers and managed to strike back with unrelenting fury that sank or seriously damaged at least one or two of its tormentors.

And while the ship had been gravely mauled, it was still afloat and could move under its own power, however slowly and noisily, with the grinding sound of broken propeller shafts and rudder competing weirdly for the ear with the explosions and the cries of wounded men. The rudder had to be moved manually with a pulley, and the man operating it got his orders via sound phone from Lester Zook, who got his from the bridge. A "quiet joy" seized Zook. What could be more satisfying than to see the crew working so efficiently under fire?

If Swenson felt any joy, it certainly sprang from the relatively low number of casualties the crew had suffered, though the exact figures weren't in yet. Yes, most of his wonderful sons were still alive. And now there was no reason for any more of them to die. The captain thus gave orders for his crippled ship to creep away from the battle area. In a kind of farewell nose-thumbing gesture, the *Juneau* loosed a couple of torpedoes toward the Japanese battleship it had so brazenly dueled with and was answered by a shell that arched over it and fell harmlessly into the sea. Other enemy missiles missed, too, and struck Japanese ships—a parting symbol, it seemed, of the total chaos of the battle, which, as one sailor would say, was like a "deadly barroom brawl after the lights were turned off."

With its own lights turned off and hardly anyone daring to speak above a whisper, the *Juneau* silently extricated itself from the jaws of death, chugging eastward along the shore of Guadalcanal to Indispensable Strait, where it would turn south through Maramasike Pass, which separated Guadalcanal from San Cristobal Island, to the open sea.

What had happened to the other ships in the task group? Since the *Juneau* had lost its TBS, Swenson had no way of knowing. But with light beams still flashing, shells still roaring, and bullets still singing, it was clear some were still fighting, and that was a good sign. Commanders like Gil Hoover would fight like hell, even as they agonized over each spilt drop of American blood. Hopefully, they would all meet in Espíritu

Santo, the nearest U.S. naval base, en route to Nouméa, farther south.

Meanwhile, as the *Juneau* struggled ahead in the lonely darkness, Swenson had plenty of time to ponder the miracle of survival and wonder how many more miracles would be needed to get him and his men back to their loved ones.

CHAPTER

· 10 ·

Lullaby of Death

JUST BEFORE DAWN ON NOVEMBER 13, AT THE SOUTHEAST END OF Indispensable Strait, the *Juneau* crew saw a suspicious shadow suddenly loom from the murk, moving in a parallel direction. If this was a Japanese ship, Captain Swenson would need another miracle. The *Juneau* was grinding forward at about eighteen knots, little more than half of its potential speed, and, because its steering mechanism didn't work, could not maneuver out of a torpedo's path. Nor could his men, in their utter exhaustion, fight effectively any longer. Hitting the *Juneau* would be as easy as shooting a lame elephant.

The crew was at Alert 3, which permitted many members to leave their stations and rest. But now Swenson, though well aware of their condition, gave the order for Alert 1, used during the battle, and told his signalmen to challenge the "dark shape" with a signal light. As Swenson and his men held their breath, a signalman reported:

"It's the *Helena!*"

Of course! With Gil Hoover commanding, Swenson knew the valiant *Happy H* would come through. And it did, apparently with minimal injury. Its 6-inch guns had pounded an enemy ship that was about to finish off the *San Francisco*. Its 5-inch guns had poured shells into a destroyer. And its heavy machine guns had forced a cruiser to flee the scene of battle.

With the *Juneau's* TBS communications system knocked out, Swenson, it seems, was unaware that his friend Hoover had assumed command of the remnants of Task Group 67.4 after a shell from the *Hiei* destroyed the bridge of the *San Francisco*, killing Admiral Callaghan and several other officers while gravely wounding Captain Young. Since Admiral Scott had died on the *Atlanta*, Hoover became the senior officer in the force. He now informed Swenson of developments by blinker signal, repeating to his friend a message he had received earlier from the *San Francisco*. That ship was being commanded by Lt. Comdr. Herbert E. Schonland, the damage control officer, though Schonland was so busy putting out fires that he temporarily relinquished his duties to Lt. Cmdr. McCandless, the navigator. McCandless's message was:

"Admiral and all of staff except one killed x Captain seriously wounded x Hundreds of casualties x Can use two turrets six five-inch and make twenty-eight knots steering from conn x Urgently need all medical assistance you can spare."

Swenson told Hoover by blinker signal of his own troubles: "Torpedo flooded forward engine room and fire room x Plotting room out of commission x Down by the head four feet x Estimate eighteen knots speed x Flooding under control x All forward fire rooms personnel lost x No TBS no ECM expect gyro in commission later." He would now follow the *Helena* southward directly to Espíritu Santo, Swenson said.

Actually, the *San Francisco* was in even greater trouble, as Swenson and his crew would learn after a second unidentified ship challenged the *Juneau*. Signalman Zook started to answer the challenge by blinker, but Swenson, still fearing a suicidal clash with the enemy, ordered him to desist.

As the dark sea sparkled with the first sunbeams, the mystery ship, hovering on the horizon, grew recognizable—the *San Francisco*. And silhouetted just behind it were three destroyers: the *Fletcher*, the *Sterett*, and the *O'Bannon*. The *Helena* had been the first in a line of ships to leave the battle scene, and now there were six.

When the tiny, battered flotilla drew to a halt after daylight to permit the *San Francisco* to make temporary repairs and obtain medical aid, the *Juneau* sailors crowded to the railings and stared in shock at the sight of this monument to the ferocity of the battle. How could the vessel remain afloat? they wondered. The hull, superstructure, and turrets were a mass of torn, twisted steel, punctured with huge, jagged holes, and the whole ship looked like one big junkyard. Its human cargo had been ripped apart, too; the men watched as sacks containing parts of bodies were thrown overboard.

The *San Francisco*, as the flagship cruiser, had become a prime target of almost every Japanese warship. But it also became the nemesis of many. It helped to turn the battleship *Hiei* into a blazing inferno and, together with a friendly destroyer, had caught the Japanese destroyer *Akatsuki* in a cross fire that sank it with almost its entire crew. The battleship *Kirishima* then took on the *San Francisco* and its 14-inch guns delivered the deadly blows that ended the life of Admiral Callaghan and almost every man on the bridge.

Torpedoes might have ended the life of the ship itself if Commander Hara had not made what he would call a "stupid" miscalculation. Hara suddenly saw a large ship materialize yards in front of his destroyer, *Amatsukaze*, which swerved just in time to avoid a collision.

"I wondered what ship it could be," Hara would later say. "We passed so close I could not see its whole shape. . . . It had no turrets, but it was not a merchant ship. It was familiar and yet I couldn't place it. . . . The next moment I realized . . . this must be an enemy ship."

Hara jumped up and cried, "Gunners! Torpedomen! Stand ready to port!"

But then he wavered again. Was it really an enemy ship? To find out, he ordered searchlights, and they laid bare an American cruiser.

"Open fire!" he yelled.

Four torpedoes immediately sped toward the ship, and all six 4-inch guns roared. But while almost every shell hit the target, setting scores of fires, the torpedoes did not explode. Hara suddenly realized his mistake. Every Japanese torpedo had a safety device that prevented it from detonating if the target was less than five hundred meters away so it wouldn't damage the attacking ship together with the enemy vessel. And his target was closer.

"I cursed my stupidity," he would say. "Through haste I had lost the chance to make a certain sinking."

Well, maybe the shells alone would do it.

"Finish it off!" Hara ordered as the phantom ship—the *San Francisco*—continued to wobble along, vomiting smoke and fire.

It was now that Captain Hoover came to the rescue with his *Happy H.*

"Commander," an officer reported to Hara, "another cruiser is sniping at us from seventy degrees to port!"

Hara "stood frozen from head to toe." He realized he had made another mistake—keeping his searchlights on and thus attracting this new enemy ship.

"Douse searchlight!" he cried. "Stop shelling! Spread smoke screen!"

Two shells then hit the *Amatsukaze*, almost throwing Hara off the bridge. When he dazedly stumbled to his feet, he found himself surrounded by death. One of his officers lay dead at his observation post, another had been blasted from the ship, leaving behind only one of his legs, and everyone in the radio room was lifeless. By the time the action was over, forty-three men had died.

Hara was devastated. Because of his blunders, one enemy cruiser had escaped oblivion and another had almost sent his own ship there. He now wondered if he was worthy of his grandfather's samurai sword after all.

Hara's ill fortune and Hoover's good timing had thus saved the *San Francisco*, though the men on the *Juneau*, gazing at the vessel with startled eyes, could only wonder if reduction to a scrap heap could be defined as salvation. Nor could they know that the man who had almost sunk it had launched the torpedo that nearly consigned their own ship, with its battered bridge, bent screw, and apparently broken keel, to an underwater graveyard.

Almost as shocking to the *Juneau* crew was the shrunken size of Task Group 67.4—only six of thirteen ships had apparently

crawled away from the battle area. The guns of the battleship
Hiei, Admiral Abe's flagship, had, in short order, sent the destroyers *Cushing* and *Laffey* to the bottom of the sea, with many
swimming survivors from the *Laffey* blown to pieces when the
flaming hulk exploded; the cruiser *Portland*, its structure
twisted and bent by a torpedo, kept going around in circles; the
cruiser *Atlanta* was in such ruins that it was later scuttled; the
destroyer *Aaron Ward* lay dead in the water after a storm of
shell blasts; the destroyer *Barton* sank with almost all aboard;
and the destroyer *Monssen* was turned into a floating torch after
its commander, mistakenly thinking a starshell that had burst
over the ship was friendly, switched on his fighting lights and
became a prime target for enemy missiles.

The destroyers that had joined the cruisers *Juneau*, *Helena*,
and *San Francisco* in exodus from the battle were more fortunate. Though its steering gear would no longer work, the *Sterett*
finally stopped the *Yudachi*'s bull-like charge into the melee
after the *Juneau* had already taken a terrible toll. The *Yudachi*
was then finished off by the *Portland*. Even so, Commander
Kikkawa had succeeded in removing the blot on his honor sustained during those first moments in battle, apparently with suf-
ficient zeal to get him into heaven. He and his crew would be
awarded a glowing commendation for their conduct in this action. As for the *Sterett*, it was soon crippled by 14-inch shells,
but managed to sneak off to safety.

Only two ships survived the battle almost unscathed. The destroyer *O'Bannon*, with just its sound equipment damaged, had
boldly loosed missile after missile at the *Hiei* while dodging
almost every one sent its way. And the *Fletcher* had threaded
a path through the maelstrom of ships, its guns firing furiously,
and with the incredible skill, it seemed, of someone avoiding
raindrops during a downpour, emerged virtually untouched.
This was the ship that the *Juneau* crew was glad not to be on
because it was riddled with the curse of the number thirteen.

It appeared clear that the Japanese had won a tactical victory,
for they had emerged from the battle with fewer losses than
the Americans. Still, the damage to their fleet was severe. Two
destroyers, the *Yudachi* and the *Akatsuki*, were sunk, and Com-

mander Hara's *Amatsukaze* was so crippled that it could not sail in a straight line and had to zigzag all the way back to Truk.

Most of the other Japanese ships were wounded in varying degree, with the battleship *Hiei*, the Americans' main target, gutted from stem to stern. Admiral Abe was injured and so convinced that the enemy bristled with overwhelming power that, after about ten minutes of flaming anarchy, he signaled his fleet to withdraw from the battle. When daylight came, Abe, seeing that the *Hiei* was easy prey for swarming American planes, ordered its scuttling.

Shortly, Abe was "retired" in disgrace. He had not only lost a prize battleship, but had failed to destroy the enemy fleet and bombard Henderson Field, his vital objective. Admiral Yamamoto sensed that these failures meant he had lost his great gamble, and though he would try the very next day to achieve the same objective, he would fail again. He could not reverse the momentum of the war. Or his personal misfortune. As he had foreseen, he had not long to live. In April 1943, an American pilot shot his plane down near Bougainville, sending him to a heaven that had not helped him on earth.

It was perhaps a merciful ending, for while the battle of Friday the thirteenth was another tactical victory for his Navy, it would seal Japan's fate.

The long-term implications of the battle, however, were not on the minds of the *Juneau* sailors as they stared at the shambles of the *San Francisco* and ruminated over the bitterness of the struggle and the loss of many shipmates. In the early light, Joe Hartney roamed through the ship surveying the wreckage and looking for the dead. He knew the grim fate of the men in the fire room, but had many others died as well? He gazed up at the shaky bridge, hoping to spot one of his friends, a signalman, up there. When a junior officer stepped into sight, Hartney spelled out in sign language, "Signalmen?"

The officer stared down at him with a glazed look, then gestured with his hands.

"All gone!" the movement said. "All gone!"

Hartney was shattered. First, Rudy, and now another close friend. He turned away and gazed numbly toward the horizon, as if seeking an explanation in some secret message written in infinity.

He then staggered below to get a drink in the mess hall, groping his way down by the light streaming through the jagged shell holes in the hull, almost choking on the diesel-oil fumes that inflamed the nose and throat and permeated the spirit with the smell of disaster. But there was no mess hall. The deck and overhead plates were twisted out of shape, and the bulkheads had become crumpled clumps of metal.

This had been the main sick bay. Now, almost all the seriously wounded on the ship lay buried in the ruins.

But if few badly injured men aboard the *Juneau* had survived, many such men were still alive on the *San Francisco*, including Captain Young, who had apparently been hit by the shell that killed Admiral Callaghan. As that ship had urgently requested medical assistance, Swenson asked Dr. James Neff, the senior *Juneau* medical officer, to send Dr. O'Neil and three pharmacist mates to the stricken vessel.

Thus, at about eight A.M., O'Neil and three assistants stepped into a motor whaleboat sent from the *San Francisco* and headed for that ship. They waved to their comrades, expecting to return to them shortly.

At about the same time, Hoover sent the *O'Bannon* some miles away so it could radio information to headquarters without revealing the task group's location to the enemy. The *O'Bannon* could be spared, for, with its sound equipment damaged, it could do little to protect the other vessels from a submarine attack. It would report on the task group's condition and request air coverage en route to its base in Espíritu Santo. A Japanese plane had been seen shadowing the task group that morning, and an air attack could follow at any time.

Captain Swenson, as concerned as ever about the vulnerability of the *Juneau*, had vigorously requested that Hoover call for urgent air coverage, especially since the small planes that the *Helena* and *San Francisco* normally carried to patrol for enemy submarines and aircraft had been transferred to Tulagi two days earlier. Only two destroyers, the severely damaged *Sterett* and the *Fletcher*, were available to screen three damaged cruisers in dangerous waters.

Now hopeful that planes would shortly be offering further protection, the maimed little fleet resumed its journey home at 8:26 A.M., sailing at seventeen to eighteen knots, the fastest the *Juneau* was able to go. Swenson knew that if a torpedo headed his way, he could do little but wait for it to hit. For the *Juneau*, with its steering problem, could only make a wide swing. Such an evasive maneuver might be futile, but to make sure he could try it if necessary without colliding with another American vessel, Swenson signaled the *Helena*:

"Would like to remain on your starboard and to give mutual aa [antiaircraft] support and to turn quickly to stbd in view of having only one screw and one uncertain gyro x Will keep well clear."

The danger of an attack seemed to grow when, at 9:50 A.M., the *Sterett* had sound contact with a submarine and fired several depth bombs. They seemed to "clear the area"—but had the submarine escaped?

When the sound room in submarine *I-26* reported a couple of possible depth-bomb blasts some distance away, Commander Yokota gave abrupt orders:

"Depth forty. Unpowered cruising! Shift to the third shift disposition. Keep on sound patrol. Those off duty will take a rest."

Tsukuo Nakano once again felt grateful for the thoughtfulness of the commander.

"He is apparently feeling anxious about fatigue," he would muse.

The tension was great—waiting for a kill. Nakano and others thus lay in their bunks trying to relax, while some men preferred to play the Japanese games of go or shogi. With all the motors turned off, the submarine was virtually noiseless. Yet, in the silence, Nakano could hear the sounds of his imagination—the clipped chirp of the grasshopper on his farm, the wail of the samisen at the village festival, the sad lilt of his mother's voice as she hummed an old refrain while scrubbing the wash. . . . How long would he have to wait for that kill?

At ten-thirty A.M., some twenty miles southwest of San Cristobal Island, the sound room broke the silence: "Left thirty degrees, sensitivity two, a group noise."

Yokota immediately ordered, "Stop unpowered cruising! Make headway with both sides at low speed! All men to their posts!"

Then he called out, "Depth eight. Up with periscope!"

And in a moment, as he peered through the periscope: "Three masts, possibly of cruisers, in sight! Three destroyers, too!" (Actually, there were two.)

Nakano shared the commander's joy. The sea, he noted, was calm with rippling waves—ideal for a torpedo attack.

"They are worthy of my sword!" Yokota exclaimed. "Prepare for torpedo battle!"

The warm furtive sun, peeking through some clouds, smiled on a sea that waltzed gently in the windless morning, aglitter with an almost blinding tropical sheen. At about eleven A.M., the spell of eternal peace was broken when Captain Hoover's flotilla of five ships limped southward past San Cristobal in concert with the sluggish gait of the *Juneau*. Four vessels formed a Y, with the fifth flanking the tip of its stem. The *Fletcher* was at the tip of the left prong of the Y; the *Sterett* at the tip of the right prong; the *Helena* in the center four hundred yards behind the two destroyers; the *San Francisco* about eight hundred yards behind the *Helena*; and the *Juneau* about eight hundred yards to the *San Francisco's* starboard side.

The *Juneau* crewmen, frazzled from battle, remained at their stations under an Alert 2, but relaxed by their guns, some asleep, others sitting against bulkheads, clinging desperately to this interlude of perfect tranquillity. Which world was real? The one of chaos, terror, and death? Or this one, in which the only sounds were the squeals of seabirds and the lullaby of water lapping against the ship?

Even sleep could not resolve the question for many men. In their dreams, there were flashes of home, but they were quickly consumed by the flaming terrors of a bloody night. Those who preferred to stay awake and wallow in the soothing balm of a transient world at peace talked of men dying and ships sinking, while trying to meld the horror with hope.

Wyatt Butterfield leaned against his gun turret at midship and talked of the courage he had seen as the sailors slugged away at the enemy. Though drained, he felt exhilarated. A hellish battle, but it brought out the best in men.

Butterfield and his shipmates spoke joyously about the liberty they would get while the ship was being repaired.

What a great time they would have in Hawaii, said one.

"What'ya mean Hawaii? We're goin' home!"

Well, what the hell, it would be somewhere on American soil.

Then back to the real world. With the worst apparently behind them, the men could actually find humor in the torpedoing of their ship. One recounted how the lights had gone out below, and in the darkness he felt water splashing over him. The ship was sinking! he thought. He was drowning! But it was just a bucket of water that had tipped over on him.

The other men laughed. A torpedo? It might upset a bucket of water, but not the *Juneau!*

Still, not all the men were upbeat. Two of them doubted they would get home alive. It was just a matter of time.

Butterfield was furious. They were "crazy," he barked. The crew had "come all this way and couldn't miss now." Those with a will to survive would survive!

On the fantail, Allen Heyn sat against a bulkhead next to his gun and also babbled about the battle with some shipmates. Only six of the thirteen ships in their task group had made it! How many men died? Whatever the number, Heyn, like Butterfield, was sure he would emerge from the war alive and intact. Others might die, but not he. He knew it; he felt it. There was no missile that could kill him.

George Sullivan, as he lay on the deck nearby groaning from the pain in his injured back, was perhaps suffering more than most of the men. For he had to think not only of his own survival, but that of his four younger brothers. And they were all separated. Were they alive? Were they lying with wounds perhaps worse than his own? He was helpless to find out, to protect them from harm. Weren't the five Sullivans supposed to stick together—even die together, if fate so decreed? But he may have thought of the Rogers brothers; only two of them might die together.

As Commander Yokota peered through his periscope, he elatedly found himself with an embarrassment of targets. Five ships! But since only two of his torpedo launchers worked, he would have to choose the most important one. There were two destroyers up front, but why sink a destroyer when he could blow up a cruiser? And why settle for a light cruiser when he could knock out a heavy one? The first cruiser in line (the *Helena*) was a light one, and was too close, anyway—less than a thousand meters away; the explosion could endanger his submarine. He needed a distance of at least fifteen to sixteen hundred meters.

Yokota eyed the second cruiser in line, a heavy ship of the *San Francisco* class. There was still another ship on the far side of that one, partially hidden from view, but it was a light cruiser of the *Atlanta* class, again hardly worthy of his sword when there was bigger prey out there.

He would torpedo the *San Francisco*–class ship, which was just about at the right distance—fifteen hundred meters. Still, he worried about the angle of the trajectory. The perfect angle was ninety degrees, but he would have to settle for seventy degrees or the ship would be too close. And to prevent the torpedoes from smashing into the first cruiser by mistake, he would have them go ten meters underwater, beneath the ship if they went off course, and then rise to four meters in the hope they would strike any more distant vessel.

"Number of launching, two!" Yokota called from the conning tower to the launching room. "Launcher number one and four, pour water!"

The commander then blared information on the azimuth, the enemy's speed, and the distance.

As Tsukuo Nakano received these orders, he commiserated with Yokota. Too bad that at such a critical moment they were missing four launchers. If not for the grounding accident, the *I-26* would have been able to sink two or three ships.

"Now," he would muse, "with only two launchers in order,

there is no choice but to put our whole heart and soul into what we have." I-26 couldn't risk lingering to fire a second round.

There was a moment of silence. Then the commander's voice again: "Get ready! Go!"

The two torpedoes leaped out of the launchers with mighty booms. Simultaneously, Yokota ordered:

"Depth seventy! Defend against depth bombs!"

And the *I-26* dived at an angle of fifteen degrees into the sheltering depths.

Dr. O'Neil had treated many wounded and dying men on the *Juneau*, but that didn't prepare him for the horrors he faced aboard the *San Francisco*. He first began treating one of the worst injured—a black mess attendant whose entire abdominal viscera had been hanging out all night.

After operating on the man, O'Neil rushed to Admiral Callaghan's cabin, where Captain Young lay gravely wounded. With the help of the ship's senior medical officer, he was improvising an operating table when suddenly a voice cried over the loudspeaker:

"Stand by for an attack!"

O'Neil was thunderstruck. Every second was precious if Young was to be saved—but how could he operate in the middle of an attack? What in God's name was happening?

On deck, seconds before, SM2c. Victor Gibson had been scanning the sea as the *San Francisco* splashed its way southward. Suddenly, he saw two white wakes streaking across the ocean from the northwest. Torpedoes! And they seemed to be coming at his ship! But as the *San Francisco* slowed down and the alarm sounded, the missiles sped across the vessel's bow, missing it by one hundred to two hundred yards, and darted past the stern of the leading *Helena* as they carved a watery path between the two cruisers.

One torpedo vanished in the distance, but Gibson watched helplessly as the other streaked directly toward the *Juneau*. Acting Commander Schonland would later report to headquarters that there was no quick way to warn the *Juneau*. The TBS transmitter had been damaged, the halyards cut, the flag bags gutted, and all but one twelve-inch searchlight wrecked.

"It was impossible for the *San Francisco* to warn the *Juneau*," according to Schonland, "and even had all facilities been instantly available, it is most unlikely that the warning would have been sufficiently in advance to enable *Juneau* to take avoiding action."

Perhaps so, but why wasn't the *Juneau* warned by the one twelve-inch searchlight that worked, or by a semaphore message? One, after all, was sent earlier to the *Helena* informing it of the casualties and damage aboard and requesting medical aid. And why didn't the *Helena* warn the *Juneau*? Apparently there was no time. Captain Hoover himself saw the wake of at least one torpedo, yet, it seems, did not warn even his own men. In fact, as the torpedo passed the *Helena*'s stern, Lt. Michael T. Tyng, the communications officer, was sending a semaphore message to a signalman on the bridge of the *Juneau*—but it was a message from Hoover to Swenson that was unrelated to the attack.

A tense silence shrouded *I-26* as the crew waited for an explosion.

"They are advancing in a beeline," the sound room reported.

Commander Yokota, in the conning tower, frowned as he glanced at his watch and sank into a chair. The projected time it would take to hit the *San Francisco*–class cruiser had passed. The torpedoes must have missed. If only he had been able to use the four damaged torpedo launchers . . .

There would be no cheers this time when he returned to Truk. Not for a Christian who had failed.

Meanwhile, aboard the *Juneau*, Lieutenant Wang left his station, climbed down the ladder to the main deck, and walked to the port side to inspect the hole that the torpedo had made in the side of the ship during the night battle. He might have been in this part of the ship. God, he felt, was certainly with him. And shortly, so were several officer friends.

"How about going to the wardroom for a sandwich or a cup of coffee," one of them said.

"No," Wang replied, "I think I'll go back and rest at my station. They're bringing sandwiches up there."

He then returned to his battle station, sat on the deck against a bulkhead, his head propped up by a life preserver, crossed his legs, and bit into a sandwich. Couldn't be more comfortable at the seashore back home. . . . He was proud of his men. He had closely observed their reaction to death and the threat of death during the night battle, and they had overcome their fears even in that burning hell. Thank Heaven that hell had passed.

At about the same time, a man wearing a dishpanlike talker helmet with earphones plugged into a gun mount asked Allen Heyn to relieve him of the heavy burden.

"Take it for a while, will you?" he said.

As Heyn took it, the man said, "Don't forget, this is Friday the thirteenth."

"So what?"

"Didn't you know? It's an unlucky number."

Superstitious bullshit! thought Heyn, as he fitted the helmet on his head.

Then, suddenly, the man, as he glanced toward the sea, gasped and his face turned pasty.

What was the guy looking at, anyway? Heyn wondered. It figured—a ghost!

At that moment, a panicky voice cried into the earphones, "Fish! Torpedo heading toward us!"

Seconds later, at 11:01 A.M., Friday the thirteenth, it smashed into a magazine, and the *Juneau* blew up.

CHAPTER

· 11 ·

An Agonizing Vision

AFTER SETTING THE COURSE IN THE *HELENA*'S CHART ROOM, COMDR. Charles L. Carpenter, navigator and officer of the deck, walked out to the portside deck of the bridge at about eleven A.M. to breathe in the ocean air and relax. He slumped into a chair, put his feet up on a stool, and gazed at the sea, hoping to reflect on less tumultuous times. But when he glanced at the crippled remnants of the *San Francisco*, the *Sterett*, and the *Juneau*, he knew he could not for an instant lapse into reverie and forget the ravages of war. Suddenly, as he was wiping his sunglasses, he noticed a white streak slicing through the water.

My God, he thought, a torpedo was whizzing straight toward his ship!

"Hard right rudder!" he yelled, leaping up from the chair. "Torpedo to port!"

The *Helena* swung to the right just in time to evade the missile.

Moments later, as Lieutenant Tyng, the communications officer, stood beside the signalman who was sending a routine semaphore message to the *Juneau*, a huge explosion suddenly shattered the peace. The signalman on the *Juneau*, with a flag in each hand, was hurled at least thirty feet into the air before disappearing in a black mist of death. Tyng was thrown to the deck and buried at the bottom of a pile of men as the force of the blast some eight hundred yards away shook the *Helena* like a toy in a hurricane.

On the *San Francisco*, about the same distance away, a jagged piece of metal spinning through the air struck a sailor on deck and broke his arm, while another knocked out an 8-inch gun. In Admiral Callaghan's cabin, Dr. O'Neil was about to operate on the gravely wounded Captain Young when he heard "the most terrific explosion I shall ever hear." He looked out the porthole and saw "tremendous clouds of gray and black smoke," but couldn't see any survivors or debris in the water.

"What was that?" he asked an assistant.

"That was the *Juneau*, doctor," the man replied. "She's gone!"

O'Neil froze. All his comrades gone at once! And he would have been with them if he had not been sent to the *San Francisco* only a short time before. Why did God single him out to be saved?

With tears in his eyes, O'Neil went back to the operating table, where Captain Young lay unconscious. He lifted the dressing from a back wound and, by the odor of the colon bacilli, knew that Young's intestinal tract had been perforated. The captain had also been injured in the head. It was too late to operate— he died on the table. O'Neil's tears soon dried up, but his heart bled. Was it his punishment for living to see life torturously ebb from every wounded man he touched?

On submarine *I-26*, Commander Yokota sat back in his chair nervously contemplating the cold reception he could expect if he returned to base without having sunk a single ship. Suddenly an explosion reverberated throughout the craft, ending his anxious speculation. And the shouts of joy aboard the *I-26* echoed almost as loudly as the deafening blast.

A hit!

Elatedly, Yokota sprang from his chair and rushed to give orders to dive to greater depth and prepare for an enemy bomb attack. Certainly the other ships wouldn't leave until they dropped bombs and picked up survivors. Why, he wondered, did the torpedo hit the *San Francisco*–class cruiser so late? Finally, he calculated that it must have struck the lighter *Atlanta*-class cruiser behind it.

Well, the victim was, after all, a cruiser. Yes, worthy of his sword.

When, after twenty minutes, no retaliatory depth-bomb explosions vibrated through the deep, Yokota ordered that the submarine rise from seventy to eighteen meters, periscope depth. Excitedly, he peered through the periscope and saw not "a shadow of the enemy." Strange that there had been no search for survivors. If they were trying to evade his second round of torpedoes, they had no cause for concern. He wouldn't loiter in the area if depth bombs were exploding around him. He wasn't suicidal.

This called for a celebration. And shortly the crew was sitting at a victory banquet, gobbling red rice and canned delicacies, washed down with sake. The men then communed with Amaterasu, the Sun Goddess, while their Christian leader offered homage to a God they were beginning to feel must have some good in Him despite His foreign origin.

Tsukuo Nakano silently thanked his mother, too. Her spirit had helped him survive to enjoy this glorious moment.

Joe Hartney, nauseous and weary, was just about to drag himself away from his lookout station at Battle Station 2, where he had been scanning the sea with his searchlight, when the explosion lifted him off the deck and sent him shooting through a narrow hatch. Amazingly, he sailed through it without his body touching the ship's structure.

Landing on the floor of a lower compartment, Hartney staggered around in complete darkness, without a ray of light coming through the portholes, though it was almost noon. Had his eyes been blown out? In terror, he rubbed his hand over them and felt something warm and sticky. Blood! He was dying! He felt his cheeks, his ears, his nose—more blood! But a few drops of the substance dripped into his mouth, and with enormous relief he realized that he was covered not with blood but with fuel oil, which rained down from the clouds of smoke rising from the ship and blotted out the sun.

Hartney groped his way back through the hatch, but as he was emerging amid the screams of men he couldn't see, his dungarees caught on a jagged piece of metal, and when he reached down to free them, he felt the water swirling around his feet.

"My God," Hartney thought. "The ship is going down right under me!"

He was unaware that the stern, where he was stationed, had been torn away from the rest of the ship when a torpedo apparently entered the wound Commander Hara had inflicted and exploded a magazine. That forward part of the ship was already completely submerged, and now the stern was sinking as well. He finally succeeded in tearing his trousers loose just as the water reached his knees. In seconds, he found himself in the grip of a swishing gurgling suction that was pulling the ship down, and him with it. Powerless to kick himself free, he went down, down, down . . .

"The pressure from the depth," he would later say, "began to close in upon me, to squeeze my brains like a giant vise, and to crush my lungs. . . . There was a great roaring in my brain and dots and streaks of fire seemed to sear my eyeballs. I knew that it was the end."

Then, a new explosion beneath him sounded in his ears like the thunder of a thousand drums.

"Depth charges!" he thought. "Now I *am* done for!"

A hatch would also help to shape Wyatt Butterfield's fate. As soon as Butterfield heard the alert, he scrambled into his gun mount, put on the earphones, and pushed the button for director control. At that moment, a torpedo hit blew him out of his seat and sent him smashing into a hatch door. The door flew open and his arm fell across the opening.

In the blackness not a sound could be heard. Had everyone abandoned ship? Butterfield wondered. No, they couldn't have moved that fast. The ghastly silence, he realized, meant the other eight men in his gun crew had been killed instantly.

After a few seconds, there was another explosion, and the hatch door slammed shut on his arm. Butterfield was trapped in the inky darkness of the mount while the water rose to his waist, and finally to his neck. He frantically tried to force the door open with his free hand and even banged his head against it, but to no avail.

"Oh, boy, I'm dead!" he thought.

Well, might as well get it over with. And he started to swallow water and oil. At that moment, a strange thought crossed his mind:

"My poor parents. Not only will they have lost their son, but here I canceled my life insurance because I couldn't keep up the payments. Here was their chance to get rich, and I blew it!"

Why was there an alert? Lester Zook was puzzled, for he was standing lookout at Battle Station 2 and he hadn't seen any sign of an enemy threat. Just as he was waiting for the ship's executive officer, who had taken charge of the station, to answer his question, the torpedo struck and suddenly draped the world in black.

Zook toppled to the deck and found himself waist deep in oil and water. He tried to swim away, but his foot got caught in the rigging of the mast, and as the ship went down, he was dragged underwater with his lungs only half full of air. He pulled at the rope, twisted it, tried to unwind it, but it only grew tighter around his ankle. Zook, the dedicated sailor, was being drawn to his death—but to an honorable one like that of his father, who had died with a mail sack on his back.

Shortly before the ship exploded, Frank Holmgren had been working below in the ammunition room as a handling man. During the night battle, he had helped to pass ammunition to the gunners on the fantail above. Now he had time to come topside and enjoy the ocean breeze. But since he hadn't eaten breakfast, he decided first to get a sandwich in the galley up forward.

The *Juneau*, Holmgren felt, was now largely out of danger. With the ship in need of an overhaul, he might even get a leave to go home. Would he soon be sitting again by the fire in Eatontown borough hall with Joyce beside him? Why not? He still carried her wishbone in his shirt pocket, and it had brought him luck so far. He'd been through all that fighting but didn't have a scratch.

Just as Holmgren started to walk forward, the ship blew up, and he went tumbling through the air. He landed with a thud on the deck in a haze of black smoke, with water flooding over him. His heart nearly stopped. The ship was going down, and he couldn't swim a stroke. There was no way out; he would die!

With all hope gone, his hand suddenly touched something soft and bouncy beside him—a life preserver! Leaning against a 20mm gun mount, he wrapped the life preserver around him, but before he could tie it he heard the roar of the ocean as it poured into the disintegrating ship, and he saw the fantail rising to an almost vertical position.

As Holmgren toppled from the deck into the water, he shouted, "I'm gonna die! I'm gonna die!"

And even the wishbone, it seemed, was powerless to save him.

Lieutenant Wang was resting against a bulkhead at his battle station nibbling on his sandwich when the *Juneau* exploded. He nearly choked on the food as he soared through the air and landed on his back—to face almost certain execution. The ship's radar antenna was spiraling straight down toward him!

Wang instinctively doubled up with his knees under his chin and shut his eyes, but though he was sure he would be hit, the seconds sped by and he felt nothing. The antenna must have missed him, he concluded as he opened his eyes and found himself caught in a swirl of fuel, smoke, and water spray. But when he tried to stand up, his right leg collapsed under him, and he realized that the antenna had, in fact, broken his leg. Since he felt no pain, however, why worry about it at this critical moment?

What was happening? The alert had somehow failed to come over his phone circuit, and he had had no warning at all of any approaching torpedo. He tried to make contact over a sound-powered phone, but it was dead. Suddenly, he felt the ship pitching forward. It was going down, and he had to jump overboard. With enormous difficulty, he lifted his broken leg over the four-foot-high splinter shield around the control station, then his other leg, and hung by his hands for a moment, trying to touch some support with his feet. Finally, he let go and dropped.

Wang landed on the main deck about thirty feet below—in about five feet of water, which fortunately broke his fall. But a few seconds later, he was completely submerged in water boiling and surging all around him. For one horrible moment, he thought he had fallen through a hole in the deck and landed in a compartment below, with the exit blocked. For as he tried to fight his way to the surface, he ran into all kinds of obstructions, from cots to corpses. With the last remnants of his breath gradually dissipating, he thought:

"What a way to die, like a trapped rat!"

And he wouldn't even have the opportunity to record his reactions.

Arthur Friend was dozing off by his 1.1 and 20mm guns at Battle Station 2 just before the explosion. He needed the sleep after the exhausting night of battle—and it offered relief from the pain in his back, which he had injured when Commander Hara's torpedo sent him crashing against a bulkhead.

Besides, sleep would help him to conserve as much energy as possible so he could maximize his chances of survival. After all, at any moment in this war his life might hinge on how quickly and decisively he acted.

The moment arrived sooner than he thought. Someone woke him with the cry, "Alert!" and in seconds the explosion hurled him through the air. When he landed on the sharply tilted deck, he could barely keep from rolling into the sea. Finally, he saw no point in hanging on, for the ship was quickly going down. To survive, he would have to get off, not stay on. And so he let himself roll to the edge of the ship, then grabbed the lifeline and threw himself overboard.

As Friend plunged into the water, he realized that, despite his expertise in the art of survival, he had made a grave error. Why the hell hadn't he been wearing a life preserver? He smashed into the sea on his previously wounded back, and the pain grew worse. His legs hurt him even more, for he had apparently injured them critically when he hit the deck. There was no time, however, to dwell on a little physical discomfort as suction pulled him ever deeper into the sea; he hardly noticed when his eardrum burst from the mounting pressure. Nor would Friend even consider dying. He would hold his breath until he could somehow save himself, even if he had to "break the world's record" for this feat.

When the torpedo struck, Heyn was thrust headfirst against his gun mount and knocked unconscious. A moment later, as he began to recover, dazed and bewildered, he removed his helmet and was aghast to see that it had been crushed, accordion-like. Although it had saved his life, the blow had fractured his skull. In his confusion, he thought it was raining, but when he wiped his face and looked at his hand, he saw that oil, not water, was showering him.

Heyn glanced around and, in the darkness, saw bodies sprawled all over the deck. But not for long, for they slid off into the sea as the stern rose grotesquely in a last-gasp salute to the gods of war. Some men, screaming and weeping, were trying to walk up the deck to jump into the sea from the fantail, but it was too slippery with oil. So they crawled to the side, held on to the lifeline, and leaped, bumping into each other during the fall.

Heyn, his mind still hazy, slowly realized that the ship was sinking. He had to get up and jump over with his shipmates. But when he tried to rise, he felt a sharp pain in his right foot and saw that it was pinned to the deck under a heavy slab of steel, apparently from the splinter shield. As water closed in around the ship, Heyn found himself trapped on a contracting little island. In a few seconds, the little island was gone, and water had risen to his waist. There was nothing he could do but go down with the ship.

Then, suddenly, he saw a life preserver floating past him. Desperately, he reached out, and though it seemed just beyond his grasp, he stretched his aching body just enough to pull it to him. But before he could tie it around his waist, he shot downward into the sea past the cadavers and the debris, his foot still clamped under the slab of steel.

Heyn pressed the life preserver to his chest, even though he realized that it could hardly save him while he was, in effect, a part of the ship.

"And so I gave up," he would later say. "I just thought there wasn't a chance at all. Everything just run through my head." His mother had said he was too young to die, that he'd miss a lot of fun.

Meanwhile, in the chart room of the destroyer *Fletcher*, which was churning ahead almost a mile in front of the *Juneau*, the skipper and his executive officer were about to break a rigid naval regulation as they lifted to their lips a paper cup brimming with forbidden whiskey. Capt. William Cole and Comdr. Joseph C. Wylie had reason to be joyous, for the *Fletcher* was the only American ship to survive the night battle without casualties or damage—despite the curse of the number thirteen. And they could thank not only their luck, but the masterful maneuvering and rapid reflexes of their crew.

The ship appeared to be doomed at one point when it was hemmed in by two Japanese destroyers to port and two to starboard. But a *Fletcher* signal officer played a trick on the enemy. When he saw one of the Japanese vessels on the port side blink a coded signal to his ship asking it to identify itself, he ran to the starboard side and flashed the same signal to one of the Japanese ships there. Thinking the inquiring ship must be friendly, this Japanese craft signaled a reply and steamed away. The *Fletcher* then raced through the gap the departing vessel left in the deadly gauntlet.

Yes, there was plenty to celebrate. But before Cole and Wylie could wet their lips, the ship trembled with the greatest explosion they had ever heard. Putting down their drink, they dashed out of the chart room and looked aft to see an enormous pillar of smoke where the *Juneau* had been. In shock, they saw tumbling toward them, in an arching trajectory, the same 5-inch gun mount that Captain Hoover had watched in disbelief as it flew over the *Helena*. When it landed about a hundred yards astern of the ship, the two men looked at each other aghast and one of them cried:

"The welders must have touched off a magazine!"

They had been sent over earlier from the *Helena* to repair the damage on the *Juneau*. The two officers then suspected that an enemy submarine was the likely culprit.

While Wylie ran to the microphone and shouted for all hands topside to take cover, Cole ordered, "Emergency flank speed ahead," then, "Right full rudder."

And the *Fletcher* turned outboard to head back to the spot where the *Juneau* had sunk so it could look for survivors and bomb the submarine if it could be found. Cole acted instinctively even though both officers agreed that no human could have survived that explosion.

But when the ship had turned almost 180 degrees, it received an order from the *Helena* by TBS: "Resume screening station."

The two commanders were dismayed. How could they leave without checking for survivors—if, by some miracle, there were any? But they had no choice. The ship turned around and resumed screening.

Shortly, Captain Hoover, apparently realizing the *Fletcher* officers would be upset, sent them an explanation: a torpedo passing between *Helena* and *San Francisco* had hit the *Juneau*, and three more submarines, it had been reported, were stealthily sailing along their route.

Wylie, at least, was mollified. Hoover, he thought, should break radio silence, but he could understand why the captain was reluctant to search for survivors. Hoover had two total cripples, *San Francisco* and *Sterett*, in his charge. And his own ship, the *Helena*, seemed to be the only relatively combat-ready cruiser in that part of the South Pacific. Yet he had just one undamaged destroyer—the *Fletcher*—to protect these ships against several submarines that might be waiting for prey. Hoover was especially worried, Wylie felt, because the Japanese submarines had a good direction-finding system and could locate the American force with relative ease. Wylie would later describe Hoover's decision as one of the most courageous of the war.

Cole, however, was skeptical. War was full of risks, but one had to take them sometimes. And this seemed like one of those times. What if there were men out there in the water? Should they be left to die?

Cole and Wylie returned to the chart room, still in shock from the momentous tragedy and wondering whether there might be survivors waiting to be rescued after all. Now the two officers really needed a drink. But some alert quartermaster or signalman had lived up to the crew's reputation for seizing the moment, in this case, the whiskey. It was gone. The commanders would have no relief from the searing vision of that monstrous cloud rising into the heavens with the souls of nearly seven hundred men.

About forty miles to the south, the crew of a B-17 patrolling bomber gazed at the cloud in bewilderment. This was no ordinary explosion. Could a single ship have gone up in that much smoke? Trouble ahead.

First Lt. Robert L. Gill, the pilot, was not unduly surprised. It was Friday the thirteenth, and the day had started out accordingly. Members of the crew, based in Espíritu Santo, had crawled out of their cots at three A.M., washed while a downpour leaked through their tent, slogged through slush to the mess hall, sat in the rain until a truck took them to their plane, and stood under the wing, chilly, sleepy, and miserable "like cattle in the lee of a barn," according to the navigator, 1st Lt. George Walker, waiting for the order to board. Finally, at eight A.M., they made a dangerous instrument takeoff, with the far end of the runway cloaked in mist and rain.

And then there was the Navy guy aboard. Thought he knew everything. Ens. Forrest C. Tanner, a Navy aviation navigator, had been sent on this special mission of the 198th Bomb Squadron, Eleventh Group, because he knew the terrain and could identify enemy ships. The plane's mission was to find the cruiser *Portland*, which was missing in the previous night's sea battle, and to spot the Japanese naval force that had fought in the battle. But in Gill's view, Tanner's advice was not really necessary. What business did a Navy man have on an Army Air Corps mission?

Gill was especially galled by Tanner's orders, which gave the ensign the final word on navigational matters in case of a difference in views. And a difference soon jelled as the plane, flying through thick clouds, approached a hilly island. Tanner was afraid the plane might hit a mountain and asked Gill to turn ten degrees to port.

No need to, Gill replied, according to Tanner.

But the mountains on the island were higher than the plane was flying, Tanner argued.

Gill finally agreed, and Tanner's assessment proved correct. The mountains were higher.

With Friday the thirteenth making so auspicious a start, the billowing black cloud in the distance seemed to Gill almost a symbol of the disquieting day this was surely destined to be. Still, the cloud could offer a hint of where the Japanese fleet might be. And so Gill resignedly headed toward the new source of trouble. Tomorrow, after all, would be another day, perhaps free of clouds and kibitzers.

A crewman of the Helena, after seeing the Juneau vanish in seconds, would write: "It was almost too much for many who saw (the Juneau) die. A man needs some kind of mental and physical reserve to accept such a disaster when not prepared for it, and we had exhausted our reserve during the night. This was not good. It was a shock to overtaut nerves and morale. In battle, with hell erupting on all sides, a man conditions himself to accept such things, but the battle had been over for hours, the sea had been peaceful, the sun shining, the white birds flying, and men's thoughts on peace and relaxation. Many a man aboard the Helena walked the deck for the following few hours in a kind of trance, brooding and frightened. The man who felt it most, perhaps, was Captain Hoover himself."

On the bridge of the Helena, Hoover stood looking back, his eyes reaching beyond the bubbly white wake of his ship to the site of the catastrophe. His face remained ashen and wooden. Like most other men who viewed the blast, Hoover was overwhelmed by the image of that awesome cloud emanating, it seemed, from the guts of the ocean, maybe from hell itself, raging, roaring, smoldering, seething, churning. For aside from the atomic bomb, which would be dropped on Japan almost three years later, this was perhaps the greatest single explosion of the war.

Little wonder that the image so brutally seared Hoover's mind and soul. For in the context of this tragedy, he was not just a man, but God. He alone had had to decide whether to go back and look for possible survivors or leave them in the water, perhaps to die. Hoover, of course, lacked the omniscience of the Almighty, and he probably did not regret this imperfection. He could not know for certain if there were any survivors floundering in the water and was therefore able to convince himself that there weren't any. How much more difficult it would be if he knew for sure that he was leaving some behind, perhaps, among them, his old classmate Swens.

But even if there were survivors, how could he save them at the risk of dooming hundreds of men on his own ship and on the others he commanded? When he had served in the Atlantic earlier in the war, he saw what the German U-boats and "wolf packs" (a group of submarines) could do.

In his struggle with his conscience, Hoover was grateful for the support of his officers and men. They couldn't all be wrong. "Let's get the hell out of here!" they cried—even though some officers wanted him to break radio silence and call for immediate help. These pleaders didn't quite realize, apparently, that the Navy was driven by rules. And the rule here was: radio only when an enemy task force was spotted or enemy planes dropped bombs. The Navy, after all, was bigger than any individual.

In any case, Hoover's crewmen were loyal and they loved him, as he loved them, and this mutual feeling was a source of great strength at this devastating moment. He only wished his own son were as respectful, disciplined, and obedient. . . .

Gilbert Jr. never did meet his father's expectations. And Gilbert Sr. never did act like the father the son pined for. Home was run like a naval academy, with the son and his two sisters by a later marriage expected to obey unquestioningly the father's every order. And woe to the one who chewed gum or made his or her bed with a wrinkle in it.

The father even demanded that Gilbert Jr. call him "sir," until the boy rebelled, insisting it was not normal for a son to address his father that way. And though the son hated military regimentation, he was expected to—and did—attend the real Naval Academy, for which his father had been training him since he was ten.

It was at this early age that Gilbert Jr. went to live with his father and stepmother. The boy had been living with his grandparents since he was one year old—from the time his mother was institutionalized for a mental disorder after she tried to kill his father. As a child, he idolized his father and would do anything to please him.

As the son grew older, however, he found it ever more difficult to please the man. He could never adjust to the strict, authoritarian demands of the Navy culture and resented the Waspish society, with its perceived clannish and prejudiced code of values that his father happily embraced. So proud was Gilbert Sr. that he falsely told his son that his mother had died when he was an infant. Not until Gilbert Jr. was twenty-seven did the elder Hoover reveal the truth. After all, madness and divorce were not the kind of family history that went over well in the father's circles.

And yet, beneath the shell of the martinet and social snob, Gilbert Jr. knew, with a tormenting ambivalence, was a man who was gentle, kind, and sensitive, a companion who would take him hunting and fishing. The father he had worshiped as a child. . . .

When Hoover first boarded the *Helena* in September 1942, crawling through a coal bag slung on a line between his old ship, a destroyer, and his new one, the crew immediately saw him as that man—fishing rod and all. As a *Helena* sailor would write:

"In his leather jacket, he looked a little like a middle-aged suburbanite about to go for a walk in the woods, with a trout rod tucked under one arm. But that room [the captain's cabin, where he met with some of the men] was a calm and confident place, mellowed already by the captain's personality. Captain Hoover belonged in it."

And this seemed especially true during the night battle. His men remembered when he placed his hand on the shoulder of a frightened, weeping young seaman and said, "Don't worry, son. I'll get you out of this."

And he did.

Now he would get his men out of this imbroglio, too. He

would not risk giving an enemy submarine the opportunity to send them to their death—even if other men might have to die.

While Captain Swenson had apparently seen each of his sailors as the mirror image of the son he had, Captain Hoover seems to have seen each of his as the son he wished he had, the son who would gladly take orders and proudly address him as "sir," showing the unstinting respect needed for a loving paternalistic relationship.

Hoover was thus buoyed by the knowledge that his men requited his love and were grateful to him for taking them out of danger, instructing their ship and the others still afloat to move swiftly in order to thwart any new submarine threat—actually faster than before, since they were no longer restricted in speed to that of the previously crippled *Juneau*. Yes, the *Helena* men loved their skipper—though it was not clear if their eagerness to "get the hell out of here" made them wonder whether they were especially worthy of their own love.

Suddenly Hoover heard a familiar sound in the distance. He looked up and saw to the north a speck in the sky. A B-17! Let the pilot take the responsibility for breaking radio silence! He ordered his signal officer to send a blinker message to the aircraft, and as soon as it came close enough, a signalman flashed the message:

"*Juneau* torpedoed and disappeared lat. 10 degrees 32 minutes S. long. 161.2 degrees 2 minutes E at 1109 x Survivors in water x Report Comsopac [Commander, South Pacific]."

Of course there were no men out there, but someone should look anyway.

Hoover felt better now. No one could charge he had abandoned survivors, even those who did not exist.

As the black cloud in the distance dissipated in the steamy morning air, Lieutenant Gill and his B-17 crew reached the motley collection of mutilated ships, about twenty-five miles southwest of the channel between Guadalcanal and San Cristobal. They were stunned to see such destruction. The worst hit of all appeared to be a near-wrecked heavy cruiser listing sharply, with its wake a series of half-moon or crescent-shaped swirls instead of the straight normal V. Clearly the ship tended to turn and was being pulled back constantly on course. What a beating those vessels must have taken. But where were the Japanese ships that had caused the damage, the task force they were supposed to find?

While Gill circled the tiny flotilla, his radio operator, Sgt. Arvid Einer, monitored all radio frequencies available for use, but not a word emanated from those ships. Then, suddenly, the crew saw blinker flashes coming from the second, less-damaged cruiser.

"Take it down!" Gill exclaimed over the intercom system.

And he and other crew members strained to decipher the message—but in vain. It was being transmitted too fast for even a Navy man like Tanner to understand. Air Corps men received less training in blinker code, and sometimes none at all.

But minutes later, Einer called Gill; he had managed to copy part of the message. Turning the controls over to his copilot, Gill rushed back to the radio compartment to see the partial message. Einer had been able to catch the word *torpedoed*, and the latitude and longitude where a ship had apparently gone down. But that was all. The message was obviously referring to the site of the black cloud they had seen.

Einer had not been trained in sending blinker signals, but he did know how to send the word *Roger*. And so he flashed it— even though he could only surmise what the whole message said.

Although they couldn't be certain, there were probably survivors, Gill and Tanner agreed, unaware of the sudden disintegration of the torpedoed ship. But what should they do—radio their home base at Espíritu Santo or fly to Henderson Field on Guadalcanal, about forty-five minutes away, and report the sinking in person?

"To me," Tanner says he told Navigator Walker, "this is important enough to break radio silence." And he asked Walker to convey this view to Gill.

But Gill was in no mood to take advice from a know-it-all Navy guy—especially since he would be putting his own neck on the block. He had received strict orders not to break radio silence unless he sighted an enemy task force or got caught in an air raid. The Japanese had broken the code a number of times, even though it was changed every few days, and they had learned information "harmful to us." So he wasn't going to risk divulging such information. In any case, if the commander of those ships "wanted this reported by radio, he would have sent it himself."

Since this wasn't a navigational problem, Gill, not Tanner, had the final word now. And he decided to head for Henderson Field, from where PBY seaplanes could be sent to the area. Also, there were PT boats on the neighboring island of Tulagi.

"This alternative," Gill replied to Tanner, "is the best solution."

But first he would fly over the area where the sinking took place—now about fifteen miles away—to look for survivors so he would know what to report.

Gill hoped all this hopping around would not take too much time. Headquarters, after all, had given him an urgent mission, and he had barely started on it.

CHAPTER

· 12 ·

The Echo of Despair

PLUMMETING INTO THE DEPTHS, JOE HARTNEY WAS SURE HE WAS headed for his grave when a violent explosion in the water far beneath him made the sea tremble. But the blast, apparently triggered by the flooding of the ship's boilers with cold water, sent him hurtling to the surface "like a shot out of a cannon." He was thrown into the air, and when he plopped back in the water, he stuffed his lungs with oxygen and floated on the waves gasping and gagging from fuel oil, which coated the sea like a six-inch layer of soft tar.

Hartney's head throbbed as if it had been struck with a wrecking ball, and every muscle in his body ached. But he couldn't just let himself be carried from wave to wave. He wiped the oil from his eyes and saw through the fuzz a boxlike object, which he could hang on to. Though a good swimmer, he now barely found the strength to paddle over to it and hook his arm around it.

Then, before his blurry eyes, he saw a rubber raft some yards away with several men clinging to it. With his free arm, Hartney moved toward it, when suddenly something blocked his path. Still half-blind, he couldn't make it out but pushed it aside, only to have the waves send it right back. What the hell was it?

Hartney wiped his eyes again and stared at the thing. My God! A headless, naked torso! Like some gimmick in a horror show, it rammed against him, receded with the waves, then struck him again.

"Panic gripped me," he would say, "so that I wanted to yell. I fought it off. It might—it might be someone I knew.... I couldn't get around it. I couldn't get away from it.... All the horror of the past few hours seemed concentrated in that one lifeless piece of flesh." Just as it had been in that circle of floating Japanese heads he had seen during the night battle.

Hartney was glad the cadaver didn't have a face. Yes, it might be someone he knew—perhaps himself. And he didn't want to feel he had died again.

Wyatt Butterfield was already underwater in his tomblike gun mount when suddenly the fast currents loosened the door that had pinned his arm to the hatch. He struggled to the surface, "alternately praying and cursing," and right there, within arm's length, was an oval-shaped "doughnut" life raft made of balsa wood with an underwater floor of wooden slats and support ropes dangling from a foot-high rim. Empty. Maybe he was the only survivor. Butterfield heaved himself onto the raft and instantly began to vomit the oil and water he had swallowed.

Heads then started to bob up through the oil slick and the debris—mattresses, rolls of toilet tissue, clothing, anything that could float. As he pulled these survivors aboard, he was sickened to see their wounds. They were mutilated, blind, half-mad with pain. One sailor's scalp had been almost completely severed from his head, and he kept pushing it back from his face. Another man's calves had been blown off his legs, and in minutes he bled to death. Butterfield himself had a long, open gash in his arm caused by the hatch door, and his back and legs were peppered with metal fragments.

Yet, because the water level in the raft was so high, the men could not lie down—they could only stand, sit, or kneel while leaning against the rim. They gazed at each other like strangers, unable to recognize their shipmates, for oil covered the face, the hands, the clothing, everything; it seeped into every pore. They knew someone's identity only when he spoke or wiped his face with the dry inside sheets of toilet paper, taken from the rolls that littered the sea like tiny buoys.

Soon about twenty men had crowded onto this little floating oasis while others bobbed in the water holding on to the ropes dangling from it. Finally, a net from the ship, kept afloat with corks, was tied to the raft and the seriously wounded could lie down until they died and found peace in the engulfing sea, making room for newcomers.

Frank Holmgren was one of the newcomers. His wishbone had finally come to the rescue, and he had not died, after all, when he slid from the deck into the sea, even though he didn't know a butterfly stroke from a dog paddle.

Holmgren kept plunging into the depths, then suddenly slowed down and started rocketing back. But was he already dead? Resigned to being a corpse, he thought it would be appropriate to act like one; he shut down his mind and felt nothing.

When he reached the surface, however, he decided this couldn't be heaven, not with all the navigation charts, bottles, trash, and toilet paper floating around to remind him of earthly needs. But he did thank heaven for the life jacket that he had found under his hand when the ship was about to go under. Without it, he might still be diving to bedrock. He would also be eternally grateful to the blessed chicken that had supplied the wishbone.

But what would he do in the middle of the ocean, alone and immobile? Even if he saw something he could cling to, he couldn't swim to it. If his wishbone would work once more . . .

It did. As Holmgren looked around, he saw only a few yards away a raft crowded with men.

"Come and get me!" he yelled.

"You paddle over here!" someone replied.

While doubtful that he could, even with his life jacket, Holmgren wildly flailed his arms and finally splashed his way to the raft that Wyatt Butterfield had found. But after being pulled aboard, he didn't stay long, for the raft was so overloaded that no one could move. He dragged himself onto the safety net that was tied to the raft, along with Charlie Hayes, his closest friend back home in Eatontown, who might now have wished he had not tried so hard to work off those extra pounds to meet Navy enlistment requirements.

As they sat among the dying, thoughts of the living flashed through their minds, thoughts of old friends and old times. And Holmgren kept imagining he was back with Joyce sitting by the fire in borough hall. Maybe he would be soon. Only minutes had passed since the sinking. Surely one of the other ships in the task group would pick them up.

As Lester Zook plunged ever more deeply into the ocean, he finally managed to extricate his leg from the rigging of the mast, but he was drowning, for he had been pulled underwater so swiftly that he did not have a chance to fill his lungs with air. He tried to swim to the surface, but there was so much suction that he soon gave up. With his breath about gone, he was resigned to death. Suddenly he started to rise involuntarily, faster, faster, and he broke through the oily surface.

Though barely conscious, Zook made out the fuzzy outline of a raft nearby and, without a life jacket, dog-paddled toward it, dragging his severely injured leg.

"Over here! Over here!" a voice called out.

When Zook reached the raft and saw there wasn't room even on the net, he decided he'd be more comfortable in the water hanging on to a rope. He had little strength and his leg throbbed with pain, but he could hold on, he was sure, until one of the other ships came—perhaps in half an hour or so.

Lieutenant Wang did not die like a "trapped rat" after all. His right leg was useless after the radar antenna had fallen on it and he had leaped from his battle station to the main deck, then into the water. But he fought relentlessly to stay alive, even after being sucked down by the currents almost, it seemed, to the bottom of the sea. He still had the strength and will to swim back through an obstacle course of 5-inch gun mounts and depth-charge projections that left him out of breath and with deep gashes on his face and head.

He popped to the surface just in time. There he met two other men, and together they swam toward a net still rolled up in canvas. As they clung to it, Wang cut off the canvas with a knife and the three unrolled the net. Shortly, it was swarming with survivors, almost all horribly wounded—legs severed or broken, skulls split open, muscles torn away.

Wang had studied medicine, and he wanted to help these men, but there were no drugs, no splints. He couldn't even help himself, though he was in pain. His broken leg was bleeding, with the shinbone, the tibia, fractured near the ankle and protruding. The fibula, the smaller bone on the side of the leg, was broken as well.

To stop the blood, he tied his feet together with his shoelaces and placed them on a plank he had grabbed as it floated by. When that didn't work, he held the leg down in the churning water and the bleeding finally stopped. Eventually his raftmates put a tourniquet on his leg above the knee with a piece of white line that Wang had in his pocket. But the pain maddeningly persisted.

Now he himself would be a guinea pig in this grotesque laboratory for studying the human mind and body under unendurable stress. Fortunately, with the other ships coming to rescue them soon, the research period, he felt, would be short.

Arthur Friend may not have broken the world's record for holding one's breath underwater, as he had vowed to do if necessary, but he held it long enough to swim to the surface with his powerful arms and achieve his aim—survival.

By the time he came up, three rafts were floating nearby. Just as he had planned. He had helped cut them loose from the ship, thinking this might happen. Well, it had happened, and now there was no question about it; he would come through this war alive.

Friend swam over to the nearest raft and climbed in. Anybody he knew? He couldn't tell, for every survivor, like him, had an oil-blackened face. But he did recognize one man—Albert Sullivan. A nice guy. Glad he survived.

Friend was glad all these guys survived. But did they thank him for saving their lives? Hell no! Never mind, he'd outlive them all.

As Allen Heyn went down with the ship, his foot still caught in a vise of steel, he clasped his life jacket to his chest, but was sure he'd be anchored to the bottom of the sea forever. He never quite reached there, however, for as he was about to pass out, his foot came loose in the buffeting currents, and the life jacket sent him shooting back into the world he was too young to leave.

"I couldn't see anybody," Heyn would say. "I thought, gee, am I the only one here?"

As he contemplated populating a whole world alone, he put on his life preserver and paddled around, looking for some object that would support him, a potato crate or anything, until he could find a more permanent home. Who would be looking for one man in the middle of the ocean?

Though his head ached and his whole body was sore, Heyn didn't yet realize that his skull had been fractured and his torso pocked with shrapnel. His mind was so hazy that he "didn't think a thing about the other ships." Then, suddenly, an empty raft "just popped right up in front of me." Heyn grabbed it and held on, but then heard someone crying for help. He swam over to a man who was about to go under and saw that his leg had been blown off.

"Shoot me! Shoot me!" the sailor pleaded.

But Heyn didn't have a gun. With the man in tow, he swam back to the raft, where other survivors who had just climbed on sat in shock, one apparently half-mad; he was distributing all his soggy dollars to his companions. The last ones to arrive had to hang on to the ropes. George Sullivan was among them.

"Am I glad to see you," Heyn said. "How'd you get off?"

He had been on the fantail when the ship capsized, George said, and had worked his way over to the side, grabbed a lifeline, and jumped into the sea.

"Have you seen any of my brothers?" George asked anxiously. "No."

George then reached up and wiped away the oil from the men's faces with toilet tissue just to make sure. No luck.

"Well, I'm going to try to find them!" he exclaimed.

And George, though in pain from his back injury, swam away to two rafts nearby, the only other ones in sight, to ask the same question: Had anyone seen his brothers? Nobody was really sure, for it was hard to distinguish one black face from another.

So again he assaulted them with toilet tissue, once more without success.

As he swam around, George called out the names of his siblings: "Frank, Al, Matt, Red! Are you here? This is George!"

And the names kept echoing in the breezeless emptiness.

Finally, according to Heyn, George found Albert hanging on to a rope attached to Heyn's raft. The younger brother was in shock and had not answered to his name, while Heyn had not recognized him under his black mask.

What happened to Frank, Red, and Matt? the two brothers asked each other. In mutual despair, neither could answer.

Perhaps they should have asked Arthur Friend, who was on Heyn's raft and says he saw not only George and Albert, but Red, who was, Friend claims, sitting in one of the other rafts. He recognized this Sullivan, as apparently no one else did, despite his blackened face.

"I gave him enough haircuts," Friend would explain.

Red's head had been split open, according to Friend. If Red had indeed survived the explosion, he must have died soon afterward, for Friend says he did not see him after the first day in the water. Sadly enough, despite the claims of Red's motorcycle pals that he had "nine lives," he proved to have but one.

When Heyn asked Albert how he managed to get off the ship, the youngest Sullivan stammered, "I don't know. All of a sudden, I was in the water."

As he had been as a child, with his four elder brothers, when their mud-patched boat sank in the Cedar River. God had saved them then. All of them. But where was God now?

That was what many of the men were asking as they watched the other ships recede toward the horizon. Betrayed!

"You sons of bitches!" one man yelled. "Get back here! Guys are dying here!"

Hadn't the men on the *Juneau* risked their necks to pick up survivors from the *Wasp* when it was going down? Why now were they being left to die?

Still, few doubted that the ships would be back or would send help within hours. After all, this was the U.S. Navy.

And, in fact, even before the flotilla was out of sight, the men heard the rumble of a plane growing ever louder. A PBY sea-plane was coming to save them!

The plane was actually Lieutenant Gill's B-17, and as the group of survivors loomed larger, the crew, staring through the windows, was stunned. First, they saw what looked like two tiny dolls splashing around and waving at the edge of a huge oil slick.

"There they are!" someone cried over the interphone.

Floating in the slick for about a mile was debris of every size and color—black, gray, white, yellow. And amid this wreckage were several rafts, each crammed with oil-covered men. And then there were, as Navigator Walker would write in his diary, "many, many tiny black coconuts floating in the mess like pea-nuts in brittle—men floating, swimming to rafts and pieces of wreckage. . . . All of them were waving their arms at us or . . . what looked to be pieces of cardboard. We could see the white-gray of their faces where they had wiped off the oil. Otherwise they were black and bedraggled."

The plane circled this scene several times looking for signs of the submarine, then roared low over the survivors at 180 miles an hour. The crew tried to count the men, and the average count was about 180. The survivors themselves estimated that they numbered from 125 to 140. The aerial calculation was per-haps the more accurate one since the total picture could best be seen from the air. If so, many more men died in the water than history would record, some undetected by those who would survive.

Meanwhile, Navigator Walker computed the exact position of the survivors in the water, marked it on his navigation chart, labeled it, and entered it in his log. No one suggested dropping rubber rafts or supplies to the men.

Ensign Tanner advised Gill, "We should send a message to the ship that signaled us telling them how many are in the water."

"No," Gill replied, "we can't open up on the radio unless we see a Jap carrier at least."

"How about sending a blinker?" Tanner then suggested.

"We don't have anyone aboard who's trained to do it."

"I am," said Tanner.

Gill then agreed, and the plane thundered back to the *Helena*, whose identity the crew still did not know. Tanner would say he flashed the message. At least 150 men were afloat, he repeated over and over again, and they had little floating equipment.

The *Helena* blinked a *Roger* and continued on its way, together with the other ships in the task group.

Captain Hoover now apparently knew that the "impossible" had proved possible. He had left scores of men behind, perhaps to die. But he would not turn back. Even so, the number of people in the water must surely have shaken him, for he could no longer ease his conscience with the rationale that a search for survivors would have been fruitless, as well as dangerous. Nor did he see any greater need now to break radio silence. The plane crew, after all, had seen the survivors, and the pilot would certainly radio for help with a firsthand description of the scene.

But Lieutenant Gill still planned to head for Guadalcanal and report on the tragedy personally. As Walker would write in his diary:

"There was nothing they could do; the sub was no doubt lurking in the vicinity waiting for rescue ships. There was little we could do either."

En route to Guadalcanal, the plane "returned to the pitiful sight" and circled over the survivors. Again, no one thought of dropping rubber rafts or supplies.

While many of the men in the water cursed once more those who would "heartlessly" abandon them, Lester Zook, always the pragmatist, was more tolerant. The plane, he felt, was obviously gathering information for rescue crews, and the survivors would shortly be picked up. He could understand why the ships did not stop and come back for them. After all, there was an enemy submarine out there. One had to make some tough choices in war.

After hanging on to a rope for about two hours, Zook found some space on the raft next to John Grycky, the violinist, who had also cheated death. Zook wasted no time helping to organize the survivors into a viable community. Only three officers were still alive, including the severely wounded Lieutenant Wang. The other two were Lt. John Blodgett and Ens. Jock Pitney, who had suffered less serious injuries.

Captain Swenson was nowhere to be seen and had evidently gone down with his ship. He had died proudly after engaging in fierce battle with the enemy, though it isn't likely he died happily. So many of his sons had gone down with him, among them the Coombs brothers, Russell and Charles, who had sailed together on the *Juneau* after Charles survived the sinking of the *Wasp*; the Rogers brothers, Patrick and Louis; and the Sullivan brothers, Frank, Matt, and possibly Red. And while no one would ever again besmirch the captain's name, his daughter, still hostile toward him, apparently did not feel pride in that name.

Blodgett, as the most senior surviving officer, thus took over command of the group, and Zook eagerly helped him. The lieutenant was a Naval Academy man, a forceful, efficient officer in Zook's discriminating eyes, the kind of man he admired. And the other men greatly respected him as well.

The sailors in the three rafts, using the paddles they found in them, rowed toward one another and tied the rafts together. Ten nets were attached to the last one in line, and they fanned out like peacock feathers. All the nets would serve as floating beds for the severely wounded. Each of the three officers manned a different raft to maintain discipline and see that food and water tucked away in his raft were equitably distributed, even though Wang, in his agonized state, was in no position to make decisions or to help anyone, even himself. A first class petty officer, George Mantere, was put in charge of the nets, and he tended to the wounded as best he could.

Having helped to achieve a semblance of order, Zook turned to bookkeeping with his usual penchant for accuracy. Who was dead and who was alive? How fast were they dying of their wounds? He removed a soggy little pad and a pencil from his shirt pocket and began counting heads—20, 50, 100, 125 ... Perhaps more, since the waves impeded his vision beyond a certain point. Then he tried to learn the identity of those on the rafts and nets and in the water. But they were dying fast, and it was sometimes difficult to tell whether a person was dead or simply unconscious. Some expired while climbing from raft to raft, falling into the water and drowning.

As soon as one looked dead, he was cast into the sea—though George Sullivan argued that there should be some kind of reverent ceremony first. The body was, he argued, not just a hunk of flesh, but a human being with a soul. Some of the religious teaching George and his brothers had absorbed as youngsters, despite their indifference at the time, had apparently taken root.

There was, however, no time for such formality. Men were still in the water clutching ropes, and so the bodies, dead or apparently dead, had to be quickly disposed of to make room for the living, especially since there was a growing fear that sharks would soon be joining the party. Everyone prayed that rescue ships would arrive first.

About forty miles from Guadalcanal, Lieutenant Gill and his B-17 crew detected a faint haze of smoke, and under it a small vessel. Was this part of the Japanese task force they were supposed to be searching for?

Gill swooped down to investigate, but the craft simply disappeared, leaving a slick of oil on the sea. The crew realized then that the ship was a submarine, probably the one that sank the American vessel.

"What we wouldn't have given to have machine-gunned it," Walker wrote in his diary.

But it was too late.

As the plane neared Henderson Field with flaps down, the crew could see trucks, jeeps, and men racing across it. Two of the men ran to the end of the runway and waved the plane off, pointing to the sky. An enemy air raid was in progress!

Was it too late to dart back into the sky? In near desperation, Gill "poured the coal" to the motors and they roared, but the big plane, lumbering now with its airspeed gone, dropped ever lower. As the toylike trees at the end of the runway swiftly matured into giant hands greedily reaching for the aircraft, the crewmen braced for what seemed certain death—not only for them, but for the men in the water.

*　　*　　*

LEFT TO DIE

On the first day, these men were not entirely without food, water, or cigarettes. For on each raft there were six cans of corned beef, one five-pound tin of hardtack, three beakers of fresh water, and several tins of cigarettes. Unfortunately, however, the men couldn't smoke the cigarettes because they might accidentally set the oil-blanketed water on fire; they could drink only a little of the water because the spigots wouldn't work, and salt water had seeped into the containers anyway; and they couldn't eat the corned beef because the cans had fallen into the water while the men were asleep. To make matters worse, those who had earlier tasted the corned beef became thirstier than ever.

That night, however, hunger and thirst were the least disturbing of the miseries plaguing the men. A rainstorm late in the day was welcome, for they would hold out empty cigarette tins and trap at least a few drops of water. But with darkness, the tropical heat turned to icy cold, and some on the rafts jumped into the much warmer water, drowning if their wounds had greatly weakened them. In fact, the night hideously rang with the screams of men dying an agonizing death. Every few minutes, it seemed, a body would be thrown into the sea.

Some of the survivors still consoled themselves with the "certainty" of imminent rescue.

"They'll be here soon," Heyn assured his shipmates. "They'll come."

But another man cried, "They won't come! We're finished!"

And these seesaw assurances echoed tormentedly across the ocean.

Daylight, it seemed, would never come. The rescuers probably couldn't spot them in the dark. The dead, all were dreadfully aware, could take the living with them. For their bodies might draw the sharks that lurked ever more terrifyingly in everyone's mind.

But then hope overcame despair. The ships in the task group and the planes that flew overhead earlier in the day had surely informed headquarters of their plight. The men didn't realize that the same plane had flown over twice.

*   *   *

As this plane now screeched over Henderson Field, Lieutenant Gill jerked back the wheel at the last moment, steering the plane over the treetops at the edge of the runway "with a foot or so to spare." In a moment or two, the aircraft regained proper speed and the wheels and flaps were up. The crew groaned a collective sigh of relief.

Gill was now in a quandary. Should he return all the way to headquarters at Espíritu Santo to get help for the survivors, even though he had been sent on a special mission of vital importance? Or should he continue on that mission? He still would not break radio silence. His mission, he finally decided, had top priority.

Gill thus flew toward Tulagi to the north, searching for the missing *Portland* and the elusive Japanese task force. He turned and flew by the north side of Savo Island, then scanned the waters around the islands of Santa Isabel, New Georgia, and Rendova. No success anywhere. At about one-thirty P.M., two and a half hours after the sinking, Gill's conscience took command.

"The hell with this!" he exclaimed. "We're going back to Espíritu and report the sinking of our cruiser."

The homeward path once more took the plane over the survivors. The scene seemed more terrible than ever, since the airmen themselves had just barely escaped disaster and had tasted the fear of dying. What terror must be seizing the minds of those men down there. They had already been in the water almost three and a half hours.

As he made three passes over them, Gill felt helpless—until Staff Sgt. William R. Entrikin, the radio operator, suggested, "We got two extra rubber life rafts. Let's drop them and some rations."

Gill would later say he wondered why he "didn't think of it." A good idea. And he dropped two extra yellow inflatable life rafts containing some metal watertight boxes with food and medical supplies wrapped in life preservers.

Then, at about two-thirty P.M., on to Espíritu Santo, where the plane would roar in at approximately five-thirty P.M., six and a half hours after the *Juneau* had sunk into its grave.

* * *

LEFT TO DIE

On the following morning, November 14, Allen Heyn awoke from a brief sleep and surveyed the tiny community of rafts and nets. Many of the ropes attached to the rafts were dangling in the water, and the nets, which had been carpeted with writhing flesh the night before, had become sparsely occupied. The wounded still alive were consolidated on three or four of them; about fifty men had died of their wounds during the night and had been tossed into the sea by their buddies. The rafts were home only for the living. Now no one had to remain in the water.

Among the men missing was Albert Sullivan, who had apparently been clinging to a rope. George, who had swum off looking for his other brothers, had not noticed he was gone until daylight, when he climbed on the raft.

"Where is Al?" he asked everyone in desperation. "Where is my brother? What's happened to him?"

He had apparently lost his other brothers. Had he lost Al, too? Although he didn't know it, he may have lost Red as well during the night—if Arthur Friend had actually seen him the day before on another raft, as he claimed.

Could not Al and his other brothers be alive on some raft out of sight? George despairingly suggested to Heyn. It was a big ocean, wasn't it?

"Al, where are you?" George again cried out with a pathos that moved even men who were themselves at the edge of death. "Red, Matt, Frank, answer me! Where are you? It's your brother George."

How could they leave him alone? What would he tell Mama? Tears mixed with oil streaked down his face.

Heyn and the others were bitter, too. Those fifty or so guys might still be alive if they had been picked up the previous day. The rest of the survivors would have to be rescued this day, for they had almost run out of fresh water and food and had no medicine; the rafts and supplies dropped from Lieutenant Gill's B-17 had apparently fallen out of reach.

But the sharks would not go hungry.

As soon as Lieutenant Gill landed in Espíritu Santo, he rushed to the Quonset hut of the Eleventh Bombardment Group

Headquarters to report the sinking of an unknown cruiser. But as he was describing the scene, the debriefing intelligence officer, a captain, interrupted him:

"Yes, but what happened on the mission?"

Gill was "disturbed." Didn't the captain care about all those men out there? He had flown to Guadalcanal in order to inform headquarters of the sinking, he explained, but had been waved off when he tried to land because of an air attack. He had then searched for the *Portland* and the Japanese task force, but had not found any trace of them. . . . Now, those men in the water . . .

All right, the officer said testily, what had he seen?

Gill then described the plight of the survivors and told of his brief communication with a cruiser (the *Helena*). He didn't know what ship had been sunk, but it was also a cruiser, he was sure.

"Okay," said the captain when told the exact location of the survivors at the time of sighting. "That'll be all."

And Gill departed, fearing that the man would not act urgently.

Gill's account, in fact, was treated just like any routine item, buried in the Daily Operations Report of the Eleventh Bombardment Group Headquarters for November 13, 1942. No one apparently noticed the single short paragraph or was even curious about what ship went down. After all, it was the sixth and last item mentioned under the heading "Unidentified."

According to Gill's radioman, Sergeant Entrikin, the intelligence officer later told him that he had delayed sending the report to naval headquarters aboard the seaplane tender, the *Curtis*, until all patrol aircraft had returned that evening and filed their reports with him. Then he threw the whole batch into one bag, and delivered it to the tender by regular courier service—though Gill's report, the officer claimed, was labeled "urgent priority."

Why hadn't the officer sent the report by special courier? He was short of men, he explained, and had no one to run errands. He didn't explain why he failed to radio the information. The task group was no longer in the area and would not have been endangered.

Nor is it clear why Gill did not personally report to the naval

commanding officer so he could give him a firsthand account
of the tragedy and make sure action was taken urgently. According to Ensign Tanner, he should have, though Tanner made
no effort himself to generate action, relying on Gill to do so.

In any case, with so many routine reports to review, no one
got around to sending a rescue mission on Friday the thirteenth.

The following day, Joey Rogers heard aboard his supply ship
that a "big battle" had been fought off Guadalcanal and suspected that the *Juneau* was involved. He asked the radio operator, who was monitoring all reports:

"Dominique, tell me what's happened in the battle."

"All right, Joe, I will," the operator agreed, knowing Joey had
two brothers serving on the ship. "The *Juneau* was in it. Hell
broke loose."

"Anything about the ship?"

"No, but I'll let you know when there is."

A little later, Joey asked if there was any new information.

"Couple of ships were hit, but not the *Juneau*."

Still later: "Joey, come here. I just heard the *Juneau* was hit
up forward and listing forward. But it's still under way with
one screw. It's headed, it seems, for Espíritu Santo for repairs."

"Fast or slow?"

"It can't go very fast."

A moment later, the operator cried, "Jesus Christ, Joe, wait a
moment. It's just been hit again—amidships. It's blown up and
gone under like a volcano!"

"Jesus Christ!" Joey exclaimed, his face a gray mask. "Any
survivors?"

"I don't think so, Joe. It went up like a volcano. Right out of
sight."

Joey didn't shed a tear. Somehow the news did not seem real.
It couldn't be. He felt only a terrible numbness. Yet he knew it
had happened; in fact, it was supposed to happen. Kill or be
killed—wasn't that war? As in the ring, it was hard to escape
that one knockout punch. It was a miracle that he and Jimmy
had not gone down with their brothers. But how could he tell
Jimmy? He might crack up.

In a daze, Joey went to look for his brother.

"Jimmy," he called, "come here. I got somethin' to tell ya."

"What you gonna say?" Jimmy asked, suspecting that something was wrong.

Joey put his arm around him and said, "Jimmy, it happened. The *Juneau* got hit."

"What happened to Pat and Louie?"

"I don't know, Jimmy. They say the ship went right down."

"Oh, bullshit! They're all right."

"I don't know, Jimmy. I hope so. But I think they're gone."

"Naw, they're all right."

Joey wanted to believe it, too. Maybe Pat, at least, was thrown clear of the ship; he worked topside. But Louie, no. He was below.

Oh, God . . . No, he didn't believe in God. . . . How could he face Pop? . . . Why couldn't he weep, as he did after taking that dive? Just one tear to ease the pain. But none would come.

CHAPTER

· 13 ·

Just Another Day

SHORTLY AFTER TEN P.M. ON NOVEMBER 13, CAPTAIN HOOVER USED the TBS to finally inform Admiral Turner, aboard the USS *McCawley*, that the *Juneau* had been sunk. But strangely, he said nothing, it seems, about the B-17 sighting survivors in the water and did not request a search for them. In any case, no search was ordered.

Late the next day, the task group sailed into the port of Espíritu Santo and Hoover immediately radioed Admiral Halsey in Nouméa that his flotilla had arrived, but simply listed the ships without mentioning either the sinking or the survivors. He apparently thought that Turner had already informed Halsey of the tragedy.

Hoover then handed a report on the sinking to Rear Adm. Aubrey W. Fitch, Commander, Air, South Pacific, who was also based in Espíritu Santo.

Had he received the blinker message the *Helena* had sent to the B-17 about the sinking? Hoover asked.

No, he hadn't, Fitch replied.

Hoover was bewildered. The B-17 must have reported his message and its own sighting, he felt. But apparently the report wasn't given a high priority.

His bewilderment was understandable. Fitch had either not received the November 13th Daily Operations Report of the Eleventh Bombardment Group Headquarters or had received it but failed to read it. And no one brought the item to his attention. Nor had Turner passed on to Fitch the information he had been given by Hoover the night before. The air commander thus knew nothing about the sinking.

But even now, after learning of it from Hoover himself, Fitch did not urgently put the rescue machinery into motion, though he must have presumed there were survivors out there.

When Joe Hartney had finally managed to wiggle past the headless corpse, he swam to an overcrowded raft some distance away. He hung on to a rope dangling from it and gripped it all that day and night. The next morning he climbed aboard the raft, which was tied to the two other rafts and the ten cork nets, and found himself nursing the badly wounded Lieutenant Wang, who was hallucinating. Hartney and another man sat on either side of Wang as he lay on the rim and held on to him so he wouldn't fall overboard. When the lieutenant fell unconscious, Hartney stretched him across his lap.

Later in the day, a DC-3 Army transport plane flew over and dropped an inflatable rubber boat about one hundred yards away. Damn it! Too far! It was almost impossible to paddle that far with the currents moving against the men. Still, the rubber boat dropped from heaven was a sign that a ship would soon be coming to pick them up. Sure . . . the Navy wouldn't just let them stay out there and die.

Hartney, however, was impatient. He looked down at the sweating face of Wang, who needed fresh water, food, medicine. Maybe there was some wrapped in that big yellow bundle. But how could he get it? He scanned the sea, and suddenly he saw a dorsal fin, then another, cutting through the water. With the little armada of rafts finally clear of the oil slick that morning, the sharks had begun to arrive to feed on the dozens of bodies littering the sea—perhaps on the men aboard the rafts and nets, too.

These predators were six- to ten-foot-long man-eating sand sharks, the kind that lurked off the tropical coasts. They were

After a ferocious sea battle off Guadalcanal on November 13, 1942, the USS *Juneau,* an antiaircraft cruiser, was limping along with the vestiges of a thirteen-ship task group when suddenly a torpedo fired by Japanese submarine *I-26* crashed into it. The ship exploded into bits and vanished in seconds. The four remaining vessels in the flotilla raced ahead, abandoning about one hundred forty survivors to sharks and other terrors of the sea. Only ten out of almost seven hundred men were rescued—more than a week after the disaster. *U.S. Navy*

The nearly seven hundred members of the USS *Juneau* crew pose at the commissioning of the ship in February 1942 in the New York Navy Yard. They could not have imagined that only ten of them would be alive nine months later. *U.S. Navy*

Capt. Lyman Knut Swenson, the *Juneau*'s skipper, knew that his frail craft was extremely vulnerable to enemy fire and not suitable for ship-to-ship combat. But he fought with great courage in the Battle of Friday the Thirteenth, the most chaotic and deadly sea clash of World War II. *Courtesy of Robert Swenson*

Capt. Swenson (left) poses with his son, Robert (right), and a friend at the U.S. Naval Academy, where Robert was a midshipman. After a messy divorce, Swenson's wife had kidnapped their son and daughter and the captain did not find them until they were teenagers. He drew very close to his son but was shunned by his daughter, Cecilia, who was thought by family friends to have been brainwashed into believing he had abused her as a child. He was devastated when Cecilia refused to see him before he left on his last voyage. *Courtesy of Robert Swenson*

Capt. Gilbert Hoover, skipper of the USS *Helena,* took over command of the depleted task group when its top commanders were killed. Seeing the *Juneau* blow up, he had to make an instant decision: send one of his ships to search for survivors, or rush on before the attacking submarine could sink another vessel. He chose to rush on, a decision that led to his disgrace. *Courtesy of Ann Wood*

Capt. Hoover and his family (from left to right): Mrs. Hoover; daughter Ann; son Gilbert, Jr.; daughter Katherine; and Hoover. Gilbert, Jr., rebelled against his martinet father, who demanded that the youth address him as "sir." The captain thus looked to members of his crew for the "respect" he craved. They were especially grateful to him for refusing to risk their lives by lingering in the area of the *Juneau's* sinking in order to look for survivors. *Courtesy of Gilbert Hoover, Jr.*

The five Sullivan brothers (from left): Joseph (Red), Francis (Frank), Albert, Madison (Matt), and George. They persuaded the Navy to assign them all to the *Juneau,* and all of them died together in the greatest family disaster in naval history when the ship was sunk. George, the eldest, was the last to die—ripped apart by three sharks after vainly churning the waters in search of his drowned brothers. For days his voice could be heard pathetically calling out their names. *Waterloo Courier*

The Sullivan family—standing, from left, Albert, George, May Abel, Madison, Joseph, and Francis; sitting, from left, Katherine Rooff, Alleta, Thomas, James, and Genevieve. Mother Alleta, the backbone of the family, reluctantly accepted the decision of her five sons to serve on the same ship. Their death killed her spiritually. Father Thomas, a less forceful character, left his railroad job after the disaster and drowned his grief in alcohol. *Courtesy of Murray Davidson*

Margaret Jaros wrote Joseph Sullivan on a dare from her friends after seeing his picture in a newspaper. They met when he went on liberty, immediately fell in love, and became engaged. Margaret had a premonition of disaster when a friend told her on seeing a pearl ring from Joseph that "pearls bring tears." With Joseph gone, she married after the war and was widowed many years later, but she says she mourns Joseph more than she does her husband because "that was an unfinished romance."
Courtesy of Margaret Jaros Woods

Beatrice Imperato begged her fiancé, Madison Sullivan, to request a transfer from the *Juneau* to another ship for fear that all the brothers might perish together. But he refused, saying that they would fight as one and, if necessary, die as one. Like Margaret Jaros, she is still in mourning for her lost love, and one of her grandchildren was named after Madison.
Courtesy of Beatrice Imperato Ferreri

The four Rogers brothers (from left): Joseph, James, Louis, and Patrick. All talented boxers, they also joined the *Juneau* crew together, even though their mobster father wanted them to fight only in the ring. Joseph and James transferred to another ship shortly before the *Juneau* was sunk and had to live with the question of why God had spared them and not their brothers. *Courtesy of James Rogers*

Lester Zook, shown with his wife, Mary, was one of the ten men who survived the *Juneau* disaster after floundering for more than a week in the sea. A tough-minded pragmatist, he was obsessed with the need to excel in the performance of duty—his own and that of his shipmates—remembering that his father, a postman, had died "with a mail sack on his back." He helped to direct the struggle for survival.
Courtesy of Lester Zook

Allen Heyn, barely seventeen, was the youngest sailor on the *Juneau,* and so was viewed by his shipmates as one of the least likely men to survive. But he remained alive in the water longer than any of them, being picked up after sharks and madness claimed his raftmates. He desperately tried to save the last one, who had been grabbed by a shark, but lost out to the shark in a grotesque tug-of-war.
Courtesy of Allen Heyn

Arthur Friend, the son of an impoverished sharecropper, was a master of survival and refused to give up even when a shark bit into his buttocks. He coolly jerked out one of its gills and the predator released him. But he couldn't save the only other survivor on his raft, though he had rescued him after a shark had bitten off the man's feet. *Courtesy of Arthur Friend*

Wyatt Butterfield had always dreamed of being a "hero," and he had his chance when a rescue plane dropped supplies near his raft. He dove into the water and swam back with the supplies while fighting off attacking sharks with a knife. When he wounded one of them, the others, drawn by the smell of blood, cannibalized it, permitting him to escape with his precious booty.
Courtesy of Wyatt Butterfield

Frank Holmgren, who carried a wishbone that his girlfriend had given him, miraculously survived without an injury either from the explosion or from the sharks. But he had some close calls. As the *Juneau* went down, he was sucked into the depths and almost drowned. And though he could not swim, he shot to the surface and was able to grab onto a raft that floated by. His wishbone kept protecting him up to the moment of rescue.
Courtesy of Frank Holmgren

Lt. Charles Wang, the only officer to survive the disaster, joined two other men on a rubber boat that they hoped to paddle to the nearest island. After several horrific days, with Wang nearly dying from a severe leg injury, the three reached the island and were greeted by natives reputed to be cannibals.
Courtesy of Marie Wang

Joseph Hartney, defying the sharks, swam out to retrieve the rubber boat after it had been dropped from a plane. As he helped to steer the craft through typhoons and deadly coral reefs en route to the island, he vowed not to die without seeing his unborn child—and he kept his vow.
Courtesy of Lucy Hartney

John Grycky, a sensitive violinist who dreamed of joining the Philadelphia Orchestra, had his shoulder torn off by a shark. Though finally pulled to safety by his raftmates, he leaped back into the water, apparently after he saw the horror in their eyes, and was again grabbed by sharks. *Courtesy of Stanley Steciw*

Lt. Laurence Williamson risked his life and the lives of his crew landing his seaplane in rough water to save survivors of the *Juneau.* Incredibly, the Navy did not send him on this mission until seven days after the ship had been sunk. *Courtesy of Laurence Williamson*

Juneau survivors, their savior, and their wives were reunited in Juneau, Alaska, in 1987. Standing, from left, are rescuer Laurence Williamson, Lester Zook, Frank Holmgren, Alaska governor Steve Cowper, Wyatt Butterfield, Allen Heyn, Arthur Friend, and Robert Swenson, the captain's son; sitting, from left, are Mrs. Holmgren, Mrs. Zook, and Mrs. Swenson. *Courtesy of Robert Swenson*

Lt. Robert Gill piloted a B-29 that flew over the *Juneau* survivors minutes after the ship went down. He did not inform headquarters for hours, fearing to break radio silence, and when he returned to base with the information, the Navy launched no serious rescue effort for more than a week. *Courtesy of Robert Gill*

Adm. William Halsey, commander of the Pacific fleet, was outraged when he learned that survivors of the *Juneau* had been abandoned, but his orders to rescue them were little heeded. Due to naval and Army Air Corps apathy and negligence, planes simply overflew the men, dropping a few supplies, and didn't bother to inform a rescue ship where to find the survivors. *U.S. Navy*

Admiral Isoroku Yamamoto, supreme commander of the Japanese fleet, hoped the Battle of Friday the Thirteenth would clear the path southward to Australia and New Zealand and establish Japanese supremacy in the Pacific. The *Juneau* played an important role in thwarting this effort. *U.S. Navy*

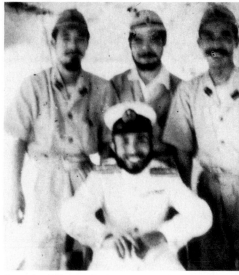

Comdr. Minoru Yokota, seen here with three of his submarine *I-26* crewmen, blew up the *Juneau* by mistake. He had aimed his torpedoes at a heavier cruiser, the USS *San Francisco,* but they missed. Yokota wished to fire more torpedoes at the flotilla, as the U.S. commanders feared, but fortunately for them, most of his launchers had been damaged in an underwater accident earlier. *Courtesy of Minoru Yokota Hasegawa*

Tsukuo Nakano, a torpedo technician on the submarine, was confident he would survive the confrontation with the Americans after seeing a vision of his mother on the water. Her spirit had come to protect him. Whatever impact this vision had on his will to survive, he managed to escape death even though, at one point, he was nearly asphyxiated when the submarine hid deep in the ocean to avoid enemy depth charges. *Courtesy of Tsukuo Nakano*

far more aggressive than those in the open ocean and in more temperate waters. With their large, sharp teeth and powerful jaws, they could easily sever a man's torso or limbs at a snap, though they usually tore off pieces small enough to swallow easily. When a shark found a victim, the scent of blood lured others to the scene.

Now, no one would risk hanging on to ropes in the water or dangling his legs over the rim of the raft. Still, there weren't too many sharks—yet.

Hartney eyed the yellow bundle bouncing in the waves as if it were some hypnotic charm. It protruded from the sea like a stubby, beckoning finger, the ultimate challenge in the struggle for survival.

"I sat there the whole morning looking at the boat, looking at the sharks, and looking at the wounded men," Hartney would say.

He was a good swimmer and had regained some of his strength, though he hadn't eaten for forty-eight hours. But the sharks . . . One of them had already torn a net. He had noted, however, that if he splashed the water vigorously, they slid away.

Finally, Hartney made up his mind. He would go for it, he told a raftmate, twenty-two-year-old Sea2c. Victor James Fitzgerald. A native of Manchester, Connecticut, Fitzgerald was a handsome youth with a strong chin and rather sad Irish eyes. He was still shaking from the vision of the *Juneau*'s twin propellers gradually dropping in the water, poised to crush him. But he had somehow evaded them and was saved by the same underwater explosion that had saved Hartney. He, too, was tossed up through the oily water— "like a toothpick." When he reached the surface, he swam for about three hours, and just when he was ready to quit, thinking he was the only survivor, he spotted the raft that carried Hartney and Wang.

The rubber boat and the supplies aboard could save Lieutenant Wang and all the others, Hartney pointed out to Fitzgerald. How about the two of them making a dash for it and bringing it back? They would be paddling with the current on the return trip. And those damn sharks were "cowards," anyway, and would beat a quick retreat if faced with any turbulence.

The two men agreed; they would swim out together. Hartney touched the pocket where he kept his wife's picture for good luck, and the pair dove into the sea. They swam as fast as they could, but before they had gone ten yards, the sharks "rose swiftly out of the depths" and "the long shapes closed in" from three sides. . . .

As late as the morning of November 15, Admiral Halsey did not know that the *Juneau* had been sunk, for Admiral Turner had, for some reason, bypassed him when he received word of the sinking from Captain Hoover. Turner reported directly, it seems, to Admiral Nimitz in Pearl Harbor, and Nimitz passed the news to Washington about the time Hoover arrived in Espíritu Santo on November 14.

The following day, Halsey realized that something was wrong. The *Juneau* was not on the list of arrivals that Hoover had sent him the day before. He called in his chief of staff, Captain Browning, and asked:

"Where's the *Juneau*?"

"I don't know, sir," Browning replied. "I'll have to check."

He apparently checked with Admiral Turner, who had just arrived in Espíritu Santo aboard the *McCawley*. Turner was welcomed with bad news. A report from a patrol plane was handed him saying that about "60 white men in water posit 10-30 south 161-05 east at 1100 (-11) 14th x dropped 1 yellow life raft"—the boat, obviously, that Joe Hartney was so determined to retrieve. Turner apparently checked the report with Hoover, who had earlier told him of the sinking but had not mentioned survivors. The admiral then fired off a reply to Halsey's query: the *Juneau* had been sunk.

"Upon my arrival Button [Espíritu Santo]," Turner radioed, "I find that Task Group 67.4 made no attempt rescue *Juneau* survivors . . . x Recommend destroyer in that area be sent to arrive daybreak tomorrow x Cactus [Guadalcanal] air cooperate x [Destroyer] *Meade* suggested after completion bombardment."

The failure of communication that had caused the prolonged agony in the water shocked Halsey. Especially since it soiled the glory of the November 13th battle. Almost all of his ships had been damaged and a few sunk, including the *Juneau*, but the Japanese had failed to demolish Henderson Field or to land large reinforcements and supplies on Guadalcanal. This, Halsey thought, could very well be the turning point of the Pacific war. His men had put up one hell of a fight, and Admiral Callaghan, who had led them into battle, deserved, posthumously, he felt, a Congressional Medal of Honor—and would receive one.

Thus, not surprisingly, Halsey's elation now melted into rage. Admiral Nimitz might even hold him responsible. Halsey had always urged his commanders to rescue survivors of a disaster if possible, even at substantial risk to their own ships. For if the men knew they wouldn't be abandoned, their fighting spirit would never lag.

Halsey immediately ordered the destroyer *Meade* to steam to the area where the survivors had been sighted and pick them up—as soon as it finished shelling Japanese positions on Guadalcanal. Meanwhile, someone's head would have to roll. And it wouldn't be his.

"Yes, I was scared!" Joe Hartney would confess.

He couldn't imagine a more terrifying nightmare—shark fins sailing toward him from every direction, it seemed. And it was too late to turn back. Still, he remained cool; he had planned what he would do if they came for him. As he swam ahead, he violently thrashed the water with his hands and feet. Within seconds, he would know if this strategy worked. If it didn't, well, once again, bye-bye, baby!

It worked—for Jim Fitzgerald, too.

"They flirted away," Hartney would report, "scattering like a bunch of minnows frightened by a stone tossed into a pool."

But the "minnows" soon swished back, and he was almost too exhausted to continue on, with still about fifty yards to go. He and Fitzgerald beat the water again, splashing and kicking. And once more the sharks veered off, with powerful flips of the tail.

"This could not go on for long," Hartney would say. "I had to reach that raft—and soon. I made another dash forward, longer this time, until the brutes were so close that my heart caught in my chest."

Frantically, the two men churned the water. "I felt it swirl

around me as a killer passed inches under my pumping legs,"
Hartney would recall, "so close that I could have touched him
as he slid past me."

But the swimmers scattered the sharks again and raced toward
the bobbing bundle before the predators could close in another
time, not daring to glance back.

Hartney grabbed the plunger of the rolled-up boat, pulled it
fiercely, and a loud hiss sounded with all the rich sweetness of
a symphonic orchestra. In seconds, the boat was taking form,
like a yellow rose blossoming forth in the sunshine.

As the pair scrambled into this bouncing oasis, Hartney "felt
the jolt of a heavy body as a shark streaked by the spot where
I had been a moment before, and his rough scales scrunched
under the thin canvas bottom. I lay there for a long time without
moving a muscle, completely exhausted, letting the sledge-
hammer in my chest quiet to the normal beating of my heart."

But as Hartney raised himself on one elbow and glanced
around, he had a problem with his heart again. It sank. All he
could see were collapsible aluminum oars, a can of carbon diox-
ide to inflate the boat, a patching kit, and a bailing bag. No food,
no water. Had he risked his life for nothing?

"God, how I'd hoped for water!" he lamented.

Well, there was no use crying. At least they had a boat with
a waterproof bottom and good oars.

As the two men paddled back to the other rafts, Hartney had
an idea. They didn't know when they would be rescued, he told
his companion, and Wang was badly in need of water and medical care. He was one of the few critically wounded still alive
and would surely join the dead if he didn't get help soon. So
why not put him in this boat and try to make it to shore? The
doughnut rafts were unwieldy and would never reach land.
Anyway, during the night, a couple of men who were paddling
fell asleep and dropped their oars into the sea.

San Cristobal was the nearest island, Hartney said, pointing
to some dimly visible cloud-capped volcanic hills in the distance, about fifty-five miles away. As a signalman, he knew
enough about navigation to make the trip and "with any sort of
luck" could reach it in two or three days. If rescuers arrived in

the meantime, they could follow the boat's course. Naturally, the three men would send back help if they reached land first.

He would propose this idea to Lieutenant Blodgett, Hartney said. If Blodgett agreed, would Fitzgerald come along?

Sure, replied Fitzgerald. It was better than hanging around in the ocean doing nothing and waiting to be eaten by sharks.

As soon as the pair reached the rafts, Hartney asked Blodgett if the rubber boat could take off alone for San Cristobal.

Better for all the rafts to try to reach land together, Blodgett answered.

And so, with the rubber boat in the lead, the tiny flotilla tried to edge its way forward but, as Hartney had predicted, could make little headway because of the waves and the drag of the nets. Besides, only six or seven of the men on the three dough-nut rafts had paddles, and most of them were too weak to wield them effectively. Thus, they would gain a yard and then lose a foot or so. Finally, Blodgett said:

"We can't make it in this group."

And, according to Hartney, the lieutenant told him, referring to the three-man plan, "Go to it! You can't lose anything by it, and at least you'll be doing something."

Blodgett was especially eager that Lieutenant Wang go along since he was severely wounded and, as an officer, could guide them with some expertise, though even the most expert guid-ance might not be enough to propel them to shore. For one thing, there wasn't enough food for them to take along, and only a little water, which was contaminated from the sea anyway.

Hartney and Fitzgerald then pulled the rubber boat alongside Wang's raft and, with great difficulty, lifted the lieutenant into it, placing him carefully in the stern. In his shock and pain, Wang, now in a trancelike state, had, in his more conscious moments, felt a sense of guilt for "holding back a whole group," and several times that morning he had been "on the point of slipping into the water quietly and drowning." Once, he halluci-nated, fantasizing that a freighter had come alongside the rafts and hoisted them all onto its forecastle. He thought the transport plane had dropped two rafts, one blue and the other yellow—though planes didn't carry blue ones. He also fought imaginary sea battles, drew up elaborate offensive plans, and married a woman from Connecticut.

"It was hard to leave the raft and the men on it," Hartney would say. "Just twenty-four hours ago there had been seven hundred of us. Now there was only this pitiful handful. I knew that chances were I would never see some of them alive again, and my throat was tight as I pulled away. There were no fare-wells. I doubt that more than one or two of them realized what was happening."

One who did was Arthur Friend, who would claim that Blod-gett instructed him to choose the men who would leave in the rubber boat. He thus chose Hartney and Fitzgerald "because they were in good physical condition," and Wang "because he really needed medical help." When some of the other men who wanted to go threatened to throw him off his doughnut raft, Friend would claim, he waved an imaginary knife and roared:

"If you try to, I'll cut your guts out!"

According to Allen Heyn, some of the men were indeed furi-ous that the three men were leaving them behind.

"All these fellows that was on the doughnuts who were very sick and wounded didn't want that," Heyn would say. "They wanted to be put in the rubber raft and all stay together. They felt, well, it was much easier there than it was on the doughnut. And why should those three go . . . and leave us here? It looked like we would just be goners that way."

And Heyn blamed Wang most of all. The lieutenant, he would charge, had "pulled his rank" and asked Blodgett to let him go. Even if this was true, Wang was hallucinating at the time, and Blodgett didn't need to be persuaded anyway.

Wyatt Butterfield would recall: "Two survivors inflated the raft, put themselves and a badly wounded officer in it, and took off without a word. Not even, 'Go to hell, you bastards!' "

As the rubber boat pulled away, Heyn would approvingly note, the men cried, "Bastards, come back!"

But the boat soon faded away in the glare of the afternoon sun, while the doughnuts sluggishly crept forward in its wake.

That night of November 14 was "rough," Wyatt Butterfield would recall. "We couldn't see the sharks because it was so dark out there on the water.... All we could hear were the sounds of winds and waves, and here we were on what felt like an endless roller coaster, wondering where the hell we were and how long it would be before dawn came. We'd doze off, awaken freezing, duck into the water in the raft to try to warm up, then come up and doze again."

To sleep in greater comfort, Butterfield decided to dare fate—and the sharks—and swim to one of the nets, though he could have taken a more laborious route, climbing from raft to raft to the net.

"I almost lost it in the dark," he would say, "and, boy, was I scared."

Then, when Butterfield finally reached it, he found there was no more room.

"I swore to myself," he would say, "but thought, Oh, well, I'll just put my head on [someone's] chest and try to get some sleep, too. I dozed off, but before long I suddenly woke up, realizing that the chest I had chosen as a pillow was hard as a rock. It was too dark to see the man, but I touched his arm, and it, too was like stone. He was dead. At dawn, we sent another of our crew into the Pacific."

On November 15, the third day in the water, "the condition of the wounded was rapidly becoming worse," George Mantere, the net superintendent in charge of the wounded, would later write in a report. "The ones who were delirious became restless and kept swimming around or hanging onto the rafts and nets and disturbing the wounded by grabbing hold of their broken arms and legs."

And Butterfield would recount: "As we drifted, our legs started to swell badly because of continual exposure to water. We all had to try to sleep standing up, which made the first days almost intolerable. Then the thirst hit. Our tongues swelled, we couldn't swallow or salivate. Our eyes were almost totally closed by the combination of oil and the intense reflection of the sun on the water. To obtain some warmth during the night, we would urinate down the legs."

With the somewhat contaminated fresh water having run out, a growing number of men were becoming delirious, mainly from drinking pure salt water. They tasted a little at first, then gulped the "poison" down until their stomachs were bloated. Madness soon overcame them, and some jumped into the sea to go "below" on watch duty, to get fresh water and a sandwich, or to swim to shore. Some lay on wooden planks that had floated by and tried to paddle there with their hands. One man who leaped in was Ensign Pitney, who, although "in command" of one of the rafts, had never quite recovered from the shock of the explosion and had been largely ignored by his raftmates.

Apparently no one told the men not to drink the salt water.

"Why should anyone have?" Butterfield would ask. "It was just plain common sense. After they went crazy, they just jumped in the water not even thinking of the sharks. Many felt they were going to die anyway."

And they did—quickly. The sharks were waiting, hundreds of them now, frenzied by the blood and the bodies, the abundance of human flesh. Nevertheless, the water, so cool and caressing, was inviting, even to those still of sound mind.

"We grew bolder," Butterfield would recall, "to the point where we would entrust at least part of our anatomy to the cool water."

One man, a muscular weight lifter from York, Pennsylvania, climbed on a plank and was rowing along with half a paddle when a shark leaped up and swallowed his arm, paddle and all.

"He's got my arm!" he cried. "He's got my arm!"

The man then tumbled into the water, and the sharks devoured the rest of him.

Even so, some of the madmen still dove in on missions of fantasy. Butterfield and others tried to hold them back at first, "but the strength of such men was amazing." Gradually, as time went on, few of the sane survivors made any attempt to stop them. They were too weak, and besides, death—from wounds, drowning, or shark attacks—had become so common that, as Butterfield would explain:

"We were beginning to take death in stride. We'd gotten used to it. Just another day. No one got excited. We felt that those who had died were perhaps lucky to have had their suffering ended."

Butterfield even lost interest now in being a hero. Since this experience had so devalued human life, what was so great about saving it? Still, he was determined to survive. He remembered his father's words before he left home:

"Remember, son, never give up! You're a Butterfield, and the Butterfields never die young."

Wyatt almost felt that he was singled out for survival. Somehow, he figured, he would get through this, whatever happened to the others. He thus resisted the temptation to drink seawater—but he hallucinated anyway. He imagined he saw his father's car and, being very cold, started to climb into it and turn the heater on. As he was about to go overboard, someone slapped him a few times and snapped him out of it. This man had saved his life. How many lives had he himself saved?

Butterfield and many of the other survivors could not help but admire, and even envy, a slight, skinny loner of a man named Moore, who aboard ship was the favorite butt of the gibes and practical jokes of the tougher guys, who felt he didn't fit into their boisterous, macho circle.

But Moore showed his hidden strength when he picked up a life jacket that had been floating by and a big, burly sailor demanded he hand it over. "It's mine!" Moore retorted, and the man began beating him up. But Moore stood up to him and kept the jacket.

He would need it. Twice he answered calls for help from men who had gone about thirty or forty yards out, quietly slipping into the water and dragging them back to his raft.

"The other men on the raft," Butterfield would say, "would, meanwhile, be thinking, we're all going to die anyway, so why hasten the process by trying to save some idiot out there?" He would add, "Some of the so-called strong men turned to jelly when faced with real danger."

Was he one of those strong men? he might have wondered. Moore was the hero that Butterfield had wanted to be. And he began to feel a certain kinship with the man he had once laughed at.

"Moore," he warned the youth, "you keep going back in and you're going to get it."

"I gotta help them," Moore replied. "I can't watch them die like that."

"You keep going, you're gonna die with them," Butterfield repeated.

Shortly, a third man was screaming for help, and Moore dove into the water once more and swam to the man. Just as he grabbed him, three or four sharks struck.

"There was just one scream," Butterfield would recount, "then silence. The sharks got 'em both."

Butterfield was distraught. "I told him," he muttered. "I told him." But he couldn't afford to mourn too much. It was, after all, "part of the day." Foolish, going after some idiot out there. . . . Who wanted to be a hero anyway?

Butterfield's struggle with guilt intensified after a second trauma. Another man he admired, "a really fine guy" named Alvin Berman, showed him a locket with his mother's picture inside.

"You're going to make it," Berman said, "but I know that I'm going to die. When you get back, I'd like you to give this locket to my mother. Tell her what we went through, and tell her that I was thinking of her at the end."

Deeply moved, Butterfield took the locket but protested, trying to convince his friend that he would survive, too. But Berman insisted:

"No, I'm going to die."

Then, after guzzling down salt water, he crawled over the rim of the raft before Butterfield could stop him. He was just going for coffee, he said. And in seconds, the sharks devoured him.

Butterfield glanced at the locket. He vowed to fulfill Berman's wish—and he would. His friend had been sure that he, Butterfield, would survive and had admired him for his toughness and will. He was a champion boxer, a strong man . . . Idiot!

"Survival, not friendship, was the order of the day," Butterfield would say, even as he watched his two comrades die.

This order was reflected not only in the acceptance of other men's deaths as nothing to get excited about, but in the daily relations between the men.

"From the beginning," Butterfield would report, "there had been a lot of dissension. . . . [The rafts were] crowded, and if one man complained, another would say, 'Go and find your own damned raft!' The response would be, 'You go, you son of a bitch!' "

Lester Zook thought he saw a head in the water when suddenly he realized it was a coconut. With no more food left on the rafts, "four or five men," according to Butterfield, "were ready to kill each other for it." Zook managed to keep the coconut and, after cutting it up, took the first piece and passed the rest around.

"Charity," Zook would pragmatically explain, "begins at home."

This was a sentiment expressed more violently by another seaman who was less a sharing type. When a raftmate found a pineapple floating in the water, this man, according to Butterfield, "beat the shit outta him" and grabbed the precious fruit for himself.

The next day, November 15, Lieutenant Gill was given new orders; he was to resume his search for the *Portland*. And, to his dismay, Navy Lieutenant Tanner would go along again so he could identify any Japanese ships the crew might spot.

As Gill flew low a few miles south of the area where two days earlier he had seen the survivors of an unidentified cruiser that had been sunk, he and his men were speechless as they stared out the window. For there were still survivors floating on rafts down there. This time, however, the number had dwindled to about one hundred, little more than half the number they had originally seen.

"What kind of Navy would leave men in the water for days?" Gill groaned. "It's a hell of a Navy that would do that!"

But again, Gill continued on his mission without radioing headquarters. Some hours later, on the trip home, after failing once more to find the *Portland*, Gill intercepted a radio report that bitterly reminded him of his sighting that morning. Some survivors, the report said, were floating at a position about five miles away from where he had seen them two days earlier.

Another day and they were still there!

On landing in Espíritu Santo, Gill reported to the intelligence officer again and told him of his sighting, repeating the lament he had expressed to his crew. The officer, according to Gill, still seemed little impressed. After all, the previous day, November 14, he had included in the Daily Operations Report the sighting by a plane that had dropped a life raft to some "white men," who were observed climbing aboard. The report indicated that a "radio aircraft code message was sent to all stations, describing contact." Of course, the sighting appeared as the third item on page two, after reports of an unsuccessful search for enemy shipping and two aircraft contacts with the enemy in which there was "no evidence of serious damage" to either side!

Now, the following day, the intelligence officer would squeeze in an item refecting Gill's new sighting. The item this time was number four on page three, appearing after another "negative" search for Japanese shipping and the sighting of several Japanese seaplanes off a beach.

Meanwhile, Gill would share his anger with other members of his squadron.

"Since our bomb group was assigned to Admiral Bull Halsey's command and all of our reports were to be sent to it," he would say, "we naturally felt hostile towards their negligence."

But he still did not protest to higher authority.

Allen Heyn thought he had found a way to confuse the sharks, while keeping warm at night and avoiding sunburn during the day. He remained fully dressed, with oil-soaked shirt, dungarees, socks, and sneakers. Since the sharks couldn't see the whiteness of his skin or smell his flesh because of the oil, perhaps they would ignore him if he fell in the water.

Other men who had thrown their clothes away in the blistering heat of the day soon realized they had compounded their torture. They stewed under the sun and froze under the stars and trembled in fear of sharks all the time. Among these men were the bullies who had tormented and humiliated Heyn aboard the *Juneau*, beating him and attempting to rape him.

Two of them accosted Heyn on the raft they shared and demanded that he give one of them his clothes and his knife.

"Hell, no!" Heyn exclaimed.

One of the men then struck him in the jaw, knocking him into the water. Heyn swam away and the man dived in after him. Then he turned to confront his tormentor. After a violent struggle in which each tried to push the other under the surface, Heyn managed to hold his antagonist's head down long enough to drown him. And the body floated away.

Heyn swam back to his raft and climbed in. None of his raft-mates, not even the second bully, openly reacted to the killing they had witnessed. Another shipmate dead? How many did that make? Nor would the dead man's buddy bother Heyn again.

But if Heyn would kill a man in self-defense, he would save a man for self-respect. When one sailor drank seawater and grew "dopey," Heyn held him in his arms all afternoon so his head wouldn't fall into the water. Toward night, however, as the man grew stiff, Heyn said to his raftmates:

"Well, how about taking him awhile? I can't hold him any longer. I've got all I can do to hold myself."

No one responded, but Heyn soon realized that it didn't make any difference.

"I felt his heart and his wrist," he would say, "and I couldn't feel any beating."

The man was apparently dead.

"Well, I'm going to let him go," Heyn said.

But George Sullivan, who had begun to hallucinate, once more protested in the name of human dignity, "You can't do that. It's against all regulations of the Navy. You can't bury a man at sea without having official orders from some captain or the Navy Department or something like that."

Some of George's raftmates agreed, but Heyn would say, "I knew [George] was delirious and there was something wrong with him and all, but they wouldn't let me let [the dead man] go. I said to them, 'Well, you hold him,' and they wouldn't hold him. So it went on that way for a little while. [The dead man's] legs were hanging down in the water a little way below mine when a shark bit his . . . leg off right below the knee. He didn't move or say anything. That was enough for me. I figured, well, I'm going to drop him. There isn't any sense holding a dead man. So we took his dog tags off, this one fellow did, and said a prayer for him and let him float away."

Meanwhile, George Sullivan was growing more unstable by the hour, apparently from the effects of drinking salt water, but also from the heartbreak of failing to find his brothers. And by the evening of November 15, he was no longer calling out their names.

Contributing to George's madness was the burning sun, for his shirt had been torn off in the explosion and his skin was raw from the relentless rays. As Heyn would later describe the man's misery:

"The fellows that didn't have shirts on, the sun burned them something awful. It burned their skin all off, and their back. It was just like as if you shaved them with a razor or something, all raw, and some of them just decided they weren't going to try anymore. They said they'd rather drown themselves than suffer like that. So that night after dark George Sullivan said he was going to take a bath."

"I'm going to swim over to the island," he said to Heyn, apparently referring to San Cristobal Island, over fifty miles away.

Heyn and others tried to reason with him. The island was too far, they said. Wait and they would all be picked up soon.

"No," George said. "I'm going to the island and get some buttermilk and something to eat."

Before anyone could grab him, George jumped into the water and swam away. And in the deepening shadows of dusk, the men watched while, about twenty-five yards away, three sharks splashed violently around him as he screamed:

"Help me! Help me!"

George's head bobbed up and down as the sharks tore him to pieces.

The sea then settled into the whispering calm of night, and George Sullivan found his brothers at last in a joyous reunion along the banks of an eternal Cedar River—perhaps just as he had planned in some rational inner sanctum of his mind.

After Admiral Halsey learned that the *Juneau* had been sunk and survivors were still floating in the water, his reflexes were swift. He ordered Captain Hoover to sail the *Helena* to Nouméa immediately. When it arrived there the next day, November 16, Hoover felt uneasy as he rode to Halsey's headquarters, well aware from the abruptness of the order that his career was in jeopardy. And he could have no doubts about this when he walked into Halsey's office.

Actually, the admiral had ambivalent feelings toward Hoover, for the man who had fueled his fury was a person he greatly admired, one with an outstanding record. How many officers had been awarded three Navy Crosses for courage? Nevertheless, the strain of prolonged combat, Halsey felt, may have impaired his judgment.

"Guts alone were keeping him going," he would remark, "and his present condition was dangerous to himself and to his splendid ship."

And Captain Browning, perhaps wishing to deflect from his boss any hint of blame for the survivors' plight, apparently helped to influence this assessment. Still, Halsey would give Hoover his day in court.

Why had he left those men in the water? Halsey asked him.

He felt the action was justified at the time, Hoover explained, giving his reasons.

After "interrogating [Hoover] thoroughly," Halsey dismissed him and called a meeting of his advisers—Rear Admirals Fitch and Turner and Vice Adm. William L. Calhoun. Shortly, Hoover was ordered back and grilled at length by this group, which also studied all relevant documents, then debated the merits of the captain's decision.

CHAPTER

· 14 ·

The Cruelest Logic

WHILE ADMIRAL HALSEY'S ADVISERS CONSIDERED CAPTAIN HOOver's fate, the skipper boarded the *Helena*, anchored at Nouméa, and anxiously sat in his cabin waiting for orders from the admiral. Orders, he knew, that could destroy his career and forever taint his reputation. He relived over and over again each horrible moment of the *Juneau*'s demise. He could still envision that great pillar of smoke and dust rising into the sky like a blasphemous fist aimed at God.

Hoover realized from Halsey's probe that the admiral was outraged by his decision to steam ahead without looking for survivors or the enemy submarine. Halsey kept asking why, why, why? The implication seemed clear: for all his explanations, Gilbert Hoover was yellow! After being awarded three Navy Crosses—yellow?

The captain was crushed. What would happen to him? If he was relieved of command and humiliated, how could he face his family? What would his son think after all his efforts to be a role model for him, to inculcate in him, despite the boy's damned resistance, the naval ethic and way of life, the pride in uniform, the resolve to perform exemplary service and accept adversity without a sign of emotion? How could he go home?

LEFT TO DIE

Some officers in his flotilla, Hoover knew, thought he had made the most courageous decision yet reached in the war—resisting an all-too-human temptation to save survivors for the greater good of cause and country. Why couldn't his superiors understand that he might have saved hundreds of lives by fleeing the scene of the sinking?

But Hoover also thought of the lives he didn't try to save. Was Swens one of the survivors? If he was, would his old friend agree that he had no choice but to leave him and other survivors to possibly die? And what would people say if the famous Sullivan brothers had not gone down with the ship, but had died in the water—the only naval family of five ever to be wiped out at a single blow? Would history blame him? And even if he was exonerated, could he ever escape the ghosts that haunted him day and night?

That day, November 16, Joe Hartney wondered whether he might soon join the ghosts as he and Jimmy Fitzgerald knelt in their little rubber boat paddling toward the promised land of San Cristobal, while the wounded Lieutenant Wang lay delirious on the canvas floor at the rear of the craft. As Hartney would say, "the oil that coated our bodies seemed to catch and hold the heat until we felt encased in red-hot armor." But hardly had their oil-caked lips begun to swell and crack when a cool breeze ruffled the water and darkness descended suddenly, turning the red-hot armor into a sheath of ice.

Fitzgerald pointed into the night and said, "There's land over there, Joe. Let's tie the boat up to the barn."

Hartney was dismayed. They were in the middle of the ocean and he alone was rational! How could he handle the boat without Jimmy? Fitzgerald's "teeth were chattering like castanets, and spasms of shivering twitched across his body," Hartney would recount. Perhaps the contents of the small canister of brackish water they had brought along had driven his comrade mad.

"Jimmy," he exclaimed, "there's no barn here! We're out at sea!"

"Aw, come on, Joe, let's tie the boat up to the barn," Fitzgerald repeated.

Hartney pulled him from the inflated ledge where he had been kneeling as he rowed and put his arms around him to shield him from the chill wind.

"Jimmy," he pleaded, "I need your help. Don't you understand? We're out at sea."

As they huddled for warmth at the bottom of the boat, Fitzgerald ranted incoherently for a while, then finally fell asleep. In despair, Hartney, wondering if his two companions would be alive in the morning, sighted the three-quarter moon against two stars and, using the heavenly bodies for navigation, tried desperately to keep the lunging, unstable boat on a path to the island.

Suddenly, a rain squall bore down, blotting out the moon. The boat was bouncing from wave to wave, but where was it going? Even if he knew, could he, without help, control it or keep it from overturning in the raging wind and driving rain?

The sea, it seemed, might claim him after all.

The storm struck with equal fury at the rafts and nets Hartney and his two companions had left behind.

"What a terrifying night!" Wyatt Butterfield would write. "I kept wondering what would happen if the raft went over."

But some of the men took advantage of the heavy rain, holding their mouths open to catch a few drops. Then, at someone's suggestion, they removed their wet shirts, wrung out the salt water, caught the rainwater in them, and wrung them out again—into their mouths.

"When the storm was over," Butterfield would say, "we checked and found that several men were missing. Once again, the Pacific had claimed its toll."

But if the men were less thirsty now, they were growing more fearful—of the sharks. Especially after Arthur Friend grabbed one about five feet long by the tail, cut out its gills, then slit its gleaming white stomach open as it slid by his raft. He and others pulled the shark into the raft and were horrified to see the remains of a human arm inside its stomach. It was apparently the arm of the weight lifter who, that morning, had climbed on a large board that had floated by and tried to paddle to shore. But at a time of starvation, the arm would be ignored.

Although the men were ready for a feast, the shark wasn't dead yet. It contemptuously slapped Friend with its tail and slithered back into the sea, leaving a trail of blood. And now other sharks converged on the bleeding one and cannibalized it, then circled the rafts by the score hungering for a second course.

This did not stop the wounded and crazed sailors on the nets from swimming toward imaginary islands or diving to the *Juneau* for a hamburger and a milk shake, only to be consumed themselves. As each net grew more sparsely populated, the remaining occupants crowded on a few of them and discarded the rest so that the rafts could more easily pull them forward in the swirling currents.

In Lester Zook's raft, John Grycky, the violinist, grasped an oar with the hands of a potential master, hands now blistered from wielding the paddle against a reluctant sea for about four hours without relief. He knew that the little flotilla wasn't really going anywhere. But at least he was helping to raise the morale of the men, making them think that they were getting closer to shore.

Each man in the raft took his turn paddling. When he turned over his oar to someone else, he would continue paddling with his hands. Grycky was about to do that when Zook, his superior, noted that he was exhausted and told him to go back to a net and lie down for a while.

Grycky was well liked by his shipmates, as he had been by his friends and students at home in Pennsylvania. He was not as tough and rugged as some of them, nor profane like many. And some were a bit uneasy trying to communicate with a musician whose music they didn't understand. They had more in common with the boxers. Yet, most respected and admired Grycky for his quiet dignity, his cheerfulness, even in adverse circumstances, and his interest in everyone he met. He offered advice on personal problems and tried to ease the stress of sailors less cool, confident, or courageous than he with his optimistic predictions.

"Never give up!" he would say.

They should think about their loved ones at home who were

praying for them, about one day taking them in their arms and living a happy life.

And Grycky took his own advice. Though apparently still pained by his girl's Dear John letter, he constantly talked about home. What a reunion he would have with his loving parents, his mischievous little sister, his trumpeter brother, and those wonderful fellow Knights of the Square Table. With death all around him, his mind was surely eased by the thought that if anything happened to him, the surviving Knights would look in on his parents and help them if necessary for the rest of their lives.

But why think of death when there was so much to live for? He could still imagine himself playing for the Philadelphia Orchestra, sitting on the stage immersed in the beauty of Beethoven or Bach, helping to express that beauty.

Now he would lie down on a net and lull himself to sleep with some great work he would turn on in his mind like an echo from home. Usually, a man would crawl from one raft to another until he got to the nets. But Grycky was sweating profusely after four hours of paddling, and the cool, bubbly water looked so inviting. Why not swim directly to the net? It was only about five yards away. He'd get there before any shark could attack, and besides, he couldn't see any dorsal fins skimming the surface.

Grycky dived into the water and started to swim toward the nearest net when suddenly a shark swooped up from the depths. And in a swirling boil of water and blood, vise-like jaws clamped shut on Grycky's right shoulder, removing all of it and leaving his arm suspended only by a couple of tendons.

Only then, as the shark streaked away, did Grycky scream. He looked at his raftmates with an agonized expression and, paddling back to them with one arm, grabbed the rim of the raft. Zook and another man held the arm while they wrapped an oily life jacket around the massive cavity in his body in a desperate attempt to stop the blood. But it kept gushing out.

"There was no way at all of saving him," Zook would say. "He looked at his shipmates there and realized that he was making them nauseated, that he was driving them crazy by just being there, and the sharks were getting around close in the water because of his blood being around ... He knew he couldn't stay there and have sharks trash the raft."

And the men knew it, too. Should he die by inches—or get the pain over with instantly?

"In all our minds," according to one raftmate, "his wound was fatal. Should we risk our lives for a dead man?"

Grycky continued to stare at the men for a moment and apparently knew what they were thinking. Yes, he was, in a sense, already dead. For the hand that might have helped to create magnificent music had virtually been torn from his body. And was not this hand an instrument of his soul?

What happened next is disputed. According to Wyatt Butterfield, "We could only push him back into a watery grave—we had nothing to ease his agony." But Zook would say that Grycky voluntarily broke loose. In any event, he started paddling away with his one usable arm and had gone only about six feet when two sharks sank their teeth into him again while the men on the rafts watched in horror through a screen of reddish spray.

This time Grycky did not scream. Perhaps because he knew he would be playing forever in an orchestra of sublime repute.

The rainstorm that had threatened to capsize the little yellow boat manned by Joe Hartney, Jimmy Fitzgerald, and Lieutenant Wang turned out to be a blessing. For it somehow refreshed Fitzgerald and edged him into the rational world again, while snapping Wang out of his delirium, or so it seemed. The downpour also brought drinking water. Until now, all they had to drink was measured out in drops from the small keg of brackish water Lieutenant Blodgett had given them.

Fitzgerald sat up and, tipping back his head, opened his mouth and let the rain splash over his face. Hartney followed suit and felt his swollen tongue soften, "absorbing water like a sponge." He then caught some rain in a bailing bag and gave it to Wang. Hartney was joyous. Moments before, he had been lost and alone, but now it was sunrise, a new day, and he had company and a fellow paddler. And he could navigate by the sun, which soon "knocked the shivers out of our bones."

But Hartney's joy was short-lived. The higher the sun rose,

the more intense was the sudden heat, which caused him and his companions to "literally (fry) in that skillet of canvas." And with all water exhausted, "our tongues would swell until speech was just a matter of croaking sounds." At the same time, hunger stabbed at them mercilessly.

Then, once more, Wang fell into a trance, groaning and muttering, almost unintelligibly, tales of the past and future. He was getting married and even answered the questions asked him at the wedding ceremony. On the third day aboard the rubber boat, however, Wang woke fully rational.

"What the hell am I doing here?" he wanted to know, the shock of his wound having worn off. He could remember nothing after the explosion that had sunk the *Juneau*.

He was amazed when told. He had missed the whole thing! Who had survived the sinking? How did they react? How did he react? Damn! He would never really know.

Wang's sudden rationality actually led to a state of despair— and pain. His leg had swelled and was black from the toe to the hip. It had a foul odor, too. He thought gangrene had set in and pleaded with his raftmates:

"Cut it off, will you, please! I'll show you how."

But they refused, arguing that it was impossible in the boat.

Looking down into the water, he would recall: "I felt an impulse to let myself slide down. I could . . . look down and see the cool green depths below and wish that I just felt myself letting myself go down into the cool, clean depths of that green. I could just see myself floating there in utter peace. It seemed to me the ultimate in release. Several times I caught myself and pulled myself back. Then something came to me and I began to pray. The prayer I said was, 'Oh, Mary, who conceived without sin, pray for us who have no recourse today.'

"I said that several times, and within a very short period of time . . . a certain feeling came over me, a feeling of determination. The feeling of despair left me and I figured we were gonna make it."

And this feeling grew when Wang remembered reading a book about some airmen who had been downed in the Pacific and survived after floating on a raft for a thousand miles in thirty days before reaching shore. So "this was certainly no time to quit and we were gonna die trying rather than just sit there crying about it."

In his mind, Wang even listed some of the reasons why he had to survive:

"(1) I knew how keenly my mother would be affected if I were lost; (2) I wanted a large pitcher of ice water and a glass, and was determined to get it; (3) I wanted one of my mother's good, home-cooked meals, especially her pineapple upside-down cake, which I was also determined not to be robbed of; and (4) a large milk shake."

Hartney was cheered once more by Wang's awakening and sudden upbeat mood. Now there were again three fully conscious men in the boat, and the lieutenant could assume some of the burdens of command. He did, telling the two others how to judge the tides, when to paddle, when to conserve their energy. In this brighter atmosphere, Hartney and Fitzgerald even took to singing as they paddled along. Thus, a medley of tunes, mostly Irish, echoed over the calm waters—"I'll Take You Home Again, Kathleen," "Sidewalks of New York," "The Bowery," "My Wild Irish Rose," "Mother Machree." Despite his pain, Wang smiled and applauded.

"Keep it up, boys," he laughed. "It's not good, but it's loud."

As their strength ebbed, however, so did their high spirits, and food became an obsession. Wang tried to catch some "pretty little blue and yellow fish" in his handkerchief, but they always managed to escape. Equally frustrating was an attempt to catch fish with Wang's collar pins, which the lieutenant bent into hooks and attached to his shoestrings. But then, off in the distance, the three men saw a round object floating in the water. They paddled over to it and jubilantly found a coconut. But when it was cut open, a terrible stench permeated the air. So much for their dinner.

At this black moment, meat suddenly dropped from heaven as a sea gull swooped down on them, barely rustling its wings. Fitzgerald whacked it with his aluminum oar, and, emitting a shrill cry and beating its wings, it flopped into the sea about five feet away. Who needed a coconut now? The men paddled over to the stunned bird, but it recovered and flew off just as a hand reached out for it.

"We were beyond tears in our disappointment," Hartney would lament.

And Wang would say, "If you've ever seen your Thanksgiving dinner go flying off a table and out the window, you can imagine how we felt."

But then they realized they might have been lucky. Some of the blood from the bird would surely have spilled in the boat. And when water was bailed out, this blood would get into the sea and attract the sharks, which they saw ominously circling under them. This rather convoluted rationale somehow eased their hunger.

Then . . . land! No longer a smudgy vision in the distance but almost, it seemed, within reach. There were sudden visions of steaks smothered in mushrooms, frosted glasses of malted milk . . . a new life!

As Fitzgerald paused to take a bearing, he added to the elation.

"Planes! Look, over there!" he shouted.

The aircraft were coming for them! Hartney and Fitzgerald stood up and waved their paddles.

"They've just gotta see us!"

But Fitzgerald then froze.

"Good God!" he gasped. "They're Japs!"

No one could mistake those silhouettes. And they seemed to be heading directly toward them. Nor was it likely that a bright yellow boat would escape their detection. It stood out against the sea like a lantern in the night. A perfect target!

Search for survivors of the *Juneau*. . . .

Lt. Comdr. Raymond S. Lamb, skipper of the destroyer *Meade*, was exhausted when he received this order from Admiral Halsey. His ship had just played a key role in blasting the enemy in a second naval battle of Guadalcanal, which raged on November fourteenth and fifteenth, following the night battle of the thirteenth. The *Meade* sailed up and down the coast of Guadalcanal, setting afire three transports loaded with Japanese troops who were trying to land, and raking the beach with bullets and shells. Then Lamb picked up the survivors of two American destroyers that had been sunk in Ironbottom Sound.

Hardly had he completed this mission when he got the order to sail off and look for the survivors of yet another ship—the *Juneau*. Would his men, who hadn't slept for two nights, ever get to rest?

But orders were orders, and so the *Meade* steamed toward the spot where airmen had sighted the survivors in the water, arriving on November 17. Lamb and his lookout scanned the sea, but aside from an oil slick, not a hint of human presence came into focus. Nor, apparently, did Lamb request that an aircraft help him in his search. How long was his combat-fatigued crew expected to comb the area, anyway?

Lamb, thus impatient, headed back to Espíritu Santo, where he and his men could finally rest. And at seven P.M., he radioed Halsey in Nouméa:

"Arrived Button 1900 L (-11) x No personnel found reference COMAIRSOPAC 150653 x Searched area Achard Point Cape Jackson San Cristobal westward to longitude 160-54 x No debris some oil vicinity 15 miles south Achard Point."

When Halsey received this message, he was aghast. What could have happened to the survivors? Had they all perished since they were last sighted? On November 18, he rushed a message to his air commander, Admiral Fitch.

"Conduct additional air search for survivors area west of San Cristobal and Guadalcanal x Utilize *Shaw* and *Nicholas* as rescue ships as required."

Though several aircraft had sighted the survivors, and reports tracked their movement almost daily, days thus went by and no unit gave rescue priority or bothered to coordinate its efforts with any other. No PBY seaplane tried to land; no aircraft kept circling over the survivors to guide a rescue ship to them; and only one ship was spared to conduct a search—when it finished a higher-priority mission.

After all, there was a war going on.

By the morning of November 17, the fifth day in the water, only about forty men remained alive after most of the wounded had died and others had swum away to their death. The living removed dog tags and personal articles from the deceased and once again eased the bodies into the sea. Then they resumed paddling, even though the currents were so strong that the rafts had actually been pushed backward during the night.

Once more, some of the paddlers had, in their exhaustion, gone to sleep and inadvertently dropped their oars into the sea. So now Wyatt Butterfield and George Mantere set about cutting up the grating at the bottom of their raft to make paddles, and with six new ones the little flotilla again attempted to fight the currents.

Lieutenant Blodgett was determined to make headway, and when someone questioned his navigational orders that night, he snapped:

"I'm navigating. The island's over that way. We'll be there by daybreak."

And shortly afterward, the men began to believe him.

"Listen," exclaimed one, "d'ya hear the water hitting the coral reefs?"

Then Blodgett described how the reefs could tear up the feet, and the jellyfish within could poison men. Only Allen Heyn, it seemed, wasn't frightened. He had already been bitten several times by jellyfish, and he was still alive, though he became sick and vomited each time. In any case, the men soon realized that their ears had deceived them. Land was still far away.

But not the land in Heyn's imagination. The land he helped to work on the family farm. How delicious the apples and strawberries were. He would pick them, then dump bucketsful into baskets. After eating some for lunch, he would go with his mother and sister from house to house selling the produce, bargaining down to the last penny. Who would not buy strawberries so large, apples so rosy. . . . His mouth watered now and he could actually taste the fruit.

By the morning of the sixth day, Blodgett was no longer giving orders. He had started to lose his mind. When someone asked him if he still thought that land was near, he now mumbled with a far-off look:

"I don't know. Don't bother me!"

Soon he lapsed into delirium, imagining that he was still on the *Juneau* and muttering that he was officer of the deck and would begin his watch after going below to take a shower. And he had to be stopped from jumping in the water when other men who had done so came up with the tantalizing "news" that the *Juneau* was about ten feet underwater and that they had enjoyed a good chicken dinner and an ice cream soda. Even some of the saner men tended to believe the story.

On the morning of November 18, the same day Halsey radioed Fitch to "conduct additional air search for survivors," Lieutenant Gill took off from Espíritu Santo once more. Just another routine patrol flight this time. Despite Halsey's order, Gill would not receive any instructions to find the survivors again. Nor had he, or anybody else, been ordered the previous day to guide the destroyer *Meade* to the men floundering in the sea.

As he flew near the area where he had twice spotted the men in the water, he could not believe what he saw. They were still down there—but now, he judged, only about fifty of them.

"My God!" Gill thought. "The Navy apparently doesn't give a damn about them! They are being left to die!"

But Gill still saw no reason to break radio silence. The Navy knew damn well that the men were there. He couldn't force it to rescue them. After completing his mission several hours later, he reported his sighting to the intelligence officer for the third time.

This new sighting did not merit even a mention in the Daily Operations Report—despite the urgency of Halsey's message to Fitch. How many times must the same item be disseminated when there were so many new ones to report?

That morning, shortly after Gill saw the men in the water, the battering wind and waves loosened the ropes tying their three rafts together, and the three suddenly drifted apart. Two of them, one with Heyn and about a dozen others, and another with Friend and five or six others, were now on their own, leaving behind Zook's raft, which was still attached to the remaining three nets.

The two detached rafts floated away even though the men struggled to paddle toward the main group against the stiff currents.

"We could just see the others once in a while at a distance on the horizon," Heyn would say. "They'd be on top of a wave and we would see them. Well, we tried to get back to them but we never could, and we didn't know what to do. We tried to paddle and we found it wasn't doing no good, so we decided just to lay there and hope that someone would find us."

Friend and his raftmates also failed to get back to the main group. The ropes, Friend suspected, had been deliberately cut.

"It was a good way to get rid of someone," he would charge—namely himself.

They would never forgive him for "helping those three guys get away with that yellow rubber boat."

Meanwhile, the men on the third raft struggled to move ahead, pulling the nets alone. This was a moment for supreme pragmatism. And Zook well understood this. With Lieutenant Blodgett delirious, George Mantere, the senior petty officer, took over command, and Zook carried on as the commander's "chief adviser." Reflecting Zook's views, Mantere would later report:

"The men on the nets were more dead than alive. They were very weak from exhaustion and exposure. As all of our food and water was gone and there were only about eight men still capable of paddling, it was decided that I, being the senior petty officer, should make the decision as to who would go on the remaining raft to make a final attempt to paddle for shore."

The others, unfortunately, would have to be left behind on the nets until they were found. Of course, if the raft was found first or if it reached shore, help would be sent back immediately.

Those Mantere picked to leave, in addition to himself, were Zook, Holmgren, Butterfield, and three other men capable of paddling—Henry Gardner, Howard Franklin, and an unidentified sailor. They would take Lieutenant Blodgett along, though in his delirium he had to be restrained so he wouldn't leap into the water.

The chosen few blessed their luck—though Holmgren was reluctant to leave his hometown friend, Charlie Hayes, who had begun to hallucinate. Hayes had already dove to the "*Juneau*" for "something to eat" and had miraculously returned.

"Make sure you stay on the net," Holmgren cautioned his friend. "Don't go anywhere."

Some plane or ship would come to their rescue.

When the breakaway group had gathered in the raft and was

about to cut the ropes tying it to the nets, the twenty-five or so men languishing on them protested with anguished fury. The strongest and most senior men were abandoning them, leaving them alone to die—just as the three men in the rubber boat had done.

"You can't leave us!" they cried. "You can't go!"

"Sorry, we're going to have to leave," one of the chosen shouted back with cruel logic, his heart barricaded against their pleas.

"You got as much chance as we have to be rescued," he added, though he would later describe the nets as "death row."

At this terrible moment, the timeless theory of the survival of the fittest seemed far more practical than death for all.

CHAPTER

· 15 ·

The Taste of Blood

As the roar of Japanese planes thundered in their ears, Joe Hartney and Jimmy Fitzgerald threw themselves across the patches of yellow on their boat unstained by oil in a desperate attempt to hide them. They prayed that the pilots would not notice the bright color against the sea.

When the roar reached a crescendo, the two men and the wounded Lieutenant Wang could almost hear the machine gun bullets whizzing by. But the planes passed on without firing, and the hum of their motors soon faded in the distance.

"Boy! That was a close one," Fitzgerald gasped.

Then he and Hartney resumed paddling, convinced they were nearing shore. But they soon realized they were making no headway at all, for a heavy current was sweeping the raft relentlessly toward the open sea, which stretched all the way to Australia. Since they couldn't fight the drift anyway, all three men went to sleep and awoke at dawn on the sixth day to find themselves at the same spot. At least they weren't heading for Down Under.

The two paddlers went to work again, and they rowed all day. Suddenly, that evening, the wind began to whistle ominously and the sea grew choppy. Another storm? The men looked into the dark sky. The prospect of drowning almost at the moment of deliverance sent chills through them.

Then, as they gazed at the threatening clouds, they saw the silhouette of another plane. They shouted in joy; this one was a PBY! The aircraft headed toward them, but as Hartney and Fitzgerald leaped to their feet, waving and screaming, it turned away and vanished in the clouds.

The two men slumped again beside Wang, their shoulders drooping, and couldn't bear to look at each other. Another disappointment. But then they heard the hum once more.

"By God, it's coming back!" Fitzgerald cried.

This time the men just sat there, not daring to raise their hopes again—until they were sure. And their skepticism proved justified. The plane veered off into infinity.

Hartney suddenly stood up and exclaimed, "I know. He's making a regular patrol. That's the end of his beat. He'll be back. Quick, where's my paddle? This time I'll flash him down."

Hartney got out his knife and scraped the oil off the aluminum oar until it shone like a mirror. He even dipped the blade in the water to give it an added luster. Now he would wait—but not for long. The familiar rumble of engines sounded in the distance and the plane swooped again into view.

Hartney held up the paddle and jiggled his wrist as he flashed it. And this time, the plane did not turn back, but circled overhead and dropped a smoke bomb to get the wind drift. It was preparing to land!

"We laughed and cried all at once," Hartney would say. "Our troubles were over. Five minutes more and he'd be down and we'd be aboard."

But at that moment of ecstasy, a geyser of water nearly swamped the raft, and the wind almost turned it around. A black squall had struck, it seemed, with the force of a hurricane, worse than the earlier storm they had survived. And suddenly, the plane disappeared from the sky—and their thoughts.

The two paddlers wanted to ride the waves, but Wang was suddenly reliving his boyhood days of surfing when he went against the waves. That experience, he felt, might now save their lives.

"Head into the wind and the waves or we'll turn over!" Wang

ordered his two companions as crosswaves hit the raft, further filling it with water. And the lieutenant, forgetting about his wounded leg, tied his shoelaces to the boat so he wouldn't fall overboard and bailed furiously while the others paddled into a wall of white water driven by a howling wind.

"The raft pitched and tossed," Hartney would relate, "every second threatening to turn over and spill us into the sea. . . . We forgot the plane, we forgot our hopes of rescue, and we only thought of keeping that bubble of air right side up."

To coordinate their battle against the sea, Hartney cried, "Backwater! . . . Pull! . . . Backwater! . . . Pull!" For hours they struggled, though "where we found the strength," Hartney would say, "God alone knows."

Finally the rain stopped and the wind relented even as the waves continued to leap about forty feet high. Now the odor of fuel oil from their oil-soaked clothing gradually dissolved into a sweet fragrance, reminiscent of the scent emanating from the jungles of Guadalcanal. The smell of gardenias! If it had been a bit sickening before, especially to Hartney, now it was the smell of life, of survival. And as the boat reached the crest of one soaring wave, Wang, his eyes feasting on greenery, cried out:

"Land! Land! We're being carried toward shore!"

The madmen on Allen Heyn's raft thought he was crazy for thinking that if they "just hung on, somebody would come and get us." Every time he would wave at a plane passing overhead, they were angry. Those guys up there didn't want to save them. Besides, who needed to be saved? The ship was right down there in the water. Some men had been down there and found cans and cans of peaches.

"Where are they?" Heyn asked.

'We left them down there."

"You show me the way," replied Heyn, who was starting to hallucinate himself.

He and the man then dove into the sea, and, Heyn would say later, he "never did find nothing down there."

On returning to the raft, he asked the man, "Well, where was the ship?"

"Didn't you see it?" the man replied.

Heyn then got his "sense again and I knew what I was doing and I didn't believe him anymore." About nine men who did believe him never came back, and now only three were left.

In their more rational moments, they talked about what they would do at home when they got there. But then they would say that "if they could get on an island, they'd stay there, they'd never go back to the Navy. . . . It wasn't fair they should be left like that!"

The men, who had not eaten for days, also talked about food. About juicy steaks, hamburgers soaked in catsup, milk shakes—and a live sea gull when one landed on the rim of the raft. They lunged at it but, to their chagrin, it flew away.

"Maybe he'll be back," Heyn said. "And as soon as he comes down, I'll grab him."

After all, he had caught chickens on his farm.

The bird did indeed return, and this time Heyn proved luckier than the men on the yellow rubber boat, who had let a gull get away. He caught this one and wrung its neck. The prey was divided among the three men, who voraciously chewed up their share, feathers and all, while drinking the blood with the joy a connoisseur might feel as he sipped fine wine.

The taste of blood gave Heyn an idea. Since the sharks were drawn by blood and were cannibalistic, why not make as many as possible bleed? Then perhaps they would devour each other. He gave a Mexican raftmate his knife, and the man slashed every predator that passed within reach. More than one ended up in the stomach of another.

Heyn's other companion, a Polish youth, having thrown all his clothes away in the heat of the day, decided in the cold of the night—the temperature had dropped about 40 degrees—to "go down to the ship and get a clean suit. I got a lot of them in my locker."

Heyn tried to persuade him not to go, and he and his Mexican companion sandwiched him between their bodies to keep him warm. But the man, slithering out of the embrace, said a prayer in English and Polish and swam away. His screams pierced the night, as a bubbly fountain of water marked the spot where a shark grabbed him.

And now, on the seventh night, November 19, there were only two.

That same day, Arthur Friend, on another raft, saw a hole in the sea. He jumped into it and slid down until he reached a bustling street hundreds of feet underwater. A whole city! . . .

Then he came to his senses and found himself alone in the raft with one man, a youth named Brown. His three other raftmates had all let themselves drift off to oblivion. And Brown, too, had lost his mind.

"I'm going below to get some ice cream," he calmly notified Friend.

And Brown swam off. About twenty feet away, he screamed. A shark had him. Friend instinctively leaped into the water, forgetting his pledge to survive at any cost, and found himself face to snout with another shark. He struck the beast on its snout with his fist and it turned tail and retreated. Friend then swam on toward Brown and reached him just as the first shark let go of him and floated away. Grasping the victim by the collar, Friend pulled him back to the raft, where he found that both of Brown's feet had been chewed off at the ankle.

Friend knew his raftmate would bleed to death, but nevertheless vowed to keep him alive as long as possible. Brown was his last companion. The thought of battling the sea all alone petrified him. Who would remind him that there was land out there, with people, horses, cows, buildings, streets. He didn't wish to look for them again under the water because he wanted to come back, to live, to see his mother and father and brother again.

Since the floor slats in the raft had been removed for use as paddles, Friend had strung a rope across the length of the open frame so the men could more easily move around. He feared that the bottomless raft would make it easier for a shark to get at them, attacking from below.

Friend now squatted on the rope just under the surface of the water and was trying to lash Brown to the raft so the man wouldn't drift away. Suddenly, he felt something "scratching" at his buttocks. He looked around and, to his horror, saw a shark that had swum into the raft and sunk its teeth into him.

"God damn!" Friend cried. "He's got me by the ass!"

Also on November 19, the day after Zook's raft drifted off on its own, Lieutenant Blodgett was still in a muddled mental state.

"Let me go! Let me go!" he implored the men holding him down.

Once, he noted the ropes trailing from the raft and asked, "Where does that ladder lead to?"

There was no ladder, the men replied. But he insisted there was and that it led to the *Juneau*.

"Let me go so I can relieve the watch!" he cried.

He was, after all, officer of the deck.

Finally, when night fell and the others dozed off, he broke away and jumped into the sea. Zook awoke at that moment and yelled:

"Come back, Lieutenant, come back! Don't be a fool!"

But Blodgett kept going until a scream signaled the end. There was the familiar sound of violently churning water and then silence. The silence of the shark.

"Well, they got Blodgett," Zook said resignedly.

And he and the others returned to their paddles. No one wept. No one thought much about it.

"We were pretty hardened by that time," Zook would explain.

The men dozed again and, on awakening hours later, found that two of them had dropped their paddles into the sea. Since the paddles had come from the floors of the other rafts, they took slats from their own raft and soon all the men were paddling again. All except two. Howard Franklin and the unidentified man swam away while the slats were being removed, and there were the usual screams. Who were those guys? No one ever got to know them. Well, two paddlers less . . .

The five men still alive kept paddling, until they saw what was surely a mirage—a destroyer and at least four transports or supply ships sallying from the southeast end of San Cristobal Island. They cleared their eyes. No, this wasn't a mirage! In joy, they waved their paddles, hoping the destroyer's radar would pick them up. But the ships sailed off into the distance. Blind again!

The men, without food or water for days, were by now almost too weak to wield their paddles. And they, like their comrades before them, were beginning to hallucinate. Holmgren burst out:

"Look! Palm trees just ahead!"

Mantere saw them, too. Yes, land!

But they couldn't stop there, they agreed—no one gave them permission.

Henry Gardner then shouted to the others, "I don't care what you guys say, I'm going to drink the [sea] water!"

Cupping some in his hands, he gulped it down and soon began retching. "Let him die!" someone said as he draped his sick shipmate over the rim of the raft. But somehow Gardner recovered, and the others began wondering if drinking salt water was "really all that bad."

Suddenly, there was a roar in the distance. Thunder in the sunshine?

"Looking up," Butterfield would recall, "we saw the prettiest PBY in the world!"

"Let's signal him!" someone shouted.

And Signalman Zook climbed on the shoulders of Holmgren and Gardner and sent a semaphore message by hand to the plane, which had begun to circle them: "We are survivors of the *Juneau.*"

The pilot replied by dropping a life jacket presumably wrapped around something.

"Water! Food!"

So excited were the men that they almost forgot the plane, which continued to circle above. But the life jacket fell about fifty feet from the raft, and no matter how hard they paddled, the currents kept carrying it away. Finally, their energy spent, they stopped paddling and no one said a word. There was only one way to retrieve it. Someone would have to swim for it. Everyone waited for a raftmate to volunteer.

Butterfield weighed the odds. He gazed at the yellow life jacket, which glowed in the sun like the proverbial pot of gold at the end of the rainbow. Then he peered into the clear blue water below and trembled at the sight of sharks crisscrossing the ocean. Suicide! Still, how could he ignore this unique challenge? He had seen so many men die, so many eaten alive. . . . Life had become almost meaningless. But was this a reason to give up his dream of glory—or to pursue it? If he succeeded, people would cheer him; if he failed, they'd remember him. So what the hell could he lose?

One might argue that, with rescue imminent, it didn't make sense to take such a risk. Yet it was precisely because of its imminence that, to him, the risk did make sense. For when would he get a chance like this again to prove himself to the world—and to Wyatt Butterfield. His whole life up to now, it seemed, had been simply a prelude leading inexorably to this climactic, defining moment. God damn it, why not? He could do it. He would do it.

Butterfield got up, shook hands all around, and said, "Please tell my parents what happened if I don't make it back."

They sure would.

Then Mantere gave him his bowie knife to fight the sharks if they tried to stop him. They wouldn't stop him, Butterfield assured himself again. He paused to gaze at the life jacket once more. Only fifty feet away, but it seemed like fifty miles. And there were a helluva lot more sharks than Hartney and Fitzgerald had had to face when they swam for that rubber boat a few days earlier. Those guys were a lot stronger, too, for hunger wasn't too bad then. It wouldn't be easy fighting the currents and the sharks on an empty stomach. But what the hell . . .

In fact, Butterfield felt good. Sort of as he did when he had stepped into the ring to fight some killer while the crowd roared. Maybe they'd even give him a medal.

And he slipped into the water while his raftmates silently watched what they thought could be the last act of madness in the tragic saga of the *Juneau*.

When Lieutenant Wang cried that he had sighted land, Joe Hartney glanced over his shoulder. "There was the island," he would say, "so close now that the trees could be easily distinguished running back from the line of the shore. The storm that had come so near to ending us had proved our greatest benefactor in the end; the wind and rushing waves had defeated the diabolical tides that had toyed with us for the past two days. Even the elements seemed destined to play a part in the strange fate that was conspiring to save us from the end that had come so suddenly to our shipmates."

With renewed hope, Hartney yelled to Fitzgerald, acting on Wang's instructions, "We've got to turn around, and when the waves come in, backpedal to take the immediate force and then ride into that lagoon there before the tide has a chance to shove us out again. Wait for a long, smooth one. Then pull like hell!"

Wang now became aware of a gradually louder roar—the crash of waves on the beach, he thought. But then he saw a white phosphorescent glow along the shoreline. A coral reef! That, Wang now realized, was causing the roar. How would they get past it? It was full of razor-sharp edges that could "cut us to pieces." But it was too late now to go back; they could never fight the waves.

Finally, a long, smooth wave. And as it hit the raft, Hartney cried to Fitzgerald:

"Pull! Pull!"

Fitzgerald put every ounce of his remaining strength behind his strokes, while Hartney backwatered "like mad." At the same time, Wang desperately searched for a wide enough channel through the coral leading to the beach—and found one. The boat was steered into it on the crest of the wave, but it turned around in the rushing current and raced on stern-first, almost sure, it seemed, to crash against the coral. Before death could strike, however, the wave lifted the boat up on a ridge of the rocklike material and, while receding, left it tilting forward at about a forty-five-degree angle. The men looked down from their precarious perch on a deep chasm of jagged coral.

"My God," thought Wang. "If that wave had not been just right, we would have all dropped into that pit and been torn to shreds."

Fortunately, another ledge of coral held the bow of the boat in place, but how could they leave the boat when the least movement could send it into the pit? Was their long, torturous journey to end with them impaled on the needles at the bottom of that pit?

*   *   *

LEFT TO DIE

Allen Heyn, who on the first day of the sinking had to cling to a rope in the water because there was no room on his raft, now, on the seventh day adrift, shared the raft with only one other man, the Mexican youth. As both men, enervated, famished, nearly mad with thirst, were dozing off on the rim of the raft, Heyn was suddenly awakened by a piercing cry:

"Help me! Quick!"

"What's happened?" Heyn called to his raftmate, who had been lying on the rim at the other side of the raft.

"Give me a knife, quick!" the man yelled.

"I already gave you mine!" Heyn yelled.

"I lost it. Something's dragging me!"

But the man finally broke loose, it seemed, and the pair, holding on to the rim, moved toward each other. As Heyn grabbed hold of his companion, the man exclaimed:

"Somebody stabbed me!"

"How can anybody stab you out here?" Heyn said. "There's nobody but us two."

His comrade swore at him, crying, "Get me to a doctor, quick!"

Half-delirious himself, Heyn immediately picked up a paddle and began rowing with the last of his waning strength.

"I didn't know where I was going," he would say. "I was just paddling, trying to get him to a doctor."

The man began yelling, Heyn would recount, "and I held his arm, and then I could see what it was. . . . A shark [had] grabbed him and tore his leg off below, just jaggedylike."

At that moment, the shark, which had careened into the raft from underneath, struck again. As it clamped its teeth around the man's remaining leg, the victim cried to Heyn:

"Hold me! He's stabbing me again!"

But the shark was now biting off the limb piece by piece, literally tearing him apart. And though Heyn tried to hold on to his companion in a grotesque tug-of-war between man and beast, the shark jerked the hysterical victim into the water, and calm returned to the raft.

Heyn was now alone.

*　　*　　*

The shark attacking Arthur Friend on another raft dragged him into the sea by his buttocks.

He was about to die, Friend thought. But then ... No, God damn it, he had survived the explosion, hadn't he? It still wasn't time! He would get loose somehow. And he suddenly recalled how he had rendered a shark helpless by cutting out its gills. Now he grabbed one of this shark's gills and desperately jerked it until he ripped it loose.

"The shark then spit me out," Friend would say.

Meanwhile, Brown, insecurely tied to the raft, had rolled off the rim into the sea and another shark "tore him up" just before Friend could reach him.

Now other sharks were drawn by the blood and zoomed toward Friend. But he climbed aboard the raft and, lying face-down on the rim, pumped his fist at the snout of any beast within reach. Finally, he tried to sit back to rest. But he couldn't. He felt no pain, but when he reached for his buttocks, he found only one. The other had become "fifteen pounds of meat floating around in my pants."

"Words can't describe the fear I felt as I approached the life jacket," Wyatt Butterfield would say. "The minutes seemed an eternity."

But he had to fetch the jacket holding the badly needed supplies that were dropped by the PBY pilot circling over his raft. Swimming swiftly through fifty feet of shark-infested water, he safely reached the life preserver, but as he grabbed it with his left hand and turned, he found that his "fear was realized."

Three sharks were heading straight for him, and "panic took over. I started slashing with the knife, and each time that one of the monsters bumped me, I was certain that I'd lost some part of my anatomy."

Butterfield gazed into the open jaw of one shark and saw its huge, gleaming teeth.

"Oh, my God," he thought, "he's gonna get my arm, or my leg!"

He kicked the water and splashed with all his might, but he could paddle with only one arm, since his other was wrapped around the jacket and its priceless contents.

"If I had thought," he would say, "I would have let the jacket go and swum like hell. But who thinks in a situation like that?"

Anyway, the jacket symbolized to him the ultimate victory, the golden belt of the champion. He could almost hear the crowd cheering him on. And, in fact, he did. As the men on the raft tried to paddle toward him, they watched with grim fascination and cried:

"Come on, Wyatt, just a few more feet, come on!"

And Butterfield, screaming in fright, finally covered those few feet and was pulled over the rim to safety, still gripping the life jacket. At the same time, the sharks he left behind were devouring one of their own.

"I had managed to knife one of the sharks," Butterfield would explain. "And the rest had settled for him instead of me."

While the other men tore open the life jacket, Butterfield anxiously felt his body "to see what pieces were missing." He discovered with relief that the only damage was a six-inch gash in one foot from scraping against sharkskin.

The life jacket held three aviator's rations, a canteen of water, and a message placed in a pocket novel, reading:

> From the plane circling over you:
> We have been ordered to circle you and stand by until a tin can [destroyer] comes to pick you up. It is on the way already. If it doesn't get here before twilight, we will shove off . . . and return in the morning.
> Cheer up lads and sit tight.
> Lt. (jg) McWilliams, USNR

The pocket novel, the men noted, was aptly entitled "The House at the End of the Road."

Ironically, the men squirreled away most of the food and water Butterfield risked his life to get—in case a rescue ship didn't arrive for another day.

The hero had good reason to wonder now: What the hell had he risked his life for? And who said the world would ever hear of his heroic act, anyway? But he still felt good. He had proved to himself, at least, that he was a pretty brave guy.

* * *

Lieutenant Wang reached a life-or-death decision. Before the next wave hit, he and his two men, Joe Hartney and Jimmy Fitzgerald, would have to get out of their boat, which was precariously perched on a coral ridge. Wang knew the risk was great; the slightest movement could send them plummeting into a chasm studded with steellike coral needles. But the risk would be even greater if they remained in the boat, for a wave might well dislodge it.

Wang cautiously stood up with the help of his companions, and the boat began to teeter slightly. He peered with white-faced terror into the abyss of death as the needles reached out to him. What a way to die! For a few seconds, the three men stood as motionless as statues. Then Wang was cautiously lifted out on one leg, and he was followed by his companions. The boat remained stable.

In nervous exhaustion, the lieutenant lay panting on the ledge, which fortunately was relatively smooth. Then, more good luck. The tide came and receded without moving the boat. Since it was impossible to walk barefoot on the coral, Wang, who had the only pair of shoes, gave them to one man while the other improvised another pair from their canvas bailing basket.

Hartney and Fitzgerald inched their way forward until they reached the fifty-yard-wide lagoon that ran parallel with the beach, the body of water they had seen from a distance. They then went back for the boat, dragged it to the edge of the lagoon, and returned once more for Wang. Making a stretcher from their paddles and belts, they laboriously carried him to the boat, and all of them boarded it again.

It was evening now, and the two men, so weak they could barely stand, went to sleep while Wang watched for the incoming tide, which they hoped would carry them across the lagoon to shore.

Were they about to be saved after all the horror? As Wang stared into the darkness, he could hardly believe the heroism and courage he had witnessed, not to mention the nautical skill of his two companions. Hartney and Fitzgerald, he would later write, "were magnificent in their conduct and ability. Without them, I feel quite sure I could not have survived."

Yes, he had learned something about men acting under unbearable stress. And his two shipmates had learned a lot about him.

Hartney would say: "The courage that man showed during those days was something marvelous to behold."

Toward morning, the tide came in and Wang wakened the men. "Stand by for the next big wave," he said. "It'll carry us into the lagoon."

And shortly they were floating.

"We shook the stiffness out of our joints," Hartney would recount, "and began to push our way in toward shore. The sun came up, spreading the hot yellow light over the sea, and bringing out the green of the trees so near at hand now. The sand gleamed white, with the grateful promise of shade under the trees behind."

At last, solid ground!

On this morning of November 19, the two paddlers climbed out on the beach and, with a rope, pulled the boat a few inches at a time out of the rising tide to the edge of a jungle, about fifteen yards from the water. The three men then collapsed in the sand and fell into the most glorious sleep of their lives.

At about noon, Hartney and Fitzgerald woke under a beating sun and staggered around in a daze. They were actually on land!

"We've got to find water," Hartney croaked.

They could barely stand and lacked the strength to go for it. But "we had to find it quickly or we might never find it," Hartney would say. For they might soon be dead from dehydration.

The two men stumbled along in the sand, "hardly able to pull one foot after the other," stopping to rest every few yards. And then they came upon a wondrous sight. Flowing out of the jungle was a stream of clear, fresh water. They fell on their stomachs, burying their faces in the stream, letting the water flow over their bruised and bony bodies.

Hartney would go on: "We drank. We rolled in it. We drank some more. We ducked our heads in it."

When they had finally quenched their thirst, Hartney filled up a patching kit, a six-inch rubber tube with a cork in each end, and brought it to Wang, who had just awakened, and he greedily gulped it down.

"Now we've got to find food," Hartney said. "Maybe there'll be some coconuts around."

And he and Fitzgerald set out once more down the beach while Wang, still in pain, dozed off again. When sometime later he opened his eyes, he saw a fuzzy figure outlined against the dark trees. Must be one of his men, he thought. But when he had cleared his eyes, he stared in shock at a figure out of some jungle film he had seen as a child—a wild-looking "savage" clad only in a meager loincloth. Wang glanced around and saw ten or fifteen more of them approaching. They were short but powerfully built and had fierce expressions on their faces.

Wang could almost hear his heart thumping. He had heard there were cannibals on some of these islands. And it was lunchtime.

CHAPTER

· 16 ·

And Then There Were Ten

ADMIRAL HALSEY'S ORDER TO ADMIRAL FITCH WAS FINALLY GET-
ting through. Rescuing the survivors of the *Juneau* had become
a priority mission at last—six days after the ship had been sunk.
Priority of a sort. No great excitement. One PBY was sent out
to search for the men so that a ship, if it wasn't already engaged,
would know where to find them.

Lieutenant McWilliams, the pilot of the assigned PBY, radioed headquarters in Espíritu Santo that he had circled a raft
of survivors until twilight, dropping some supplies to them.
Then, when no ship turned up, he flew back to base before his
fuel ran out. The destroyer *Ballard*, which was supposed to
rescue the men, had been delayed. So another PBY with a fresh
crew would be sent to guide the ship to the scene.

Lt. Lawrence B. Williamson, a highly respected twenty-eight-
year-old naval pilot, was selected to do the job. He loved flying
and had dreamed of becoming a pilot ever since he was a child.
Every Sunday he would wander off to the airfield and, while
sipping on a soda pop, gaze in awe at heroic barnstorming avia-
tors, who soared into the sky with anyone thirsting for a celes-
tial joyride. At seventeen he quit work in his family's country
store in Brookhaven, Mississippi, and joined the Navy. Assigned

to the carrier *Saratoga* in the mid-1930s, when Admiral Halsey had been its skipper, he soon became the "bridge talker," relaying Halsey's orders around the ship on the loudspeaker.

Now, as the pilot of a PBY attached to Squadron VP-72 under the operational control of Commander, Fleet Air Wing One, Williamson would once more serve as the voice of Halsey, who had personally given the order to rescue the survivors.

"We're going on a special mission and we're not going to fail!" Williamson told his crewmen at their base in Espíritu Santo.

They were not overwhelmingly enthusiastic, for they still hadn't recovered from an intensive two-day search for Japanese ships. Their reward was a day off to relax—until Williamson gave the order. But they did not gripe, for they trusted Williamson implicitly. As one crew member, Plane Capt. William Anderson, would say:

"We liked Larry. He was one of the best. He was down-to-earth, and he never took unnecessary chances. We felt safe with him. And he never jumped on us. We knew what he wanted and followed his orders without question, and he never disobeyed orders either."

But though Williamson was determined to succeed on this mission, as on every one, he had little information to guide him in the search. The operations officer of his unit simply told him:

"Here is the position report on the *Juneau* survivors. Go out and search for them."

How long had they been in the water? How many rafts had been seen? There was no background data at all. No great interest, really. But there were men out there floating in the sea, and Williamson knew that the *Juneau* had been sunk days earlier. And that his old commander, Admiral Halsey, wanted survivors rescued at almost any cost.

At five-thirty A.M. on November 19, after the crew had unloaded four five-hundred-pound bombs from his plane, Williamson was ready for takeoff. He now informed his men, without mentioning the *Juneau*, that they were to rescue crew members of a ship sunk in the Battle of Guadalcanal. Thus, while Williamson could sense the special drama of the *Juneau* disaster, to his men, the mission was "no big deal." They had searched for many survivors before, so now there were a few more. Another boring, if necessary, mission.

Williamson looked for the survivors all day, starting his search forty miles southwest of the southwestern tip of San Cristobal Island. But they were nowhere to be seen. Finally, at about five P.M., he gave up and radioed a message to his headquarters: he was returning to base. Williamson was agitated. Why wasn't the raft anywhere near the spot reported by Lieutenant McWilliams?

But as he started home in a southeasterly direction, someone shouted over the intercom:

"There they are!"

And Williamson saw a speck in the ocean that looked like a barrel. It was a raft—and there were five to seven men aboard. In joy, he circled it, then sighted a second raft with just one man on it, apparently Heyn. Three more circles, and he found a third one with a number of people sprawled across it, but no movement. This "raft" was, it seems, one of the three nets that had been set adrift. The crew did not see the raft with only Friend aboard or the two other nets with additional men.

Williamson radioed the sighting to his headquarters and received the response: "USS *Ballard* en route to area of survivors. Remain on-site until arrival of *Ballard* about 2330 [eleven-thirty P.M.]."

Like McWilliams the day before, Williamson was worried, for his fuel supply might not last if the ship was late. He had to choose: risk a crash or leave early. After dark, the rafts would be difficult to spot anyway. But how could he leave? What if the ship couldn't find them without his help? One more night out there and the survivors might all be dead. There had to be a third alternative.

And there was. With his copilot, Earl Paul, Williamson studied sea conditions and saw that the three conveyances, driven by a sixteen-knot wind, were bouncing in a line along five- to six-foot swells that rolled with tempered anger across the ocean.

"We can do it!" Williamson asserted.

He would land into the wind, pick up the five or six survivors in the first raft they had spotted, then taxi to the two others. He thus radioed headquarters and asked for permission to land.

The reply: "Use your own discretion."

Williamson then announced over the intercom, "Prepare for open sea landing. We're going in."

His men were not afraid. They knew Larry wouldn't be going in if he thought it was too risky. When one man crossed himself, Anderson joked:

"You should have thought about that when you were messing with that girl in Honolulu."

The man had abandoned her when he learned he was being sent to the South Pacific. Why bring God into this? Anderson thought. Larry knew what he was doing.

And indeed, as Williamson gently eased down for a full-stall landing, he was confident he would touch water safely even though he had never done so in the open sea, only in a bay. He would later admit that he had a "false sense of security," perhaps because otherwise he might not have attempted so dangerous a landing. In fact, his sense of security vanished when the plane suddenly lost its lift and dropped precipitously toward the heaving sea.

At the same time, another lieutenant's sense of security vanished in the heat of an imaginary jungle kitchen.

"I thought I was headed for the cooking pot," Lieutenant Wang would say later about the "cannibals" in loincloths who approached him on the beach of the island where he and his two companions had landed. "And did I give them a smile!"

The natives drew closer, then stopped, and Wang wondered if the stench from his wounded leg might have kept them back. But then one of them beckoned to him to come forward.

"This is it!" Wang thought. "They're taking me to the pot!"

He pointed to his leg, then picked up a stick and broke it in several places. And they stopped beckoning. Then, to show his friendly intentions, Wang removed everything from his pockets—nickels, dimes, keys—and offered it to them. But they remained silent with scowling faces.

What else could he offer that might take their minds off the day's menu? . . . His boat! He pointed to the craft and then to them, indicating they could have it, and they finally smiled back. Several now walked to the boat and, lifting it, started to carry it toward the jungle. But as they moved, they jostled Wang, and he cried out in pain. The others then shouted to those holding the boat to put it down.

But the scowls had returned and continued to bode ill. Suddenly Wang spotted in the group a little girl about ten years old, and suspended from her neck was "something that looked very much like a medal"—a Sacred Heart Medal! These people were Catholic!

Wang unclasped a chain hanging from his own neck and swung his Miraculous Medal in front of him.

"Now they knew that I was one of the boys," he would say.

Wang then motioned to the men to bring him something to drink, and within a minute he was handed half a coconut shell filled to the brim with coconut milk.

"It was the most delicious thing I have ever tasted," Wang would rave.

Then he counted on seven of his fingers, pointed to his stomach, and shook his head, trying to convey the message that he hadn't eaten for seven days. And after a loud hubbub went up, the little girl wearing the medal left and soon returned with a shellful of cooked papaya. It tasted like potatoes au gratin.

Wang was suddenly struck with a terrifying thought. Were they fattening him up for the kill? But he immediately dismissed the possibility. No Catholic would think of lunching on another!

While Lieutenant Wang feasted, Joe Hartney and Jimmy Fitzgerald foraged—until they, too, found themselves face-to-face with a group of "savages."

"We stopped dead in our tracks," Hartney would relate. "So did the savages. Come to think of it, we probably had them beat in hideousness."

But the natives, to the relief of the two survivors, didn't carry weapons and made no hostile gestures.

"Hell," said Fitzgerald, trying to ease his anxiety, "they're as much afraid of us as we are of them."

He then stepped forward, extending his hand and grinning.

The "savages" did not respond, but stared suspiciously at the two men while chewing on betel nuts, which they kept in little wicker baskets that hung around their necks. They would spit out the nuts in a stream of red saliva, then dig into the baskets for more.

The two Americans used pantomime to express their friendly intent and their hunger, but "nothing fazed them."

The pair were now less concerned about satisfying their own appetites than about satisfying the natives'. Finally, a little old man with wrinkled, leathery skin and sticklike limbs came forward and peered at them curiously. Unlike the others, who sported loincloths only, he was wearing a white cotton sack with holes for the arms—and a chain around his neck with something dangling from it.

Fitzgerald cried, "Look at that medal around his neck. It's a Saint Christopher Medal!"

And so, being fellow Catholics, the pair realized with enormous relief, as Wang did, that they would not serve after all as the tribe's protein intake for the day.

Fitzgerald walked up to the little old man, pointed to the medal, and tried to show admiration for it.

"Missionary," the man uttered with a toothless grin.

And now the whole welcoming party smiled and crowded around the two strangers. As communication grew easier, Hartney drew a circle—a "rising sun"—in the sand with his finger and pointed to the jungle. Any Japanese there? But the natives suddenly grimaced and muttered to each other.

"God!" Fitzgerald whispered. "They think we're Japs!"

Maybe they couldn't tell the difference because the faces of the two were smeared with oil. And it was clear these people didn't like the Japanese.

The pair pointed to themselves and exclaimed, "American! American!"

And the grins returned.

The survivors then pointed to the part of the beach where they had landed, and the feeble old man agreed to accompany them back to meet "another American." If there was a missionary on the island, perhaps this man could lead the three of them to him, and a doctor—before Lieutenant Wang had to have his festering leg amputated to avoid dying of gangrene.

Thus, after lunch, Wang saw three men approaching along the beach—Hartney, Fitzgerald, and the old man.

"Isn't it lucky?" Hartney greeted him, smiling. "These natives turned out to be from a small mission settlement and this old native is the instructor."

The man had been taught, Hartney said, by an old missionary who made frequent visits to the island.

Now the three strangers were asked to follow the group. Wang was lifted into the boat and several men carried it, following the others. The group trekked about a half mile up the beach, then turned into the jungle, and some fifty yards in came to a clearing with about ten large thatched huts nestled in the greenery.

The guests were ushered into one of them, and as they sat on the dirt floor in the shadowy emptiness, more food was brought in—papayas, coconut milk, baked yams. Wang was about to stuff himself further when a native pulled the food from him and wouldn't permit him to eat until another man came with a half coconut shell of water and washed his hands. Wang felt ashamed. He had forgotten his table manners. Then someone held a coconut dish of food and spoon-fed him.

After the meal, the three men lay on the grass-matted shelves that encircled the interior of the hut and slept for hours, while four of the hosts sat in the hut tending a fire to keep them warm. When the guests awoke that evening, more food was waiting for them, including a stringy but tasty fowl.

Then more sleep, and in the morning they opened their eyes just as a good-looking, copper-colored, young half-caste dressed in a neat pair of shorts and sport shirt walked into the hut. Grinning, he held out his hand and said in halting English:

"Good morning, gentlemen, how do you feel?"

Startled, the survivors listened as the man told them, "I'm from the neighboring island of Santa Ana. One of the boys crossed the mountain and paddled over to us during the night to tell us you were here. My name is Albert Kuper. My father is a trader. We'll get you out of here at once."

He looked at Wang's leg and said gravely, "That's bad. You've got to get to a hospital. Fortunately, I've some sulfanilamide tablets. The boy said one of you was quite badly injured."

Then, while Kuper cleaned the maggots out of Wang's wound and applied a crude splint to his leg, he continued, "[My father] is a big man in these parts. He sent me off immediately to give you what aid I could and to get you back over to the plantation so we can really help you."

Some men put Wang on a litter, carried him outside, and together with Kuper and several others, stumbled through the dark, humid jungle, which was brightened only by exotic, multicolored birds and huge blossoming flowers.

"For several hours," Hartney would report, "we swung along the mountain trails, climbing higher and higher, treading dangerous paths through yawning valleys. On the other side of the range, we were shifted into a couple of great war canoes that lay on the black, sluggish surface of a jungle river and were paddled swiftly downstream to the coast. (Wang was placed in the rubber boat, which had been carried to the site.) There in a bay lay a neat little motor launch, Bermuda rigged, with clean white sails already set."

Everyone was transferred to the launch, and each of the natives shook hands with the three survivors and said, "Good-bye, good-bye!" Then, after a three-mile trip across the open sea, the launch chugged its way to another much smaller island.

There on the beach waiting to greet them was a welcoming party of natives headed by a little gray-haired, pink-cheeked man sporting a handlebar mustache and draped in a white linen suit that might have been tailored by Savile Row.

After the sinking, the sharks, and the storms, this glittering speck of a world long lost—clean, elegant, frivolously normal— was almost the final shock. Were they hallucinating again?

One man who wished he was hallucinating was Lieutenant Williamson as his PBY nosed toward the water to rescue the men on Lester Zook's raft. As the plane, in a full stall, lost its lift and headed steeply down, his concern about survival now shifted to his own men.

The plane finally hit the water and leaped from wave to wave. Williamson slowly let out his breath—he had not crashed! But there was still danger ahead from the swells that were striking the windtip floats. The aircraft was difficult to maneuver, but gradually drew to a halt. Williamson wondered if the rough landing had damaged the plane, perhaps sufficiently to prevent a takeoff. And his worry grew when Anderson reported:

"We got a few leaks back here."

Anderson, however, plugged the leaks with sharpened pencils, and now the pilot, who had landed only about one hundred yards from some survivors—just where he wanted to be—taxied toward them. As he approached the raft, Williamson feared that the men might be trapped between the wingtip float and the port propeller. So one crewman went out on a wing and threw a line to them. Then he swung the raft around the plane to the rear, keeping it outboard of the float.

Anderson lowered a small metal ladder from the blister door, and one by one the survivors grasped it and were pulled into the plane.

"What ship you from?" Anderson asked them.

"The *Juneau*," muttered Butterfield, the first to be dragged aboard. "There's some other guys floating around here. Out of maybe one hundred and twenty-five guys in the water, we're the only ones left."

Butterfield then passed out and was carried to a cot. The others made it on their own, but collapsed on their cots like corpses returning to the grave.

Meanwhile, in the cockpit, Williamson, holding the plane as steady as he could, was in a dilemma. After rescuing these men, he had planned to pick up more in the other rafts—but that could be dangerous. He had misjudged the size of the swells, and the sea was far rougher than he had thought. The aircraft had already been punctured and might be further impaired if he taxied around. And as darkness descended, it could be hell finding the other rafts, or taking off. Besides, a destroyer was on the way and would pick up any remaining survivors.

So the logical thing to do now, in Williamson's view, was to fly his five survivors to Tulagi, refuel there, assess the danger, and return at dawn to assist the destroyer in rescuing the others. Until then, true, the ship might not be able to find them, but this was still the safest solution.

Yet Williamson was not entirely at peace with himself. Should he have landed in the first place instead of circling overhead, as originally planned? And once he had chosen to land, should he remain until all of the survivors were rescued, whatever the dangers involved?

Stupid misgivings! he decided. Of course he was doing the right thing. He had to think of the lives of his own men. And the lives of the five survivors, too. They had to get to a hospital quickly. They were starved and burned from the sun, "really bad off," the navigator told him. The men still alive out there—perhaps only that one he saw—were no doubt in similar shape. But he wasn't abandoning them, just delaying their rescue by a few hours.

And so Williamson raced his engines and plowed forward through two huge swells, with the propellers wildly churning the water. He feared that the next wave would throw the plane into the air before it gained flying speed, but the aircraft floated over a flat surface and reached the proper speed. And the next swell whisked it safely into the air.

In the rear, one of the survivors asked Anderson, "Got any coffee?"

"All we have," the plane captain said, "is some old used grounds."

"We'll take it."

Those still awake sipped the stale beverage, draining their cups.

"That's the best damn coffee I ever had," one of them commented.

"Nothin's too good for you guys," a crewman responded.

Yeah, nothing.

The following morning, November 20, Arthur Friend almost despaired for the first time. How much longer could he last in the middle of the ocean with no food or water and with a chunk of his person chewed off? There wasn't even anyone left to talk to except the sharks, and they were too busy trying to gulp him down to listen. So he just lay silently on the rim of the raft—on his stomach, since one of his buttocks was missing. He could pray, but what was the use? He wasn't religious, so even God wouldn't listen to him.

Friend's feverish mind drifted into a reverie about home. His mother was probably worried sick about him and his brother, who was stupid enough to risk his neck in the Marines. He himself had refused even to join the Army because he didn't want to end up in a foxhole "freezing my tail off." How could he have known that he'd lose half of it in the Navy? He watched the sharks float by, waiting for him to fall one more time into the water. What part of him would go next?

Suddenly, Friend heard a familiar roar. Another plane, a PBY, and it seemed to be rising from the sea. He feebly lifted his arm and waved.

"I'm here! I'm here!" he groaned.

But the plane kept on going and finally disappeared.

Several hours later, he saw something strange. Looked like a broomstick. A mast? . . . A ship? He wanted to weep but didn't have the strength.

The "broomstick" drew nearer, and when it was about two hundred yards away, it stopped and a motor launch with two men chugged toward Friend. As it slowed up and advanced to within four feet of the raft, one of the men cried:

"Don't jump!"

But Friend couldn't wait. He jumped—landing on his face in the launch. The men picked him up and lashed him down so he wouldn't fall into the water. When they reached the ship, the USS *Ballard*, the rescuers tied a rope around Friend and pulled him up. As soon as he was aboard, he asked a waiting officer:

"Where's the captain?"

"I'm the captain," the man said.

"Well, get your ship under way as soon as you can. A submarine may be using me as bait. I think I saw a periscope."

Friend didn't want another ship to sink under him. He wasn't at all sure he could take another week or so on a raft with all those fucking sharks waiting to chew him up.

Then, as several men carried him to sick bay, he lost consciousness. At last he could sleep without fear of falling into the water and losing the rest of him.

The same morning, Allen Heyn still languished on the rim of his raft, almost too feeble to move. This would surely be his last day on earth, he thought. The evening before, he had seen a PBY flying overhead and felt a glimmer of hope. But though he waved his shirt madly with his last bit of strength, it ignored him. Now he would just lie quietly and die.

But suddenly he heard the same buzz—another PBY. This time it circled around, and his hopes rose once more. But again it went away.

"Well, I gave up," Heyn would say. "I figured, well, I guess it's just like all the other planes, they ain't gonna bother, they figure you ain't worth coming for. Or maybe they didn't know what I was because I was all black. I might have been a Jap for all they knew."

And so he went back to dying—until, about two hours later, the plane returned, circled again, and dropped smoke bombs all around. They were testing the wind!

"Well, that built up my hope a lot," Heyn would recall.

And he waved his shirt again, though he could barely lift his arm.

"They waved back at me and then they went off and I could see them way off flying. And I figured, well, they must be guiding a ship to me. And that's what they were doing because it wasn't long before I could see the mast of a ship coming over the horizon and it was the USS *Ballard*. They lowered a small boat and came out and picked me up and took me aboard there."

"Who are you?" a sailor asked. "Where you from?"

"The *Juneau*," Heyn muttered.

The man seemed skeptical but then looked at the tattoo on his arm and saw the inscription USS *Juneau*.

"But we heard," exclaimed the man, "that there were no survivors from that ship."

Apparently the sailor didn't know that the man picked up about two hours earlier, Arthur Friend, was also from the *Juneau*. But the captain knew. He seemed to have been told only that a PBY pilot had sighted two rafts in addition to the one with the five men who were rescued. The *Ballard* then picked up a man on each. And Heyn, the captain felt, was the last survivor still alive. But was he?

The pilot, Lieutenant Williamson, said he saw a single survivor on one raft and what appeared to be a number of bodies on another, no doubt referring to one of the three nets on which about twenty-five weak and wounded men had been set loose. The nets were probably still afloat, and no one will ever know whether any of the "bodies" were, in fact, still breathing at the time of Heyn's rescue.

Heyn himself thought he was the only survivor of the *Juneau*, though there were actually ten. Out of nearly 700 men—the only one? Why? he asked himself. Perhaps God felt sorry for him because he was the youngest man on the ship. Heyn was plagued by a sense of guilt. Did he really deserve to be the only one?

Two sailors carried him to the main deck and cut his clothes off, then took him below and laid him on a bunk.

"Water!" he mumbled.

But they only let him wet his lips. His body might not tolerate any food or liquid yet.

In a minute, however, Heyn, dead to the world, was picking huge, red strawberries again and popping them into his mouth.

"Welcome!" said the smiling little man in a distinctly German accent as the three American survivors set foot on the island of Santa Ana.

Henry Kuper introduced himself, then his native wife and five of his half-caste children, now joined by Albert and many inhabitants of the island.

As several servants carried Lieutenant Wang to Kuper's house nearby, the other two survivors walked beside Kuper, who explained his accent. He had left Germany, he said, to escape military service and the Hitler regime.

"I am in no sympathy with the Nazis," he said.

He was happy living here in this island paradise "while the rest of the world went mad," though he played a role himself in the war. The Australian government had commissioned him as a lookout, and he was to report any Japanese activities in the area.

In Kuper's large, comfortably furnished wooden house, surrounded by a well-tended plantation carved out of the jungle, servants washed Wang's body with benzine to remove the fuel oil, while his two companions scrubbed themselves. Then, after sipping tall, cold lime drinks, the men were given silk pajamas and put to bed between clean, white sheets. They couldn't believe it. Would they wake up in their rubber boat, fighting the waves and the sharks and themselves, expecting to die at any moment and hardly caring?

Albert Kuper had gone to find a doctor and returned with him in the morning. The doctor immediately calmed Wang, who had awakened hysterically from a bad dream. But the dream was over and he realized that he was no longer in the rubber boat. Now he knew that he and his two companions had really been saved and would be going home. And that, even if he lost his leg, he would resume his medical studies with a better understanding of body and mind, of how much punishment they could take, and how much will and courage a man inherently had in facing death, dispensing death, escaping death.

Meanwhile, Henry Kuper, who prided himself on having helped save some American pilots who had earlier crash-landed nearby, would now try to get his three guests on a plane back to their base. Albert, his son, had already sent a radio message from one of the family boats to Tulagi, requesting that it be relayed to an American air base. But, the elder Kuper pointed out to Hartney, it could take days for a rescue plane to arrive. And since Lieutenant Wang was in critical condition, he had a more expedient plan.

"I understand you are a signalman," he said. "Sometimes U.S. planes fly close to the island on patrol. Not often. But let us hope that they will come soon. Your lieutenant must get to a hospital very soon."

Then, giving his guest a metal mirror, he continued, "If the planes come, you must try to flash them a message and get them to land. It is a long chance—but we've got to hope for it."

And on the second morning, November 21, an excited native ran to the house crying that he had seen two planes approaching. Hartney and Fitzgerald jumped out of bed and dashed to the beach in their silk pajamas. They were joined by Wang, carried on a stretcher.

"I searched the skies—and my heart leaped," Hartney would say, flashing the signal mirror. "PBYs again, and flying low, that peculiar, uptilted tail recognizable as far as they could be seen.

They must see my signal.... I began to tip the mirror in the sun, beaming it toward the planes."

"Land! Land! Land!" he signaled again and again.

The survivors waited tensely. Then the planes turned toward them and the men could see the sun gleaming on the blisters. In a moment, the motors were deafening and a hand reached out and waved.

"There was no doubt about it now," Hartney would joyously report. "They had seen us. Jimmy and I grinned and waved our arms like maniacs."

Hartney now was sure that he would hold in his arms the baby for whose future he had challenged the enemy, the sharks, and the most violent forces of nature.

One of the PBYs landed on the water, and shortly the three survivors were bundled aboard, to be delivered from one of history's most horrifying nightmares.

On that day, November 21, a messenger entered Captain Hoover's cabin aboard the *Helena* and saluted. Admiral Halsey and Captain Browning were boarding, he reported.

In a few minutes, Hoover was escorting the two solemn-faced men to the cabin. About five minutes later, the three emerged, and Hoover saw the visitors off, waiting by the railing until their launch was underway.

Then, as he started back to his cabin, he turned to Commander Carpenter, who was standing nearby, and coolly, without a trace of emotion, announced:

"I have been relieved of command."

Shortly, Halsey radioed Admiral Nimitz:

After analysis of the situation presented, I consider that commanding officer *Helena*, senior officer present in the task group, committed a serious and costly error in the action which he took.

He should have made radio report of the torpedoing at once. Radio silence, as a measure of concealment, had ceased to be effective since the enemy was in contact. Only positive action to keep him submerged could be expected to delay his report.

He should have instituted offensive action, together with, or closely followed by, rescue operations, utilizing at least one of his destroyers.

His failure to take prompt action on the above lines was further aggravated by lack of any follow-up to insure that senior commands were informed of the *Juneau's* loss. Commander South Pacific (Halsey) was first apprised of this fact as a result of his own inquiry into *Juneau's* status when she was not included in the arrival report of the group.

Attempts are still in progress as of this date to locate and effect rescue of any of the approximately sixty survivors who were reported in the water at the scene of the torpedoing by a search plane on the fourteenth.

In view of the above circumstances, I have this date relieved Captain G. C. Hoover of his command of the USS *Helena*, and ordered him by dispatch to proceed by the first available government air transportation and report to Commander in Chief [Nimitz] for assignment.

About that time, in Espíritu Santo, Bob Gill was urgently summoned to squadron headquarters.

"Lieutenant," a sergeant asked, "are you the pilot who saw the survivors of that cruiser that sank on the thirteenth?"

"Yes."

"They want you at group headquarters."

At last, thought Gill, they're checking into why those men were in the water so long.

He was driven to group headquarters, and as his jeep drew up to the hut, the operations officer met him and also asked if he was the pilot who had sighted the survivors.

"Well," snapped the officer when Gill had replied affirmatively, "somebody's going to pay for the delay in rescuing them!"

"I reported that we sighted them," Gil replied.

"Well, come in and tell your story."

Inside the hut, Gill was confronted by a Navy captain, who questioned him further about his identity.

"Why didn't you report the sighting by radio?" the captain then asked.

Gill explained that a Navy briefing officer had told him that he should be careful what he reported by radio because he might be giving away valuable information to the Japanese since "they had been breaking our codes."

"I reported the sighting on returning to base," Gill said, "not only on the thirteenth, but on the fifteenth and the eighteenth— to the same officer."

After a pause, the captain grunted, "That's all!"

And Gill saluted and left. Later, he would say:

"They must have thought I acted correctly, because I never heard anything more about it."

In fact, Gill was promoted to captain a few weeks later. But it seems the intelligence officer whom Gill reported to was less fortunate. William Entrikin, Gill's radioman, would recall that he saw two jeeploads of field grade naval officers enter the man's office and shuffle through his reports. Finally, one investigator exclaimed:

"Here it is!"

According to Entrikin, the man handed the document to his superior, who "looked at it and nearly bit his cigar in two." It was apparently a copy of Gill's original report, which had never reached group headquarters or else got lost there.

The investigators then stormed out and drove off. And the intelligence officer was not seen again. Someone had to pay for one of the cruelest and most devastating blunders of World War II.

But a second man would have to pay, too. . . .

At five A.M., November 22, in Nouméa, Captain Hoover stepped out on the quarterdeck of the *Helena*, his face a mask of suppressed pain. Then, suddenly, he smiled. It was like a surprise party. His sailors manned the rails and his officers were lined up in the center of the deck, every man standing rigidly at attention.

How the hell did the crew know . . . ?

Hoover was to be formally relieved at this ungodly hour precisely, it seems, in order to avoid any emotional farewell that might embarrass the Navy. The crew was not to be told the time. But somehow the news leaked out.

Earlier, Admiral Halsey had radioed the *Helena*: "When relieved Captain Gilbert C Hoover USN detached command *Helena* proceed via first available government air transportation to Pearl and report CINCPAC for assignment x per diem 6 dollars will be allowed while on an air travel status x 100 pounds excess baggage allowed."

This message had only added to Hoover's humiliation. Normally, he would be informed of his new assignment, not simply ordered to report to headquarters. And the reference to per diem expenses in this humbling context seemed only to sharpen the whip.

Hoover's officers stood traumatized and barely able to contain their tears as their captain took his place beside them. Then a representative from Halsey's headquarters read to him an official order relieving him of command and turning it over to a newly appointed officer.

Hoover knew he would never command another ship. In Pearl Harbor he would try to explain to Admiral Nimitz why he had acted as he did. But it wasn't likely that Nimitz would reverse a decision of a giant like Halsey.

Only days earlier he had longed to go home to embrace his wife, daughters, and son. Now, leave would be granted and he dreaded the thought of facing them. His whole life was being swept away with hardly less finality than the life of his friend Swens, if he had not miraculously survived the explosion. Swens would surely understand why the survivors had to be left in the water—even if they had to die.

With a silent smile, Hoover shook hands with each of his officers, barely able to look them in the eye for fear of breaking down. And after a final salute, he climbed into a launch taking him to shore, and to a life in which he would forever be haunted by the vision of a great murky cloud befouling the exquisitely structured world of pride and honor that had helped to mold his soul.

About two weeks later, on December 4, Hoover would write in a report to Admiral Nimitz that "if it had been known the despatch [Lieutenant Gill's message] reporting the torpedoing [of the *Juneau*] had not been received [by headquarters], I would have broken radio silence, despite the menace of air and submarines."

Yet even before Hoover saw the B-17, he had made the excruciating decision not to search for possible survivors or to break radio silence.

However history may judge Hoover, with his disgrace, and apparently that of the intelligence officer, the full tragic story of the *Juneau* was quietly buried. There was no need to ruin other reputations by inquiring more deeply into why the brave survivors were allowed to go mad and be devoured by sharks, to die, one by one, for up to eight days, though their presence in the water was known almost from the moment the *Juneau* blew up.

Let the *Juneau* be remembered simply as the ill-fated ship on which the five celebrated Sullivan brothers courageously died fighting when it went down, bringing new glory to the U.S. Navy.

Epilogue

IN EARLY JANUARY 1943, A NEIGHBOR BRAVED THE ICY COLD AND knocked on the door of the Sullivan home in Waterloo. She had just received a letter from her son in the Navy revealing tragic news:

"Isn't it too bad about the Sullivan boys? I heard that their ship was sunk."

The neighbor had thought it over. Wouldn't it be best to tell the boys' parents, to prepare them for the worst?

When Alleta opened the door, the caller said, "Mrs. Sullivan, I hate to tell you this, but I think you should know. My son heard that your boys went down on the *Juneau*."

Alleta turned pale. "I don't believe it!" she cried. "I won't believe it!"

The neighbor then began to cry, and Alleta awkwardly tried to comfort her, assuring her that her son was mistaken. But when the woman left, Alleta couldn't shake off a feeling of dread. Why hadn't she heard from her sons in months?

"Even though I went on with my work as usual," she would say, "I couldn't sit down to eat the dinner I cooked. And when I went to bed that night, I could hardly sleep. When I did fall asleep, I had terrible dreams in which my boys were in danger.

I wanted to help them and couldn't. In my nightmare I could even hear their voices calling 'Mother!' I woke with a start, to find that I was still lying in bed. And I thought, 'I'm being silly letting rumors affect me so. Probably nothing has happened to my boys.' "

But Alleta then remembered a letter Genevieve had received some weeks earlier from one of her brothers: "Keep your chin up, Sis, and take care of Mom and Dad. We'll be back."

Now she wondered, "Could it be that they were wrong and that they would never be back?"

About a week later, on January 12, 1943, there was another knock on the door. It was seven A.M., and Tom Sullivan was up getting his own breakfast since Alleta wasn't feeling well. Tom heard a car stop outside, then footsteps on the porch, and finally the knock. He opened the door and saw three men in naval uniform.

"I'm Lt. Comdr. Truman Jones," one of the officers said, introducing himself.

Jones had sworn in the five boys in Des Moines. With him were a petty officer and a doctor.

"I have some news for you about your boys," Jones said.

Alarmed, though he had been expecting these words, Tom asked them to wait so he could call his wife. When he had rushed upstairs and summoned Alleta, she gasped, then put on a bathrobe and slippers and awakened Genevieve and Katherine, Albert's wife, who had moved into her in-laws' home with her infant son, Jimmy, while her husband was away. Nervously, they all went downstairs with "a premonition of what the news was going to be."

As they entered the living room, the visitors stood up and Jones said, "I'm afraid I'm bringing you very bad news. You see, the way they do things ordinarily—why, you'd get a telegram right from the Navy Department, but because . . ."

Jones hesitated, and Alleta understood why.

"I knew what he was trying to tell us," she would later explain. "It was true. The boys were gone. Poor Commander Jones. I knew how hard it must have been for him to break the news."

Jones cleared his throat and went on, "The Navy Department

deeply regrets to inform you that your sons Albert, Francis, George, Joseph, and Madison Sullivan are missing in action in the South Pacific."

Alleta would describe the moment: "Genevieve turned white, and Katherine looked as if she were going to collapse. I could hardly hold back the tears, but I wouldn't let myself cry in front of the three men."

After a long, devastating silence, Tom turned to his wife and stammered, "Should I go?"

He had never missed a day's work for thirty-three years, except for serious illness. And his train was leaving in half an hour. How could he survive the tragedy if he didn't carry on as usual?

"I knew that his train was carrying war freight," Alleta thought. "If that freight didn't reach the battlefronts in time, it might mean more casualties. Dad holding up the train might mean that other boys would die, that other mothers might have to face such grief needlessly."

So Alleta replied, "There isn't anything you can do at home. You might as well go."

Tom was relieved. He groped for his hat and coat and shambled off to the railroad as soon as the three men had left. The women then trudged upstairs to Alleta's bedroom, "and there we gave way to our grief." Alleta tried to comfort the others.

"We can't be sure," she said, without believing her own words. "Commander Jones only said 'missing in action.' They may still be alive."

But hardly had newspapers and radio stations across the country blared stories on the Sullivan tragedy when the family received a letter that killed this flickering hope. It was from Lester Zook, who had returned home on leave and heard the news reports. It read:

First, let me introduce myself. I was a sailor on the *Juneau* with your boys. George was a special friend of mine. I am afraid all hope is gone for your boys.

George got off but died on the life raft I was on. [Actually, he was on a different raft and was devoured by sharks—a fact that Zook couldn't bring himself to say.] The other boys were below at the time. They went down with the ship and did not suffer. [Allen Heyn and Arthur Friend claim Albert was in the water, and Friend, that Red was on a raft, each brother disappearing on the first or second day.]

It was a sad and pathetic sight to see George looking for his brothers—but all to no avail. George and I made several liberties together and always kidded about coming home and going back on the railroad after the war was over.

I don't know whether a letter of this sort helps you or hurts. But it is the truth. I saw it. In the meantime ... I trust you to carry on in fine spirit. I truly hope your boys' lives didn't go to no avail.

I will try to avenge them for you.

On reading Zook's letter, Alleta wanted to burst into tears, to scream out her grief. But she remembered that a group of newsreel reporters and cameramen, among the countless media people who wanted an interview, would be coming any minute. She must remain composed. Despite her shattered state, she had to speak to many thousands of other mothers around the country through the newsreel.

When the newsmen arrived, Alleta broke down in the first attempt at a take. But then, suppressing her anguish, she succeeded.

"If they have gone together," she said through tears, "that is the way they would have wanted it. ... It's hard, of course, terribly hard. It's hard when you lose even one boy. But I know that they went in of their own free will and they did it together and for their country. ... We got twenty-eight Jap ships, didn't we? And aren't the Russians doing swell?"

The next day, Margaret Jaros, Red's fiancée, arrived from Pittsburgh, and the two women hugged each other and wept. Alleta had telephoned Margaret, who was in shock after hearing the news on the radio.

"I wish you were here, honey," Alleta had said.

And Margaret was on the next train. She told reporters crowding into the house, "Everything I ever hoped to have went down with that ship."

Meanwhile, in Jersey City, Beatrice Imperato, Matt's fiancée, went to work and saw a colleague reading the morning newspaper. As she walked by, she glanced at the front page and saw a photo of the five Sullivan brothers.

"Do you mind if I look at the headlines?" she asked the man apprehensively.

And then she read the head under the picture: "Five Sullivan Brothers Missing in Action."

Beatrice almost fainted. She had just received a long-delayed note from Matt saying he was fine. And now, suddenly, her whole world collapsed. She ran home, locked herself in her room, and wouldn't come out for two weeks. Finally, her mother pleaded:

"You can't bring nobody back, Bea. Please come out."

And Beatrice finally emerged from the room. She, too, would visit the Sullivans, and would never forget Alleta's words:

"They're gone, but we who are left behind are the ones who shall suffer."

To alleviate their pain, and possibly spare other families with boys at the front a similar tragedy, Alleta, Tom, and Genevieve traveled across the country at the Navy's request selling war bonds and urging defense workers to turn out military weapons more rapidly so their fighting brothers would end the war quickly and return to their loved ones.

The Sullivans would be a powerful stimulus to the war effort, for the catastrophe struck a unique chord in the American heart. Letters of condolences poured in from all over the free world, including one from President Roosevelt, who wrote that "the entire nation shares in your sorrow."

Typically, in a speech to the employees of the Philadelphia Navy Yard, Tom declared, "What I feel is this. If we had more planes and more ships out there in the Solomons, the cruiser *Juneau* wouldn't have been sunk, and our boys wouldn't have been lost. Maybe if the men and women in war plants realize what it has meant to Mom and me, and to a lot of other mothers and fathers, that there weren't enough planes and ships, they will work their level best to make sure there will be enough from now on. And then the war will be over sooner."

There were to be more Sullivan tears. Tears of pride when Alleta christened a new destroyer named *The Sullivans*; tears of gratitude when the family stood in the U.S. Senate as the whole chamber resounded with deafening applause; tears of sorrow when Genevieve, after joining the Waves, sustained a permanent back injury in an automobile accident; tears of new grief when she learned that her fiancé, who had given her an engagement ring early in the war, had, like her beloved brothers, died in battle; and tears of despair when, after marrying another man and giving birth to two children, she had to have a hysterectomy, further narrowing the future of the ravaged family.

When the war ended and the family returned to the slow-motion tempo of peace, the therapy was over, and the agonizing realization set in that the boys would never be coming home. Seldom again would laughter be heard in the Sullivan house, and even smiles would seldom grace a Sullivan's face.

The parents could never escape the vision of their sons. When they moved and sat on the porch of their new home near St. Mary's School, they stared for hours at a time at a statue of the Blessed Mother dedicated to their sons. They went for strolls in a new Sullivan Park and gazed at a memorial to their sons. They journeyed to Chicago one year to lead a St. Patrick's Day parade—and listened to speeches about their sons. Every time a government dependency check arrived, they would be reminded of their sons, and Alleta would weep. From year to year to year, she would constantly repeat how old they would be if they were alive.

At the same time, Tom's drinking problem grew despite his wife's demand that he "lay off that stuff." And once, when he was caught with a pint of whiskey on the job, he was pulled out of service—until furious railroad officials in Chicago ordered that he be put back on the trains before the world learned that the father of the five heroes had been "laid off." Everyone knew he had good reason to drink. He would retire in 1948 and die in 1965, a broken man.

Alleta's loneliness would be relieved when the remnants of the family came to see her. Genevieve and her two young sons, and Albert's widow, Katherine, who had remarried, and her son, Jimmy, were frequent visitors. Grandmother May still did most of the housework, but the older she and Alleta got, the more they engaged in petty brawls, once over whether May, now half-

blind, had served her daughter a hot dog. But then these argu-
ments would melt in mutual tears at the least mention of the
boys. May carried an additional burden; she still grieved for her
husband, who had also died before his time.

Constantly ill, Alleta would spend her last days in a nursing
home, where she would continue her verbal jousting with May,
who now resided there, too. Alleta died in 1972, and May some
years later, at the age of 105. Genevieve would die of cancer in
1975. Katherine, since losing her second husband, has lived
alone trying to suppress the memories that haunted the rest of
the family. She has refused to discuss Albert with anyone, or
even to attend ceremonies honoring the Sullivans—perhaps because Albert insisted on going to war, leaving her and Jimmy
to face the bitter consequences of his death.

At fifty, Jimmy, on the other hand, seeks to perpetuate the
memory of his father and uncles as a kind of compensation for
being "cheated out of a family." An electrician with two children in college, he has been pushing for congressional passage
of a "Sullivan Act," which would convert into law the present
informal Pentagon policy that forbids family members from
serving together in the same unit or on the same ship.

The fiancées of Red and Matt have been just as tormented by
the tragedy as the surviving Sullivans. Both Margaret Jaros and
Beatrice Imperato would eventually marry and become grand-
mothers, but the memory of their lost loves would always remain with them.

Beatrice keeps a treasured photo of the brothers on the wall
of her home, and a grandson has been named Matt. And Margaret, a widow, says that after her husband died, "I started thinking about Joe [Red] more than I did of him. It ended with my
husband, but it was an unfinished romance with Joe. I am still
so sad. And I haven't even got his ring with the pearls as a
memento—only the tears that they brought."

Joey and Jimmy Rogers did not give up hope that their brothers, Pat and Louie, had survived the sinking of the *Juneau*.
When they arrived in the Fiji Islands on a stopover, they visited
the field hospital there. Perhaps they would find their siblings,

or survivors who might know about them. They found a sailor from the *San Francisco*.

"Oh, Jesus, Joe," he said, "when that ship got hit, there was one huge explosion. It split in half, and the bow and stern were up in the air. Midships went straight to the bottom. But there were a few survivors, I've heard."

Armed with renewed hope, the two brothers now found one of them—Arthur Friend.

"Art, do you know about our brothers?" Joey asked excitedly. Maybe a miracle had happened.

But it hadn't. "No, Joey," Friend said, "they didn't get off. They went down with the ship."

Joey and Jimmy felt sick. Now, at last, they believed it, and they wept and clung to each other. How could they face Pop? Four had left home, and only two would be coming back.

By the time they came back, after the war, they found that their father had recovered from the shock of the tragedy.

"I got a telegram from the Navy Department in January 1943 telling me that my two sons Louis and Patrick had died when the *Juneau* went down," the father would tell a reporter. "We hadn't even heard that the *Juneau* was sunk until then. . . . It was heartbreaking that two of my boys were gone, but then as things worked out that the five Sullivan brothers were lost on the *Juneau*, it made what I had suffered not feel so bad."

And the father's suffering was further eased when he and his wife met Tom and Alleta Sullivan during a visit by the Sullivans to Bridgeport on their morale-boosting tour. After all, two of his own boys had returned.

But they would never be the same. Nor would their world. Joey's former fiancée, Nancy, had married someone else, and so had all his other past girlfriends. His male friends were still in the services or were dead or wounded. There were no diversions to help him suppress the trauma of losing two brothers—until he met a girl named Josephine.

"Holy Christ! What a doll!" Joey exclaimed when he saw her at a party.

And they were soon married. But when Joey looked for a job, he couldn't find one; for apart from his boxing skills, he had none. So he started training as a pugilist again and had three fights. After the long layoff, however, his timing was poor and he had lost his killer instinct. And he could never erase the nightmare of being counted out in a fixed fight. When he lost two of the matches, his wife urged him to quit the ring, and he did. He went through the next decades plastering wallpaper, delivering milk, and assisting mechanics. He retired at sixty-three.

Joey never stopped grieving for his dead brothers. And though, as a determined fighter, he had seldom touched alcohol before, for about fifteen years he would attempt to drown his grief in it. With his wife's help, however, he eventually conquered his alcoholism and would enjoy life with his two sons and three grandchildren—while finding comfort in the bittersweet memory of Pat and Louie, who, when they listened to his advice, could damn well knock out anyone their weight. Joey died in January 1993.

Jimmy Rogers was still a driven man when he returned home from the war, but also a more caring one. His fiancée, Marion, had still not recovered from the shock of a rumor that he was one of the dead. On the day the local radio broadcast the news that two of the Rogers brothers had died, she was returning home from high school when a schoolmate yelled to her:

"You lost your boyfriend, Marion. He went down with his ship."

Marion went "cuckoo." She ran home and cried to her father: "Did you hear? Did Jimmy go down with the ship?"

When he replied that it was Pat and Louie who had, she felt deep sorrow but thought, "Thank God it wasn't Jimmy."

And almost as soon as Jimmy arrived home, he married her—despite his vow to first become champ. It wasn't fair to make her wait any longer, he felt, even if marriage hurt his career. At the same time, however, he was driven now by a new incentive: Pat had predicted that he would one day reach the top, and he couldn't let him down.

Jimmy thus returned to the ring, now as a professional, and fought at least once a week, sometimes with his arms still sore from the previous fight. He kept winning, but in one bout he took such a beating that he didn't know where he was, even as the referee raised his arm in victory.

That was enough, Marion proclaimed. And Jimmy never fought again. Yes, marriage had thwarted his career, but now he didn't seem to care. Suddenly, he was repelled by violence, whether on the battlefield or in the ring. And he grew fearful when he noticed that his son had inherited his own "feeling of aggressiveness." When the youth told him he had enlisted in the Army during the Vietnam War, Jimmy rushed to the recruiting office and cried:

"You signed up my son. I lost two brothers in World War II and I don't want to lose my son, too."

To his relief, the boy was sent to Germany rather than to Vietnam. And though he would sometimes spar with his son, Jimmy dreaded the thought that he might also become a boxer.

"I went through a lot trying to be world champion," he would say, "and I didn't want him banged up, too."

Jimmy remembered when his father had urged him to get up after he had been knocked down in one fight and to "go get 'im." But where had violence gotten Pop? Or himself? Or his beloved brothers?

He opened up a restaurant in Bridgeport and found that it was great making a buck without having to trade punches with some guy out to kill him. And it was also a good place to hang up a photo of the *Juneau*—and two sailor hats right under it— in remembrance of Pat and Louie. Let everyone know that the Rogers brothers were bound by a love more powerful than their most devastating punches.

As Allen Heyn lay on a cot in a Fiji field hospital, he had, as he would put it, "very bad headaches in my head where I had been hit on the ship. And I was sick all over, and I don't know, I was sorta wore out."

In fact, Heyn was suffering from shock, exposure, a fractured skull, a broken foot, shrapnel wounds, shriveled skin, saltwater sores, hands that had turned blue from poisonous jellyfish bites, and malaria from mosquito bites. But since he had no medical records, the doctors treated him like any other patient, not realizing that he had survived one of the most ghastly traumas in the war.

Nor would Heyn enlighten them, for they might discharge him, and he would never get the chance to avenge his shipmates who had died terrible deaths, leaving him to carry the burden of guilt for surviving.

After nine months in bed, Heyn happily returned to duty. He was sent to one of the Fiji islands to work with the Seabees under the command of a desk lieutenant who sadistically chewed him out for not saluting. What did Heyn learn at boot camp? he asked. Heyn, in his fury, wanted to tell him what he had learned at sea, but he still remained silent. Out of spite, the man might send him home!

Heyn applied for submarine duty and was soon on the way to a base in Australia. And in the next year and a half, he served aboard six submarines. Finally, the Navy realized he was a survivor of the *Juneau* and in 1944 sent him on a tour of war plants to raise worker morale. It then offered him a chance to enter the Naval Academy. But when he was finally given a thorough physical examination and the doctors saw how the explosion and the eight days in the water had ravaged his body, he was disqualified. In fact, they couldn't believe that he had been serving for eighteen months on submarines without anyone checking whether he was physically fit to do so.

As Heyn had feared, he was given a medical discharge. He then headed for Detroit, where earlier, during a speaking engagement, he had met a girl named Nancy. They now married, and Heyn found a part-time job selling real estate while simultaneously earning a high school diploma and two years of college credits at Wayne University. The couple then moved to his hometown of Callicoon, New York, a few blocks away from his parents. To while away the time, Heyn built a new home and a service station lunchroom with his own hands, put in a full day for the Erie Railroad on a track gang, operated a tree nursery, and worked as a mason. In his free time, he planned a real estate business and fathered three children.

Heyn would eventually become a prosperous land developer, mainly in Michigan, and he retired in 1979. But retirement has brought little joy. For all his frenetic activity, the

Juneau experience has taken a monstrous toll. Over the years, he has been afflicted with cancer, strokes, diabetes, recurrences of malaria, and heart problems, all at least partly attributable to his ordeal at sea. He has thus spent much of his time in hospitals and almost died several times, once after a heart bypass operation in which veins from his leg were transplanted to the heart.

But Heyn's inner strength has prevailed. He was dying? On that raft, he was, too. He survived then, and damn it, he would now. After those sharks, what the hell was cancer or a bad ticker? Nothing can kill him, he believes—except maybe old age. And he's still the youngest sailor on the ship. So he will perhaps live through many more nights on the raft watching helplessly while sharks tear apart his shipmates, and wondering why he is living and they aren't.

Allen Heyn is a survivor; that's his punishment.

Unlike Heyn, Arthur Friend, who recuperated at the same hospital in the Fijis, was not eager to return to combat. In fact, he "raised hell to go back to the United States and get the hell out of the Navy." He barged into the office of the commanding officer and made his demands. No man with only half an ass, he argued, should have to fight.

But the commanding officer simply replied, "It's up to the medical officer."

And though Friend had to undergo three operations since his wound was infected and it was difficult to graft skin onto it, the medical officer still thought he would soon recover and be fit for duty.

"We're going to send you back to sea," he said.

"The hell you are!" Friend snarled. "Nobody's gonna send me anywhere! My Navy days are done!"

Eventually, Friend was sent to Treasure Island in San Francisco Bay, and there he received some shattering news. His younger brother, Ralph, the Marine, had been killed in battle, throwing himself on a grenade to save his buddies. A real hero! Friend called his mother and she was despondent. And his father would express his grief by seeking revenge against the Japanese. He joined the Navy.

His father was right—revenge! And when Friend was now given a choice of either a discharge or a new assignment, he chose the assignment.

"I want to go back to sea," he told his superiors, even though his injured buttocks and legs had partially disabled him.

And so he would go back. But before he did, he married a young woman he had picked up in his jeep. He knew her for only two weeks, but that was enough. He didn't love her, but she looked healthy enough to bear him a child, and he needed one so that part of him, in a sense, would go on living after he was dead.

Friend, however, saw little combat on the troop transport and oil tanker he was assigned to before being discharged when the war ended. In Visalia, California, he worked in a lumberyard, then for a trucking firm. Later he went to Missouri to plow earth on a farm, then back to California to serve as an ambulance driver, a policeman, a welder, an underwater salvage worker, a gold miner, and a river dredger. He would divorce his wife and marry and divorce three more times.

Friend eventually moved to a ranch near Fresno, living alone in a trailer and, with a cowboy hat planted on his white, uncut locks, performing odd jobs while entrancing visitors with the details of how he had been left behind by a "heartless" captain and left without a behind by a hungry shark.

Lester Zook emerged from the ordeal in relatively good condition, though his right leg had been severely injured when the *Juneau* went down. He was grateful, for he had decided to make the Navy his career.

As soon as his wound had healed in a hospital in Espíritu Santo, he was back on duty as a chief signalman happily assigned to a new heavy cruiser, the USS *Boston*. But before stepping aboard, he rushed off to Corona, California, to marry his sweetheart, Mary, whom he had met during the war. He had vowed in the water to do so the moment he was reunited with her—if he survived. Since he loved her, why wait? Not practical.

He would become an ensign and, by the time he retired, a lieutenant commander. Then, to make up for his mediocre academic record before he joined the Navy, he enrolled in a community college in Eugene, Oregon, and earned three associate degrees in business.

Zook found deep satisfaction in completing his education, however belatedly, a goal his father had failed to achieve because of financial problems. Anyway, since he had been among the handful of men on the *Juneau* to be chosen by God to live, it seemed logical to make the most of the borrowed time by improving himself.

Though Wyatt Butterfield suffered from a deep gash in his arm, shrapnel wounds, and severe shock that made him jump with fright if anyone even touched him, he was sent back to combat in December 1942, less than a month after he was rescued. And his new ship did little to ease his psychological problem; it was the destroyer *O'Bannon*, which had fought beside the *Juneau* in the Battle of Guadalcanal. Nor did his nightmare experience impress his new captain. As soon as Butterfield climbed aboard, the skipper called him to his cabin and said:

"I know you're a survivor from the *Juneau*. But don't expect any special favors."

In fact, when Butterfield arrived in Espíritu Santo, the Navy didn't even give him the treatment it normally accorded survivors. No one sent him to a hospital; no one examined him. He was entirely ignored and wasn't even assigned to a unit at first. Only when he went to the Seabees and asked for a place to sleep was his existence finally recognized. They gave him a place to sleep!

Eventually the *O'Bannon* would become Butterfield's home. But with the memory of the *Juneau* explosion still fresh in his mind, he refused to go below deck and slept in his gun mount instead while his shipmates brought food to him. After three months of sporadic battle, the ship returned to Espíritu Santo, and Butterfield went to see the commanding officer there.

"Sir, I just got off the *O'Bannon*," he said. "I'm a survivor of the *Juneau*. Why am I not being sent back to the States?"

The commander stared at him in shock.

"Oh, my God!" he exclaimed. "We must have made a mistake."

Butterfield was then sent back in a hospital ship and remained for three months in a San Diego naval hospital.

What did he want to do now? he was asked. Did he want a medical discharge?

A medical discharge? That was a helluva way for a hero to go home! No, he wanted to go to Lakehurst Naval Air Station for blimp reconnaissance training. And shortly, he was trained and sailing effortlessly in a blimp looking for submarines. But one night a storm broke, and as the blimp shook and trembled, so did Butterfield, and he almost jumped out. He now had to admit that "my nerves are shot and I want to go home." And so, in February 1944, he was given a discharge.

It was a glorious homecoming as he embraced his parents. His father had never lost hope that his son would survive— even after that frightening night in the bar he frequented in Trenton. A sailor had come in and told the bartender:

"Did you hear about the *Juneau* sinking with everybody aboard?"

"Not so loud," the bartender whispered. "This guy's son was on the *Juneau*."

But the father had heard the sailor's revelation.

"Make no mistake," he said confidently, "my son will survive. A Butterfield never dies young."

And his confidence was not misplaced. Wyatt was home—the first of the six brothers to return. The press pounced on him; his friends lionized him; the Navy awarded him the Bronze Star for risking his life to bring back vital supplies to his raft; and, in 1948, one of his admirers, Genevieve, became his wife and would present him with two boys and a girl who would worship him. Just as he had planned!

Butterfield worked as a salesman for Westinghouse and then as sales manager for Mack Trucks in Pittsburgh before retiring in 1982 as everybody's hero.

The price of glory, however, was high. He had two strokes, heart problems that required eight bypasses, and kidney failure that kept him on dialysis for several years, until he died in October 1991. And he never did fully recover from the trauma. But though the vision of shark's teeth about to snap shut set him trembling, he heard, until the end, the background roar of the crowd acclaiming him for his extraordinary courage.

"I got back!" Frank Holmgren cried as six arms wound around him.

Finally he broke loose from the grip of his mother, father, and sweetheart.

"Gosh, you're making me cry!" he bawled.

Everyone was crying when Holmgren stepped off the train in his hometown of Eatontown, New Jersey, to start a thirty-day leave. It seemed like a miracle—especially after the Navy had wired the Holmgren family that Frank was missing in action.

The wire was particularly cruel since it came after the family had received mail from Frank himself exulting in his survival. Had Frank died after sending those letters? Or had the Navy simply made a terrible mistake?

Frank's father, Floyd, rushed to the *Eatontown Daily Standard* with the wire, and the editor immediately contacted the Navy Personnel Department in Washington. Finally, after several days of grief and bewilderment, laced with hope, a second wire came. The Navy had erred; Frank had survived after all!

After recuperating in the Fijis, he was assigned to the USS *Oakland*, another antiaircraft cruiser, though, like Wyatt Butterfield, he agreed to fight only "topside." And now he had come home on leave. His wishbone had broken, but it had served its purpose.

Still, home was not all joy. For he had to face the parents of his best friend, Charlie Hayes. He twitched nervously and tears welled in his eyes as he told them his story. He had last seen Charlie when he had left him on the net.

"I'm still praying for Charlie," he said.

Maybe he would still turn up alive. But he never did.

Shortly, Holmgren was back in combat, fighting the enemy in the Pacific again. By 1944, however, he had had enough of battle and asked to be transferred to a gunnery school in San Diego, where he served until discharged. After the war, he worked as a civilian in a Navy weapons station near his home until he retired in 1980.

The broken wishbone perhaps symbolized the new personal life that was awaiting Holmgren when he was discharged. It was not Joyce, but another young woman, Theresa, who would marry him and help him to recover psychologically from those days of horror in the water—and from his torment over the fate of Charlie Hayes.

Still, Holmgren hasn't wanted to forget those days, and certainly not his friend. He has kept a scrapbook of the hometown articles written about him and does not mind at all if his two children occasionally peruse it so they'll know what their father did in the war.

"Arrived today Naval Hospital Mare Island, California," Lt. Charles Wang wired his mother on January 31, 1943. "Don't worry about me. My only wound is a broken leg below the knee. Am coming along fine."

But Chuck Wang's broken leg developed into a chronic bone disease that was to plague him for the rest of his life, requiring more than thirty operations and sometimes causing him unbearable pain, until he finally had it amputated in his declining years.

Yet, after two years of treatment in the hospital, Wang managed to live a full, rich life despite his constant suffering. In the early postwar era, he was still a social charmer—especially at a party where he met a pretty young neighbor, Marie. Though Wang wore a cast up to his hip, he asked her to dance and managed to limp around while the other guests gaped.

"This must be very difficult for you," Marie said. "Why did you ask me to dance?"

"Because I wanted to get my arms around you," he replied.

Then he asked her what she enjoyed doing most.

"Well, I enjoy cooking."

"What do you like to make?"

"Oh, I love baking a pineapple upside-down cake."

Wang glowed. That was his mother's specialty. On the raft it was the symbol of everything he wanted to live for. And now, he realized, it still was. Thirteen days later, Wang and Marie were engaged, and in April 1947 they were married. In the next six years they had three daughters.

Meanwhile, Wang finished his premed studies at La Salle College, then went to Jefferson Medical School in Philadelphia, graduating in 1951. He would now specialize in pathology at Lankenau Hospital in that city and become the first doctor there to introduce cytopathology, the study of pathological changes in cells. He also worked in microbiology. His laboratory efforts complemented his indelible observations of human behavior during the war, which had deepened his faith in people and in God.

"I think God meant for me to suffer," he once said while in pain.

His suffering, he felt, was a small price to pay for his survival, his marital happiness, and the opportunity to continue his quest for the secrets of man's makeup.

Still, when a fellow doctor responded that "God, it is said, 'chastises him whom he loveth,' " Wang, in his agony, replied, "Perhaps, but I wish God didn't love me quite so much."

In 1964, he joined the pathology department at the Community General Hospital in Reading, Pennsylvania, where he persevered in his work even as the pain grew worse. But though he had always been a leader, his suffering stifled his earlier aggressiveness and he kept his eyes focused strictly on his microscopic slides, never on the power and the glory beckoning from the departmental throne.

Sometimes, when the pain grew too great, his eyes couldn't even focus on the slides, and once he told his wife, referring to a pistol he kept in a drawer:

"Take it away, please! I'm afraid I might use it."

No, it was too soon, he decided, as he once had in the water. He must wait a little longer. God would reward him in the next world for his agony in this one.

Amputation helped to relieve the pain, but five years later, in 1985, Chuck Wang suffered a fatal heart attack and, his mind bulging with data on the wonders of the human organism, went to collect his reward.

As soon as Joe Hartney jumped from the train in New Britain, Connecticut, in January 1943, his wife thrust his infant daughter, Dona, into his arms. Hartney was overwhelmed with joy. He should be dead, and perhaps he was. Could this be heaven?

But Hartney soon realized it wasn't. As with Wang, the blessings of peace were curdled with the aftereffects of war. He suffered frequent headaches as a result of blows to his head that had occurred during the sinking, and the pain became so great sometimes that he would batter his head against the wall. He also had nightmares, with the sharks still chasing him.

Hartney was nevertheless determined to stay in the Navy and served at various bases in the United States until his discharge in 1946. He was in and out of hospitals thereafter even as he attended college and worked for an insurance company, in an ammunition depot during the Korean War, and as a private investigator later.

Hartney was kind, thoughtful, and loving, but his wife, who would bear him a son and three daughters in addition to Dona, would never see after the war the happy-go-lucky man she had once known—except at parties when, pathetically, "he tried to be what he was no more." He died of leukemia in 1981 at the age of sixty.

A few days before Lilyan Grycky, John's younger sister, graduated from college in January 1943, she was suddenly called out of class by the dean. Perhaps he wanted to congratulate her for her good work, she thought. Instead, he said gravely:

"Sit down. I want to talk to you. We had a phone call. You're wanted at home."

"Are my parents all right?" Lilyan asked anxiously.

"It's about your brother John."

Lilyan rushed home and found her mother lying prostrate on the sofa and her father pacing the floor. When he was able to talk, he said:

"Two men from the Navy were here. They told us Johnny's ship was lost, and Johnny is missing."

His wife started to wail, and the daughter tried to comfort her, even as her own heart was breaking. Lilyan immediately wrote a letter to Tom and Alleta Sullivan. Did they know what happened to the ship and to John?

They knew, Alleta replied, "as much as you do."

In desperation, Lilyan sought information from the Navy.

It was a military secret, the Navy replied.

All the family would ever know is that the ship went down and that Johnny was gone. His loss touched many people, especially the lone survivor of the four members of the Knights of the Square Table who had enlisted together. James Latta would write Grycky's parents:

"Words of praise will never express the place that Johnny takes in that small group of boys of which both of us were members. I am proud to consider him one of my closest friends. . . . I just can't and won't give up hope that I will see Johnny again."

But he never would. John's memory, however, would live on. For Latta established a $25,000 scholarship fund in his name, and that of his two comrades who also fell in battle, for each graduating class at Coatsville High School, which they had all attended. The scholarship is based on acts of patriotism, grades, and participation in extracurricular activities.

Latta also kept his vow to look in on the parents of all the dead Knights as long as the parents lived. From 1943 to 1988, when John's mother, the surviving parent, died, he visited each of the families on Christmas, Easter, Memorial Day, and the victim's birthday, bringing flowers and fruit.

"Johnny," Latta would say, "would give his life jacket to someone even if it was the last one. He felt it was his duty to help his fellow man. Why did God take so outstanding a man?"

Japanese commander Minoru Yokota became a schoolteacher in Fujisawa, near Tokyo, after the war, and some years later changed his name to Hasegawa, symbolizing the change in his life. It was the name of his second wife, whom he married shortly after his first wife died. He apparently wanted to blot out completely any memory of the past, especially the war. As Tsukuo Nakano, his torpedoman, would explain, Yokota "no longer wanted anything but religion in his life." He wanted to purge his soul of the guilt he felt for killing people. Being a Christian, he worshiped no god of war who could ease that guilt. Thus, he has never shown up at the *I-26* reunions or kept in touch with any of his men.

Childless by his first wife, Yokota was happy to take his second wife's three children under his wing.

"It's the first time I have been called Father," he would proudly tell his friends.

He would become like a father to many other youngsters as well when, in the early 1950s, he was appointed the director of a Bible college in Yokohama.

As for Nakano, he returned to his farm near Tokyo after the war and thanked his beloved mother for sending her spirit to look after him.

Captain Swenson turned out to be right. By going down with his ship, he laid to rest any lingering doubts about his courage and character. He was posthumously awarded the Navy Cross "for extraordinary heroism . . . during action . . . on the night of 12–13 November 1942, on which occasion the force to which he was attached engaged at close quarters and defeated a superior enemy force. His daring and determination contributed materially to the victory which prevented the enemy from accomplishing their purposes."

Swenson's son, Robert, carried on the naval tradition when he graduated from the Naval Academy in 1944 as a lieutenant and went to war. But soon after the conflict he left the Navy and earned a doctorate in business administration at George Washington University before pursuing a career in business.

Captain Swenson's final triumph came in 1944 when a destroyer was christened the USS *Lyman K. Swenson*. His estranged daughter, Cecilia, broke the champagne bottle on its bow in his honor.

"Lovable Swens" could now sleep in peace.

Captain Hoover could not. The memory of the disaster and the disgrace continued to erode his nerves. His five-year-old daughter, on opening the door of the Hoover home in Bristol, Rhode Island, could not recognize him. She cried out in shock when she saw a man with a drawn face that was almost as pale as his white uniform. Was it a ghost? She slammed the door shut. When Hoover finally entered, the whole family shuddered. He did, indeed, resemble a ghost.

It was just before Christmas 1942, and he had come home on leave. There had been an air of gaiety in the house as the lights on the Christmas tree flickered, but tears of joy at this reunion were soon replaced with Hoover's tears of guilt and depression. It was clear that he was emotionally disturbed. Especially when he went out Christmas shopping with his wife and suddenly clamped his head in his hands and screamed. Alarmed, Mrs. Hoover admonished her daughters:

"Daddy's not feeling well, so let's be good little girls."

Why was he ill? What happened in the war? Hoover refused to say. How could he tell them what happened?

"Don't bother me with such questions," he would snap. "I lived through it. I don't want you to."

One battle Hoover didn't have to live through took place in the New Georgia area in July 1943, eight months after the *Juneau* sinking. This time it was the turn of his beloved *Helena*. It was sunk by several torpedoes, and the crew abandoned ship. Almost immediately, two destroyers were dispatched and picked up almost a thousand survivors—an action that agonizingly accentuated the *Juneau* tragedy.

Hoover's naval commands after that tragedy were only on land, but he kept hoping that Admiral Halsey would exonerate him and give him another ship. He thus asked his friend Vice Adm. Robert B. Carney, who was leaving to be Halsey's new chief of staff, to persuade his new boss to rescind the order condemning him to naval oblivion.

And Hoover was hopeful after he received a copy of a letter Admiral Nimitz wrote to Adm. Ernest J. King, Chief of Naval Operations. It stated that while Hoover "would have shown better judgement if he had broken radio silence immediately to report the loss of the *Juneau*," he "was in no way responsible" for the failure of his effort to report it through a B-17.

Moreover, Nimitz wrote, Hoover's failure to seek out and attack the submarine and to look for survivors "was the result of a decision made by him when confronted by a difficult situation. . . . The necessity for getting his damaged ships back to a base was balanced against the natural instinct of every naval officer to go to the rescue of officers and men in distress and danger.

"Whatever may be the opinion of Captain Hoover's decision," Nimitz said, "he was the responsible officer on the spot and, from his war record, his courage may not be questioned. . . . It is recommended that [he] be given a suitable command at sea after he has had a reasonable rest period in the United States."

But Nimitz would not exonerate him and remove the black mark from his record. And when the captain stopped off in Pearl Harbor on his way home, Adm. Raymond A. Spruance, one of Nimitz's commanders, told him why: Nimitz did not wish to upset Halsey at this time by making it appear that he had less than full confidence in him.

Ironically, Carney persuaded Halsey that "he had been guilty of an injustice" by relieving Hoover of his command, but Halsey, using the same rationale used by Nimitz, would not exonerate him either, arguing that his commanders recommended the action and he didn't "want to kick those guys in the tail." Nevertheless, he would, Halsey said, send a letter to the chief of naval personnel requesting that Hoover "be restored to combat command," adding that "I would be delighted to have him serve under me."

Halsey would later write: "The stigma of such a detachment can never be wholly erased, but I have the comfort, slight as it is, of knowing that Hoover's official record is clean. I deeply regret the whole incident. It testifies to Captain Hoover's character when I say that he has never let it affect our personal relations."

But it did indeed affect their personal relations. For despite his conciliatory words, Halsey never did restore Hoover to a combat command. Shortly after the war, when Hoover had retired from the Navy, he was returning on a train to New York from an Army-Navy football game in Philadelphia when an officer approached him and said:

"You're Captain Hoover, aren't you?"

"Yes."

"Well, Admiral Halsey is sitting in the next car. He has asked if you will come to see him."

Hoover turned pale. The man who had ruined his career?

"No," Hoover said. "If the admiral wishes to see me, let him come here."

The two men did not meet.

On his retirement, Hoover threatened to shoot himself with his pistol, but his wife snatched the weapon away, and he checked into a hospital to be treated for "battle fatigue." And his depression was not relieved when his son, though an Annapolis graduate, left the Navy after serving for only five years and went into business. One more disappointment.

But gradually Hoover's mental health improved with the help of a deep religious fervor, and he became active again. He was elected mayor of Bristol, then served as an administrator with the Atomic Energy Commission, first at Sandia Base, Albuquerque, New Mexico, and later at the Rocky Flats installation in Boulder, Colorado. Hoover, however, was never entirely happy on these jobs. He pined for the ship that he would never see and anguished over one that he would forever see.

One day in 1955, Hoover met Robert Swenson, his late friend's son, on the tennis court at the Army-Navy Club in Washington while both were waiting to play. He sat next to Swenson, whom he had never met, and, nervously plucking his racket strings, said:

"I've been bothered ever since what happened in the Battle of Guadalcanal. I'm sorry about your father."

Robert, who says he did not then know the full story, looked into Hoover's eyes and could see the pain.

"I've read the reports," Robert replied. "I can understand why you didn't want to expose your own ship to a possible attack and took the action you did."

Hoover's face lit up, and, trying to control his tears, he stammered, "Thank you."

And the two men played each other, though neither apparently had his mind on the game.

Later, when Swenson learned the full story of what had happened, he thought that Hoover should have looked for the survivors regardless of the danger, or at least broken radio silence. But was not the man suffering enough? He would live with the tragedy the rest of his life. Even at the Navy football games. At one game in the Naval Academy stadium, Swenson noticed that a plaque was engraved on a particular seat. It was dedicated by Hoover to his old classmate.

In 1980, at age eighty-five, Hoover was afflicted with throat cancer and died. The men of the *Helena* mourned him and would always cherish his memory. Had he not saved many lives?

Notes

Full data on printed material can be found in the Bibliography. Interviewees (ints.) are identified in the Acknowledgments.

PROLOGUE

1–4 Hoover and the explosion: ints.—William R. Barnett, Charles L. Carpenter, John L. Chew, Richard L. Cochrane.

CHAPTER 1

5–6 Swenson visits Fullenwider: int.—Adelaide Fullenwider.
7–9 Swenson's background: Hein, letter commending Swenson, Oct. 17, 1940; *The Lucky Bag*, Class of 1916, Naval Academy; Russell Swenson, notes on L. K. Swenson; ints.—Fullenwider, Laura Swenson McIntire, Joseph Nevins, Robert Swenson.

CHAPTER 2

10–25 The Sullivan family: Sunseri and Lyftogt, "The Sullivan Family of Waterloo" (booklet); Christian, *The Iowan*, Winter 1988; Leipold, *All Hands*, Mar. 1944; Turbak, *American Legion Magazine*, Apr. 1982; *Chicago Herald-American*, Jan. 17–22, 1943; Fredericksburg (Ia.) *Review*, Dec. 3, 1987; *Kansas City Star*, Jan. 24, 1943; *Waterloo Courier*, Jan. 13, 1943; ints.—Hazel Ball (Peterson), Murray Davidson, John Draude, Leo Harrington, Steve Katalinich, Eileen Koch, Ruth Leet (Roe), Albert Mixdorf, John Mrzlak, Leo Rooff, Richard Schultz, Eugene R. Stephens, James Sullivan, Gene Francis Wagner, Frank Zubak.

25–26 George Sullivan and Joseph Rogers meet: int.—Joseph Rogers.

CHAPTER 3

27–34 The Rogers family: *Bridgeport* (Conn.) *Post-Telegram*, Sept. 8, 1989; *Bridgeport* (Conn.) *Sunday Post*, Nov. 12, 1978; *Darien Conn. News-Review*, Mar. 3, 1983; *Stratford* (Conn.) *News*, Mar. 31, 1988; Rogers, Joseph, manuscript; ints.—James and Joseph Rogers.

CHAPTER 4

35–37 Swenson meets his men: ints.—Wyatt Butterfield, Arthur Friend, Allen Heyn, Frank Holmgren, Lester Zook.

36 "When I say my prayers at night": Swenson, letter to friends "Nonie and Ned," n.d.

37–41 Red and Margaret: int.—Margaret Jaros (Woods).

38–40 Matt and Beatrice: int.—Beatrice Imperato (Ferreri).

41–42 Joey and Nancy:—int.—Joseph Rogers.

CHAPTER 5

43–44 Butterfield and his dream: int.—Butterfield.

45–49 The *I-26* goes to war: Nakano, *Maru* (Tokyo), Feb. 1987; int.—Tsukuo Nakano.

49–50 The *Juneau* "binge": ints.—Butterfield, Heyn, Zook.

51–52 "I would appreciate having you entice (Bill)": Swenson letter to friend "Louise," Oct. 3, 1941.

52 "If you once get your French": Swenson letter to son, Robert, n.d.

52 "Let me know how the fencing is going": Swenson letter to son, Jan. 29, 1941.

52 "It pleases me very much": Swenson letter to son, Feb. 17, 1941.

52 "Love is a grand thing": Swenson letter to son, May 5 and 26, 1941.

52 "I heard almost universal praise": Swenson letter to son, Oct. 19, 1941.

52 "I wish that you were at college": Swenson letter to daughter, Cecilia, Nov. 11, 1941.

52 "The biggest happiness": Swenson letter to daughter, Feb. 23, 1942.

52–53 "Knowing me as a stranger": Swenson letter to daughter, Feb. 27, 1942.

53 "Tell the men in the brig": int.—Butterfield.

54–55 The *I-26* and the *Saratoga* force: Nakano, *Maru* (Tokyo), Feb. 1987; int.—Nakano.

CHAPTER 6

57–58 Joey and the *Wasp*: int.—Joseph Rogers.

58–59 Swenson and the *Wasp*: ints.—Butterfield, Friend, Heyn, Holmgren, Zook.

59 The Coombs brothers: Schwartz, *Saturday Evening Post*, Feb. 25, 1950; int.—Butterfield.

59–60 The *I-26* surfaces: Nakano, *Maru* (Tokyo), Feb. 1987; int.—Nakano.

60–61 Halsey takes over command: Frank, *Guadalcanal*; Griffith, *The Battle of Guadalcanal;* Halsey and Bryan, *Admiral Halsey's Story;* Hammel, *Guadalcanal: Decision at Sea;* Hoyt, *Guadalcanal;* Lee, *Victory at Guadalcanal;* Merrill, *A Sailor's Admiral;* Morison, *The Struggle for Guadalcanal;* Potter, *Bull Halsey.*

61–64 Zook's road to the Navy: int.—Zook.

64–68 Yokota "outwits" the enemy: Nakano, *Maru* (Tokyo), Mar. 1987; int.—Nakano.

68–69 Wang and the crucible: ints.—Marie Wang, Richard M. Wang.

70–71 Heyn—the youngest man on the ship: int.—Heyn.

71–73 Holmgren and the wishbone: int.—Holmgren.

73–74 "Go to *Enterprise*": int.—Zook.

75–76 Hara and the *Analects:* Hara, Saito, and Pineau, *Japanese Destroyer Captain.*

76–78 The *I-26* in peril: Nakano, *Maru* (Tokyo), Mar. 1987; int.—Nakano.

CHAPTER 7

79–80 *Juneau's* boxing champions: Schwartz, *Saturday Evening Post*, Feb. 25, 1950; ints.—Butterfield, James and Joseph Rogers.

80–83 The Rogers split up, the Sullivans don't: ints.—James and Joseph Rogers.

83–85 The *I-26*—one mission to go; Nakano, *Maru* (Tokyo), Mar. 1987; int.—Nakano.

85 "Our mail took quite a while": Joseph Sullivan, letter to his mother, n.d.

85 "If the motorcycle racing didn't kill me": Joseph Sullivan, letter to Margaret Jaros, n.d.

85 "Dear 'Pal' Red": Genevieve Sullivan, letter to her brother Joseph, Oct. 28, 1942.

86 "Do you remember the time": Joseph Sullivan, letter to his mother, n.d.

CHAPTER 8

87–89 Yamamoto the gambler: Agawa, *The Reluctant Admiral*; Davis, *Get Yamamoto!*; Hara; Hoyt, *Yamamoto: The Man Who Planned Pearl Harbor*; Potter, *Admiral of the Pacific*; Sorimachi, *The Human Side of Isoroku Yamamoto*.

87–88 "If I am told to fight": Davis, p. 30.

88 "What a strange position": Davis, pp. 37–38.

88 "I fear," he wrote to a friend": Agawa, p. 335.

88 "Things here are proving hard going": Agawa, p. 333.

89 Hara's role: Hara.

89–91 Halsey's plan: Frank; Griffith; Halsey; Morison *(Struggle)*.

90–91 "There is every indication": Lee, p. 233.

91 "It's good to know that the old man": Lee, p. 234.

91–93 Admiral Abe's burden: Frank; Hara.

93 Hara and his grandfather: Hara.

93–97 Japanese air attack on transports: Frank; Morison *(Struggle)*; Hartney and Fay, *Our Navy*, mid-Dec. 1943; McCandless, *U.S. Naval Institute Proceedings*, Nov. 1958; narrative: Hartney, Heyn, Roger W. O'Neil, Zook; "Jenkins Report," Nov. 26, 1942; ints.—Heyn, Zook.

95–96 Hartney's greatest fear: int.—Lucy Hartney.

96 "A solid sheet of flame": Hartney and Fay, *Our Navy*, mid-Dec. 1943.

97 Marine flier downs three enemy planes: Wolfert, *Reader's Digest*, Feb. 1943.

97–99 Callaghan given command of task group: Frank; Halsey; Morison *(Struggle)*; Navy Department biographies of Callaghan and Scott; "Arison Report," Oct. 7, 1943; Nimitz preliminary report of action, Nov. 12–13, 1942.

99–100 Hartney and the smell of death: Hartney and Fay, *Our Navy*, mid-Dec. 1943.

100–01 Heyn and George Sullivan prepare for battle: int.—Heyn.

101 The *I-26* waits for prey: Nakano, *Maru* (Tokyo), Mar. 1987; int.—Nakano.

102–03 Callaghan shuffles his ships: Frank; Halsey; Morison *(Struggle)*.

103–06 Abe heads for Guadalcanal: Dull, *Battle History of the Imperial Japanese Navy*; Frank; Hara (including quotations); Morison *(History)*.

107 "We had the feeling": Hartney and Fay, *Our Navy*, mid-Dec. 1943.

107 A surprise party: int:—Holmgren.

107–09 Friend cuts rafts loose: int.—Friend.

109–10 Grycky sails on a "safe ship": ints.—Lilyan Grycky (Steciw), James Latta, Stanley Steciw.

111 Swenson and Hoover: Cook, *The Battle of Cape Esperance*; Morris, "The Fightin'est Ship"; Baird, *The Crowsnest*, Dec. 1959; ints.—Charles Cook, Jr., R. Swenson.

111 "We'll see action tonight": int.—Friend.

112 *Helena* radar picks up enemy ships: Hoover report, Nov. 15, 1942.

112–13 Pandemonium reigns aboard Japanese battleships: Hara (including quotations).

CHAPTER 9

114–15 Kikkawa expects the worst: Dull; Hara.

115–16 Parker awaits permission to fire: Hoover report (Enclosure B), Nov. 15, 1942; Parker oral history; Parker report, Nov. 16, 1942; Stokes report, Nov. 15, 1942.

116 "Stop using the TBS!": Parker oral history.

116 "What are you doing?": Frank; Hoover report (Enclosure B), Nov. 15, 1942.

116 "The *Atlanta's* turning left": McCandless, *U.S. Naval Institute Proceedings*, Nov. 1958.

116 "Stand by to open fire!": Hoover report, Nov. 15, 1942.

117 Zook's critical view: int.—Zook.

117 Enemy searchlights switch on: Frank; Morison *(History)*; ints.—Butterfield, Friend, Heyn, Holmgren, Zook.

117 "like I was naked on the stage": Schwartz, *Saturday Evening Post*, Feb. 25, 1950.

118 "Odd ships commence fire to starboard": Nimitz preliminary report, Dec. 26, 1942.

118 "You are making a mistake": int.—Zook.

118 "Cease firing own ships!": McCandless, *U.S. Naval Institute Proceedings*, Nov. 1958; Hoover report (Enclosure B), Nov. 15, 1942.

118 *San Francisco* shells *Atlanta:* Frank; Pratt, *The Navy's War.*

118 "We want the big ones": Frank.

119 Hartney sprays enemy: Hartney and Fay, *Our Navy*, mid-Dec. 1943.

119 Like in the days of John Paul Jones: Wang tape.

119 "Get those lights!": Hartney and Fay, *Our Navy*, Mid-Dec. 1943.

119–20 Two ships attack *Juneau:* ibid.

120 Rudy is killed: ibid.

120 Heyn's barrel jams: int.—Heyn.

122–23 Kikkawa the raging rhino: Dull; Frank; Hammel, *Guadalcanal: Decision at Sea;* Hara (including quotations).

123–24 The *Juneau* is torpedoed: Hartney and Fay, *Our Navy*, mid-Dec. 1943; narrative: Hartney, Heyn, O'Neil, Wang, Zook; ints.—Butterfield, Friend, Heyn, Holmgren, Zook.

124 "We closed relentlessly": Hartney and Fay, *Our Navy*, mid-Dec. 1943.

124 "All hands stand by": ibid.

124–25 Heyn and the torpedo: int.—Heyn.

126 Hartney and the tiny pearls: Hartney and Fay, *Our Navy*, mid-Dec. 1943.

126–27 The crippling of the *Juneau:* narrative: Hartney, Heyn, O'Neil, Zook; ints.—Butterfield, Friend, Heyn, Holmgren, Zook.

127–28 Leaving the battle zone: ibid.

CHAPTER 10

129 Challenging the "dark shape": Zook narrative.

130 Callaghan is killed: McCandless, *U.S. Naval Institute Proceedings*, Nov. 1958 (including quoted message).

130 "Torpedo flooded forward engine room": Swenson, blinker signal to Hoover, Nov. 13, 1942.

131–32 Hara, Hoover, and the *San Francisco:* Hara (including quotations); McCandless, *U.S. Naval Institute Proceedings*, Nov. 1958; int.—Cook.

132–34 Fate of the ships in the battle: Dull; Frank; Morison *(History)*; Hoover, report to Nimitz, Nov. 15, 1942.

134 Abe retired in disgrace: Dull; Frank; Hara.

134 Yamamoto shot down: Agawa, *The Reluctant Admiral*; Davis, *Get Yamamoto!*; Hoyt, *Yamamoto: The Man Who Planned Pearl Harbor*.

134–35 Hartney looks for the dead: Hartney and Fay, *Our Navy*, mid-Dec. 1943 (including quotations).

135 O'Neil goes to *San Francisco*: O'Neil narrative; int.—Orrel Cecil.

135 Swenson asks Hoover to call for air coverage: Swenson, blinker signal to Hoover, Nov. 13, 1942.

136 "Would like to remain on your starboard": ibid.

136 *Sterett* bombs "submarine": Coward, report to Nimitz, Nov. 22, 1942; Hoover, report to Nimitz, Nov. 15, 1942.

136–37 Yokota sights American ships: Nakano, *Maru* (Tokyo), Mar. 1987; int.—Nakano.

137–39 Mood of *Juneau* crew: Butterfield manuscript; ints.—Butterfield, Heyn.

139–40 The *I-26* fires torpedoes: Nakano, *Maru* (Tokyo), Mar. 1987; int.—Nakano.

140 O'Neil treats *San Francisco* wounded: O'Neil narrative; int.—Cecil.

140 Gibson sees torpedoes: int.—Victor Gibson.

140–41 Schonland "unable" to warn *Juneau*: Schonland, report to Nimitz on loss of *Juneau*, Nov. 15, 1942.

141 Yokota waits tensely: Nakano, *Maru* (Tokyo), Mar. 1987; int.—Nakano.

141–42 Wang savors peaceful atmosphere: Wang narrative; Wang tape.

142 Heyn relieves shipmate of burden: Heyn narrative; int.—Heyn (including quotations).

CHAPTER 11

143 Carpenter sees torpedo; int.—Carpenter.

143–44 Tyng sees explosion: int.—Michael T. Tyng.

144 Shrapnel hits *San Francisco*: McCandless, *U.S. Naval Institute Proceedings*, Nov. 1958; int.—Gibson.

144 Operation interrupted on *San Francisco*: O'Neil narrative (including quotations).

144–45 The *I-26* celebrates hit: Nakano, *Maru* (Tokyo), Mar. 1987; int.—Nakano.

145–46 Hartney blown through hatch: Hartney and Fay, *Our Navy*, mid-Dec. 1943 (including quotations); Hartney narrative.

146–47 Butterfield trapped in mount: Butterfield manuscript; int.—Butterfield.

147 Zook's foot caught in rigging: Zook narrative; int.—Zook.

147–48 Holmgren topples into water: int.—Holmgren.

148–49 Wang breaks leg, then plunges: Wang narrative; Wang tape (including quotation).

149–50 Friend won't consider dying: int.—Friend.

150–51 Heyn becomes part of the ship: Heyn narrative (including quotation); int.—Heyn.

151–53 *Fletcher* officers see explosion: Wylie manuscript; int.—William Cole II, Joseph C. Wylie.

153–54 B-17 crewmen see explosion: Cleveland (ed.), *Grey Geese Calling* (article by Entrikin); Eleventh Bombardment Group, report, Nov. 13, 1942; Gill report; Walker diary, Nov. 13, 1942; Gill career sketch; Entrikin letter to author, May 14, 1991; Gill letter to author, June 20, 1991; ints.—William R. Entrikin, Robert L. Gill, Forrest C. Tanner (all material related to himself), George Walker.

154 "It was almost too much": Morris, pp. 95–96.

154–55 Hoover as "God": Hoover report to Nimitz on *Juneau* sinking, Nov. 14, 1942; ints.—James Baird, Carpenter, Chew, Cochrane, Cook.

155–57 Hoover and his son: ints.—Gilbert Hoover, Jr., Katherine Miller, Ann Wood.

156 "In his leather jacket": Morris, p. 27.

156 "Don't worry, son": int.—William Bunker.

157 "*Juneau* torpedoed and disappeared": Hoover, blinker message to Gill's B-17.

157–58 Gill reaches Hoover's ships: Cleveland (ed.), *Grey Geese Calling* (article by Entrikin); Eleventh Bombardment

Group, report, Nov. 13, 1942; Gill report; Walker diary, Nov. 13, 1942; Entrikin letter to author, May 14, 1991; Gill letter to author, June 20, 1991; ints.—Entrikin, Gill, Tanner, Walker.

158 "To me, this is important enough": int.—Tanner.

159 "In any case, if the commander of those ships": Gill report.

159 "This alternative": int.—Gill.

CHAPTER 12

160–61 Hartney and the torso: Hartney and Fay, *Our Navy,* Jan. 1, 1944 (including quotation).

161–62 Butterfield finds raft: Butterfield manuscript; int.—Butterfield.

162–63 Holmgren drags himself to net: int.—Holmgren.

163 Zook makes it to raft: Zook narrative; int.—Zook.

163–64 Wang his own guinea pig: Wang narrative; Wang tape.

164 Friend survives as he expected: int.—Friend.

164–66 Heyn survives despite massive wounds: Heyn narrative; int.—Heyn.

165–66 Heyn meets George and Albert Sullivan: int.—Heyn.

166 "You sons of bitches!": Butterfield manuscript.

167 "many, many tiny coconuts": Walker diary, Nov. 13, 1942.

167 B-17 crew counts men in water: ibid; Gill report; ints.—Gill, Walker.

167–68 "We should send a message": int.—Tanner.

168 Tanner message to *Helena:* ibid.

168 The plane "returned to the pitiful sight": Walker diary, Nov. 13, 1942.

168–70 Survivors organize raft community: Butterfield manuscript; narrative: Hartney, Heyn, George Mantere, Zook; Wang tape; ints.—Butterfield, Friend, Heyn, Holmgren, Zook.

170 George Sullivan favors funeral ceremony: int.—Heyn.

170 Gill's B-17 waved off from airfield: Gill report, Walker diary, Nov. 13, 1942 (including quotation); ints.—Entrikin, Gill, Tanner, Walker.

171 Hunger, thirst, and cold take toll: Butterfield manuscript;

narrative: Hartney, Heyn, Wang, Zook; ints.—Butterfield, Friend, Heyn (including quotations), Zook.

172 Gill decides to continue on mission: Gill report; Walker diary, Nov. 13, 1942; ints.—Gill, Walker.

172 "The hell with this!": int.—Gill.

172 Two extra rubber life rafts: ints.—Entrikin, Gill.

172 Gill "didn't think of it": int.—Gill.

173 George Sullivan searches for brothers: ints.—Butterfield, Friend, Heyn (including quotations), Zook.

173–75 Gill reports to intelligence officer: int.—Gill.

174 Entrikin and the intelligence officer: int.—Entrikin.

175 Gill report treated routinely: Daily Operations Report, Eleventh Bombardment Group Headquarters, Nov. 13, 1942.

175–76 Joey and Jimmy Rogers learn of sinking: ints.—Joseph (including quotations) and James Rogers.

CHAPTER 13

177–78 Hoover contacts superiors; Halsey, p. 133; Hoover, report to Nimitz, Nov. 22, 1942

178–80 Hartney decides to swim for rubber boat: Hartney and Fay, *Our Navy*, Jan. 1, 1944; *Hartford Courant Magazine*, Mar. 7, 1943; Hartney narrative.

178–79 The nature of sharks: Llano, *Science Digest*, Jan. 1957; Simpkins, *Navy Times*, Sept. 24, 1975; int.—Scott Johnson.

179 "I sat there the whole morning": Hartney and Fay, *Our Navy*, Jan. 1, 1944.

180 Hartney and Fitzgerald face sharks: ibid; *Hartford Courant Magazine*, Mar. 7, 1943; Hartney narrative.

180–81 Halsey notes that *Juneau* not on arrival list: Halsey (including dialogue with Browning), p. 133.

180 "60 white men in water": Daily Operations Report, Eleventh Bombardment Group Headquarters, Nov. 14, 1942.

180 "Upon my arrival Button": Turner, radio message to Halsey, Nov. 15, 1942.

181–82 Hartney and Fitzgerald reach rubber boat: Hartney and Fay, *Our Navy*, Jan. 1, 1944; (including quotations); *Hartford Courant Magazine*, Mar. 7, 1943; Hartney narrative.

182–83 Hartney wishes to separate from group: ibid.

183 "We can't make it in this group": Hartney and Fay, *Our Navy*, Jan. 1, 1944.

183 Wang feels guilt for "holding back" group: Wang tape.

184 "It was hard to leave the raft": Hartney and Fay, *Our Navy*, Jan. 1, 1944.

184 Friend claims authority: int.—Friend (including quotation).

184 "All these fellows that was on the doughnuts": Heyn narrative.

184 Heyn claims Wang "pulled his rank": int.—Heyn.

184 "Two survivors inflated the raft": Butterfield manuscript.

184 "Bastards, come back!" int.—Heyn.

184–85 "We couldn't see the sharks": Butterfield manuscript.

185 "the condition of the wounded": Mantere narrative.

185 "As we drifted": Butterfield manuscript.

186 "Why should anyone have?": int.—Butterfield.

186 "We grew bolder": Butterfield manuscript.

186 Shark grabs man's arm: ibid. (including quotations).

186 "but the strength of such men": ibid.

186 "We were beginning to take death in stride": ibid.

187 "Remember, son": ibid.

187 Butterfield hallucinates: ibid.

187–88 Butterfield and Moore: ibid (including quotations).

188 Butterfield and Berman: int.—Butterfield (including quotations).

188 "Survival, not friendship": Butterfield manuscript.

188–89 "From the beginning": ibid.

189 Fighting for a coconut: ibid.; int.—Zook.

189 Fighting for a pineapple: Butterfield manuscript.

189 Gill sights survivors again: Gill report; Walker diary, Nov. 15, 1942; ints.—Entrikin, Gill, Tanner, Walker.

189 "What kind of Navy": Gill report; int.—Gill.

189–90 Gill reports again to intelligence officer: int.—Gill.

190 The third item on page two; Daily Operations Report, Eleventh Bombardment Group Headquarters, Nov. 14, 1942.

190 The fourth item on page three: ibid., Nov. 15, 1942.

190 "Since our bomb group": Gill report.

190–91 Heyn kills man in self-defense: int.—Heyn.

191 Heyn tries to save another man: Heyn narrative (including quotations).

191 George Sullivan protests "unofficial" burial: ibid.

191 "I knew [George] was delirious": ibid.

192 "The fellows that didn't have shirts on": ibid.

192 "I'm going to swim over to the island": int.—Heyn.

192 Sharks attack George Sullivan: ibid.

192–93 Halsey interrogates Hoover: Halsey, p. 134.

CHAPTER 14

194–95 Hoover waits for Halsey's decision: ints.—Carpenter (including quotations), Cook.

195–96 Hartney alone is rational: Hartney and Fay, *Our Navy,* Jan. 1, 1944 (including quotations); Hartney narrative.

196 "What a terrifying night!": Butterfield manuscript.

196–97 Friend grabs a shark: int.—Friend.

197–99 Grycky's tragic fate: Butterfield manuscript; Zook narrative; ints.—Butterfield, Zook.

198–99 "There was no way at all": Zook narrative.

199 "we could only push him back": Butterfield manuscript.

199 Wang and Fitzgerald become rational: Hartney and Fay, *Our Navy,* Jan. 1, 1944 (including quotations involving Hartney).

200 "What the hell am I doing here?": Wang tape.

200 "I felt an impulse": ibid.

200–01 "this was certainly no time to quit": Wang narrative.

201 "I knew how keenly my mother": ibid.

201 Hartney and Fitzgerald sing: Hartney and Fay, *Our Navy,* Jan. 1, 1944 (including quote).

201–02 Fish, a coconut, and a bird: ibid.; Wang tape (including quote on "Thanksgiving dinner").

202 The three survivors see planes: Hartney and Fay, *Our Navy,* Jan. 1, 1944 (including quotations); Wang tape.

202–03 USS *Meade* sent in search of survivors: Frank (role in naval battle); Lamb, radio message to Halsey, Nov. 17, 1942.

203 Halsey aghast at failure: Halsey, message to Fitch, Nov. 18, 1942.

203–05 Blodgett and the island: int.—Heyn (including quotations).

204 Heyn and the family farm: ibid.

204 "I don't know. Don't bother me!": ibid.

204–05 Blodgett goes mad: ints.—Heyn, Zook.

205 Gill sights survivors a third time: Gill report; int.—Gill (including quotation).

205–06 Rafts drift apart: narratives: Heyn (including quotation), Mantere, Zook; ints.—Butterfield, Friend (including quotation), Heyn, Holmgren, Zook.

206–07 Remaining raft separates from nets: Butterfield manuscript; narratives: Mantere (including quotation), Zook; ints.—Butterfield, Holmgren (including statement to Hayes), Zook.

CHAPTER 15

208 Enemy planes roar past rubber boat: Hartney and Fay, *Our Navy*, Jan. 1, 1944 (including quoted material); narratives: Hartney, Wang; Wang tape.

209 American plane sighted: ibid.

209–10 "Head into the wind": Wang tape.

210 "The raft pitched and tossed": Hartney and Fay, *Our Navy*, Jan. 1, 1944.

210 "Land! Land!": Wang tape.

210–11 Heyn and the madmen: Heyn narrative; int.—Heyn (including quotations).

211 Heyn and the sea gull: ibid.

211 Sharks devour each other: int.—Heyn.

211 Man goes down to "locker": Heyn narrative (including quotation); int.—Heyn.

212–13 Friend and the sharks: Friend letter to author, Aug. 4, 1991; int.—Friend (including quotations).

213 Blodgett swims to oblivion: Butterfield manuscript; narratives: Mantere, Zook; ints.—Butterfield, Holmgren, Zook (including quotations).

214 "Look! Palm trees just ahead!": int.—Holmgren.

214 Gardner drinks seawater: int.—Zook (including quotations).

214 PBY flies over raft: Butterfield manuscript (including quotations); narratives: Mantere, Zook; ints.—Butterfield, Holmgren, Zook.

214–15 Butterfield decides to swim to life jacket: Butterfield manuscript; ints.—Butterfield, Holmgren, Zook.

216 "We've got to turn around": Hartney and Fay, *Our Navy,* Jan. 1, 1944.

216 Coral reef causes roar: Wang narrative; Wang tape.

216 "My God. If that wave had not been just right": Wang tape.

217 Heyn's tug-of-war with shark: Heyn narrative (including quotations); int.—Heyn.

218 Friend battles sharks: Friend letter to author, Aug. 4, 1991; int.—Friend (including quotations).

218 "Words can't describe the fear": Butterfield manuscript.

218 "panic took over": ibid.

218 "Oh, my God": int.—Butterfield.

219 "If I had thought": Butterfield manuscript.

219 "I had managed to knife one of the sharks": ibid.

219 PBS pilot drops note: McWilliams, note to survivors.

220 Crossing the coral: Hartney and Fay, *Our Navy,* Jan. 1, 1944; narratives: Hartney, Wang; Wang tape.

220 Hartney and Fitzgerald "were magnificent": Wang narrative.

221 "The courage that man showed": Hartney and Fay, *Our Navy,* Jan. 1, 1944.

221 "Stand by for the next big wave": Wang tape.

221 "We shook the stiffness out of our joints": Hartney and Fay, *Our Navy,* Jan. 1, 1944.

221 Hartney and Fitzgerald search for water: ibid.

222 "Now we've got to find food": ibid.

222 Wang confronted by "savages": Wang narrative; Wang tape.

CHAPTER 16

223–24 Williamson selected to rescue survivors: Anderson,

letter to Sport Little, Aug. 21, 1989; Williamson, letter to author, Oct. 8, 1991; ints.—William Anderson, Lawrence B. Williamson.

224 "We're going on a special mission": int.—Williamson.

224 "We liked Larry": int.—Anderson.

224 "Here is the position report": int.—Williamson.

225 Williamson spots survivors: Anderson, letter to Sport Little, Aug. 21, 1989; Williamson, letter to author, Oct. 8, 1991; ints.—Anderson, Williamson.

225 "USS *Ballard* en route": Commander, Fleet Air Wing One, radio message to Williamson, Nov. 20, 1942.

225 "We can do it!": int.—Williamson.

226 "Prepare for open sea landing": ibid.

226 "You should have thought about that": int.—Anderson.

226 Williamson's false sense of security: int.—Williamson.

226 "I thought I was headed for the cooking pot": Hartney and Fay, *Our Navy*, Jan. 1, 1944.

226–27 Wang tries to "bribe" natives: Wang tape.

227 Wang discovers natives are Catholic: ibid.

227 Natives bring Wang food: ibid.; Wang narrative.

227–28 Hartney and Fitzgerald meet natives: Hartney and Fay, *Our Navy*, Jan. 1, 1944 (including quotations); Hartney narrative.

229 The three survivors reunite and go to jungle village: ibid.; Wang narrative (including Hartney greeting); Wang tape.

229–30 Food, sleep, medicine, and a trip to paradise: Hartney and Fay, *Our Navy*, Jan. 1, 1944 (including quotations); narratives: Hartney, Wang; Wang tape.

230–31 Williamson's PBY lands in water: Anderson, letter to Sport Little, Aug. 21, 1989; Williamson, letter to author, Oct. 8, 1991; ints.—Anderson (including quotation), Williamson.

231 Survivors pulled aboard PBY: ibid.; Butterfield manuscript; ints.—Butterfield (including quotes), Holmgren, Zook.

231–32 Williamson not entirely at peace with himself: int.—Williamson.

232 Survivors drink coffee: Anderson, letter to Sport Little, Aug. 21, 1989; int.—Anderson (including quotations).

232–33 Friend is rescued: Friend, letter to author, Aug. 4, 1991; int.—Friend (including quotations).

233–35 Heyn is rescued: Heyn narrative (including quotations); int.—Heyn.

235–36 Kuper hosts the survivors: Hartney and Fay, *Our Navy*, Jan. 1, 1944 (including quotations); narratives: Hartney, Wang; Wang tape.

236 "I understand you are a signalman": Hartney and Fay, *Our Navy*, Jan. 1, 1944.

236–37 "I searched the skies": ibid.

237 "There was no doubt about it now": ibid.

237 Hoover is detached: Halsey, p. 134; Halsey, report to Nimitz, Nov. 21, 1942; int.—Carpenter (including quotation).

238–39 Gill interrogated about survivors: Gill report; int.—Gill (including quotations).

239 Investigator finds Gill's original report: int.—Entrikin.

239–40 Hoover formally relieved of command: int.—Cochrane.

240–41 "if it had been known": Hoover, report to Nimitz, Dec. 4, 1942.

EPILOGUE

242–43 Neighbor tells Alleta Sullivan *Juneau* sank: A. Sullivan, *American Magazine*, Mar. 1944 (including quotations).

243–44 Another knock on the door: ibid.

244–45 Sullivans learn their sons dead: Zook, letter to Alleta and Thomas Sullivan, received Jan. 14, 1943.

245 Alleta speaks to newsmen: *Des Moines Register*, Jan. 17, 1943.

245 Margaret Jaros arrives in Waterloo: *Waterloo Courier*, Jan. 17, 1943; int.—Jaros.

245–46 Beatrice Imperato devastated by news: int.—Imperato.

246 Surviving Sullivans help in war effort: *New York Times*, Feb. 3, 1943; *Waterloo Courier*, Oct. 24, 1943.

246 "the entire nation shares in your sorrow": Roosevelt, letter to Mr. and Mrs. Sullivan, Feb. 1, 1943.

246 "What I feel is this": *New York Times*, Feb. 6, 1943.

247 The vision of their sons everywhere: ints.—Eileen Koch,

other friends and relatives listed under "the Sullivan family," Chapter II.

247 Tom pulled off job for drinking: int.—Draude.

247–48 Alleta's lonely days: int.—Koch.

248 Sullivan son pushes for "Sullivan Act": *Times* (London), Feb. 26, 1991; *Waterloo Courier*, Feb. 24, 1991; int.—James Sullivan.

248 Memory remains with Margaret and Beatrice: ints.—Imperato and Jaros.

249 "Oh, Jesus, Joe": int.—Joseph Rogers.

249 "Art, do you know about our brothers?": ibid.

249 "I got a telegram": *Bridgeport* (Conn.) *Sunday Post*, Nov. 12, 1978.

249–50 Joey's new personal life: int.—Joseph Rogers.

250–51 Jimmy's new personal life: int.—James Rogers.

251 Heyn had "very bad headaches": Heyn narrative.

252–53 Heyn's career and health problems: int.—Heyn.

253–54 Friend's career and marriage problems: int.—Friend.

254–55 Zook makes most of borrowed time: int.—Zook

255–57 Butterfield achieves his goal: int.—Butterfield.

257–58 Holmgren finally gets home: *Eatontown* (N.J.) *Daily Standard*, Jan. 12, April. 12, 1943; ints.—Frank and Alfreda Holmgren.

258–59 Wang perseveres despite pain: ints.—Willis Hoch, Marie Wang, James Welsh.

259–60 Hartney's nightmarish heaven: *New Britain* (Conn.) *Daily Herald*, Oct. 19, 20, 1943, July 30, 1946; *Passaic* (N.J.) *Herald-News*, Oct. 20, 1943; int.—Lucy Hartney.

260–61 Grycky's legacy: ints.—Lilyan Grycky, James Latta, Stanley Steciw.

261–62 Yokota teaches Christianity: int.—Nakano.

262 Swenson triumphs in death: int.—Robert Swenson.

262–63 Hoover's torment: ints.—Hoover Jr., Miller, Wood.

263–64 Hoover finds hope in Nimitz letter: Nimitz, letter to King, Dec. 4, 1942.

263 Carney persuades Halsey that Hoover is guiltless: Halsey (including quotations, "be restored to combat command" and "The stigma of such a detachment"); int.—Cook (including quotation, "want to kick those guys in the tail").

NOTES

264–65 Snubbing Halsey on train: int.—Cook.

265 Hoover threatens to shoot himself: int.—Hoover Jr.

265 Hoover's postwar career: ints.—Roswell Bosworth, Jr., Cook, Hoover Jr., Miller, Rev. Delbert W. Tildesly, Wood.

265–66 Hoover meets Robert Swenson: int.—Robert Swenson.

266 Hoover's obituary: *Bristol* (R.I.) *Phoenix*, Jan. 10, 1980; *New York Times*, Jan. 9, 1980; *Providence Journal*, Jan. 9, 1980.

Bibliography

Books

Abbazia, Patrick. *Mr. Roosevelt's Navy*. Annapolis: Naval Institute Press, 1975.

Agawa, Hiroyuki. *The Reluctant Admiral*. Annapolis: Naval Institute Press, 1979.

Benedict, Ruth. *The Chrysanthemum and the Sword*. Boston: Houghton Mifflin, 1946.

Buell, Thomas B. *Master of Sea Power*. Boston: Little, Brown, 1980.

Campbell, John. *Naval Weapons of World War Two*. Annapolis: Naval Institute Press, 1985.

Cant, Gilbert, *America's Navy in World War II*. New York: John Day, 1942.

Cate, J. L. *The Army Air Forces in World War II*, vol. 1. Chicago: University of Chicago Press, 1948.

Churchill, Winston S. *The Hinge of Fate*. Boston: Houghton Mifflin, 1950.

Cleveland, W. M., ed. *Grey Geese Calling: A History of the 11th Bombardment Group Heavy (H) in the Pacific, 1940–45*. Seffner, Fla.: 11th Bombardment Group (H) Association. n.d.

Coffey, Thomas M. *Hap*. New York: Viking, 1982.

Coggins, Jack. *The Campaign for Guadalcanal*. Garden City, N.Y.: Doubleday, 1972.

Cook, Charles. *The Battle of Cape Esperance.* New York: Crowell, 1968.

Costello, John. *The Pacific War.* New York: Rawson, Wade, 1981.

D'Albas, Andrieu. *Death of a Navy.* New York: Devin-Adair, 1957.

Davis, Burke. *Get Yamamoto!* New York: Random House, 1969.

Dulin, Robert O., Jr., and William H. Harzke, Jr. *Battleships— United States Battleships in World War II.* Annapolis: Naval Institute Press, 1976.

Dull, Paul S. *A Battle History of the Imperial Japanese Navy, 1941–1945.* Annapolis: Naval Institute Press, 1978.

Dyer, George C. *The Amphibians Came to Conquer: The Story of Admiral Richmond Kelly Turner,* vol. 1. Washington, D.C.: U.S. Government Printing Office, n.d.

Evans, David C., ed. *The Japanese Navy in World War II.* Annapolis: Naval Institute Press, 1986.

Frank, Richard B. *Guadalcanal.* New York: Random House, 1990.

Friedman, Norman. *U.S. Cruisers: An Illustrated Design History.* Annapolis: Naval Institute Press, 1984.

———. *Naval Radar.* Annapolis: Naval Institute Press, 1981.

Griffith, Samuel. *The Battle of Guadalcanal.* New York: Lippincott, 1963.

Halsey, William F., and J. Bryan III. *Admiral Halsey's Story.* New York: McGraw-Hill, 1947.

Hammel, Eric. *Guadalcanal: Decision at Sea.* New York: Crown, 1988.

———. *Starvation Island.* New York: Crown, 1987.

Hara, Tameichi, with Fred Saito and Roger Pineau. *Japanese Destroyer Captain.* New York: Ballantine, 1961.

Hashimoto, Mochitsura. *Sunk: The Story of the Japanese Submarine Fleet, 1941–1945.* New York: Henry Holt, 1954.

Hayes, Grace P. *The History of the Joint Chiefs of Staff in World War II: The War Against Japan.* Annapolis: Naval Institute Press, 1982.

Hodges, Peter, and Norman Friedman. *Destroyer Weapons of World War II.* Annapolis: Naval Institute Press, 1979.

BIBLIOGRAPHY

Holmes, W. J. *Undersea Victory*. Garden City, N.Y.: Doubleday, 1966.

Howarth, Stephen. *To Shining Sea: A History of the United States Navy*. New York: Random House, 1991.

Hoyt, Edwin P. *Yamamoto: The Man Who Planned Pearl Harbor*. New York: McGraw-Hill, 1990.

———. *The Glory of the Solomons*. New York: Stein & Day, 1983.

———. *Guadalcanal*. New York: Stein & Day, 1982.

———. *How They Won the War in the Pacific*. New York: Weybright & Talley, 1970.

Ingram, Luther Gates, Jr. "The Deficiencies of the United States Submarine Torpedo in the Pacific Theater: World War II." Thesis, San Diego State University, 1978.

Ito, Masanori. *The End of the Imperial Japanese Navy*. New York: Norton, 1956.

Jentschura, Hansgeorg, Dieter Jung, and Peter Mickel. *Warships of the Imperial Japanese Navy, 1869–1945*. Annapolis: Naval Institute Press, 1977.

Karig, Walter, and Eric Purdon, eds. *Battle Report: Pacific War, Middle Phase*. New York: Rinehart, 1947.

Kurzman, Dan. *Kishi and Japan: The Search for the Sun*. New York: Obolensky, 1960.

Lee, Clark. *They Call It Pacific*. New York: Viking, 1943.

Lee, Robert Edward. *Victory at Guadalcanal*. Novato, Cal.: Presidio Press, 1981.

Lenton, H. T. *American Battleships, Carriers and Cruisers*. Garden City, N.Y.: Doubleday, 1968.

Lord, Walter. *Lonely Vigil: Coastwatchers in the Solomons*. New York: Viking, 1977.

Lundstrom, John B. *The First Team*. Annapolis: Naval Institute Press, 1984.

———. *The First South Pacific Campaign Pacific Fleet Strategy December 1941—June 1942*. Annapolis: Naval Institute Press, 1976.

McConkie, Bruce R. *Mormon Doctrine*. Salt Lake City: Bookcraft, 1966.

Merillat, Herbert Christian. *Guadalcanal Remembered*. New York: Dodd, Mead, 1982.

———. *The Island.* Boston: Houghton Mifflin, 1944.

Merrill, James M. *A Sailor's Admiral: A Biography of William F. Halsey.* New York: Crowell, 1976.

Mickel, Peter. *Warships of the Imperial Japanese Navy, 1869–1945.* n.d.

Miller, Thomas G., Jr. *The Cactus Air Force.* New York: Harper and Row, 1969.

Mills, George. *Iowa's Amazing Past.* Ames, Ia.: Iowa State University Press, 1972.

Morison, Samuel Eliot. *History of United States Naval Operations in World War II,* vols. 4, 5. Boston: Little, Brown, 1964.

———. *The Struggle for Guadalcanal.* Boston: Little, Brown, 1964.

Morris, C. G., with Hugh B. Cave. *"The Fightin'est Ship": The Story of the Cruiser "Helena."* New York: Dodd, Mead, 1944.

Navy Department. *Almanac of Naval Facts.* Annapolis: Naval Institute Press, 1969.

———. *Dictionary of American Naval Fighting Ships,* vol. 4. Washington, D.C.: U.S. Government Printing Office, 1968.

Newcomb, Richard F. *Savo: The Incredible Naval Debacle off Guadalcanal.* New York: Holt, Rinehart & Winston, 1961.

Okumiya, Masatake, and Jiro Horikoshi, with Martin Caidin. *Zero!* New York: Dutton, 1956.

One Ship: USS San Francisco. n.d.

Orita, Zenji, and Joseph D. Harrington. *I-Boat Captain.* Canoga Park, Cal.: Major Books, 1976.

Potter, Elmer Belmont. *Sea Power: A Naval History.* Annapolis: Naval Institute Press, 1987.

———. *Bull Halsey.* Annapolis: Naval Institute Press, 1985.

———. *Nimitz.* Annapolis: Naval Institute Press, 1976.

Potter, John Deane. *Admiral of the Pacific.* London: Heinemann, 1965.

Pratt, Fletcher. *The Navy's War.* New York: Harper, 1944.

Robson, R. W. *The Pacific Islands Handbook, 1944.* New York: Macmillan, 1945.

Saki, Saburo, with Martin Caldin and Fred Saito. *Samurai.* Garden City, N.Y.: Doubleday, 1957.

Silverstone, Paul H. *U.S. Warships of World War II.* Garden City, N.Y.: Doubleday, 1966.

Smith, Stan. *The Navy at Guadalcanal*. New York: Lancer Books, 1963.

Sorimachi, Eiichi. *The Human Side of Isoroku Yamamoto*. Tokyo: Kawada, n.d.

Spector, Ronald H. *Eagle Against the Sun*. New York: Free Press, 1985.

Stafford, Edward P. *The Big E*. New York: Random House, 1962.

Sunseri, Alvin, and Kenneth Lyftogt. *The Sullivan Family of Waterloo* (12-page booklet). Cedar Falls, IA.: M & M Publishing, 1988.

Toland, John. *The Rising Sun*. New York: Random House, 1970 (Part 4).

Van Metre, Isiah, ed. *History of Black Hawk County, Iowa, and Representative Citizens*. Chicago: Biographical Publishing, 1904.

War History Series, South Pacific (Senshi Sosho, Minamilaiheiyo Rikugun Sakusen). Tokyo: Defense Agency, Defense Research Institute, Office of War History, 1968.

Willmott, H. P. *Empires in Balance*. Annapolis: Naval Institute Press, 1982.

Periodicals

The Alaska Journal, Autumn 1985. "The Day the USS *Juneau* Went Down." John McDowell.

All Hands, Mar. 1983. "Five Who Dared." Joi J. D. Leipold.

———, Nov. 1950. "Fighting *Fletcher*."

American Heritage, June 1956. "One Who Survived: Seaman Heyn's Story." Allen Heyn.

American Legion Magazine, Apr. 1982. "The Sullivan Sacrifice." Gary Turbak.

American Magazine, Mar. 1944. "I Lost Five Sons." Mrs. Thomas F. Sullivan.

Bureau of Naval Personnel Information Bulletin, Dec. 1942. "Admiral Scott's Triumph Revealed."

The Crowsnest, Dec. 1959. "The Battle of Cape Esperance." L.J. Baird.

BIBLIOGRAPHY

Erie Railroad Magazine, July 1950. "Worth the Fight." (about Allen Heyn)

The Iowan, Winter 1988. " 'If We Go Down, We'll All Go Together.' " Rebecca Christian.

Life, Dec. 1989. "Sinking of the *Juneau*." Wyatt Butterfield.

The Lucky Bag, annual, Naval Academy, Class of 1916. "Lyman Knut Swenson."

Maru (Tokyo), Mar. 1987. "An Account of the Dangerous Transport Operations of the *I-26* Submarine." Tsukuo Nakano.

———, Feb. 1987. "My Youth Aboard an Iron Whale." Tsukuo Nakano.

Newsweek, Feb. 15, 1943. "Chins Up."

Our Navy, mid-Nov. 1950. "Swing and Sway on the *Lyman K.*" H. V. LeClaire.

———, mid-May 1950. "USS Fletcher DD-445."

———, mid-Dec. 1943 and Jan. 1, 1944. "The Story of the *Juneau*" (two parts). Robert C. Fay as narrated by Joseph P. Hartney.

Reader's Digest, Feb. 1943. "A Grandstand View of Jap Naval Disaster." Ira Wolfert. (Condensed from *New York Times*, Nov. 28 and 29, 1942.)

Saga, Feb. 1961. "The Sharks Were Willing to Wait." Mark Sufrin.

Saturday Evening Post, Feb. 25, 1950. "The Terrible End of the USS *Juneau*." Robert L. Schwartz.

———, Jan. 22, 1944. "I Saw the *Helena* Go Down." C. G. Morris.

Scale Ship Modeler. "USS *Juneau* (CL-52)." Steve Andereggen.

Science Digest, Jan. 1957. "Survival From Sharks." George Albert Llano.

Sea Classics, Mar.–Apr. 1986. "The Terrible Ordeal of USS *Juneau*." John McDowell.

Shipmate, July–Aug. 1975. "Nights to Remember: The Rescue of USS *Helena*'s Survivors, July 1943." Leonard J. Baird.

Southeastern Log (Ketchikan, Alaska), Nov. 1986. "690 Died When USS *Juneau* Was Lost." Steve Andereggen.

U.S. Naval Institute Proceedings, May 1963. "Comment and Discussion." Bruce McCandless.

———, Aug. 1962. "Solomons Battle Log."

———, Nov. 1958. "The *San Francisco* Story." Bruce McCandless.

———, Nov. 1958. "Thoughts on Japan's Naval Defeat." Toshiyuki Yokoi.

U.S. Navy Cruisers at War 1941–45, Summer 1984. "America's Antiaircraft Cruisers." Preston Cook.

Newspapers

Bridgeport (Conn.) *Post-Telegram*, Sept. 8, 1989. "Harris-Rodgers: State's Oldest VFW Post Marks 70th Birthday."

Bridgeport (Conn.) *Sunday Post*, Nov. 12, 1978. "Veterans Day Poignant for Family" (Rogers). Robert Zarnetske.

Bristol (R.I.) *Phoenix*, Jan. 10, 1980. "Adm. Hoover, former Council Pres. Veteran of World Wars, Dies at 85."

Buffalo Evening News, June 19, 1980. "War Hero Found New Friends Amidst Sad Memories in WNY." Bob Curran, Curran's Corner.

———, June 5, 1980. "*Juneau* Survivor Met Parents of 'The Fighting Sullivans.'" Bob Curran, Curran's Corner.

Chicago Herald-American, Jan. 17–22, 1943. "The Fighting Sullivans" (six-part series). Basil Talbott.

———, Jan. 18, 1943. "Five Off to War Forever, a Stricken Mother Learns."

———, Jan. 15, 1943. "Five Sons Lost, Parents Keep Their Chins Up."

Chicago Tribune, 1943. "The Log of the *Mighty A*," the story of the USS *Atlanta* (14 installments). An officer of USS *Atlanta* (Edward Corboy) as told to Charles Leavelle.

Christian Science Monitor, Jan. 14, 1943. "Guadalcanal: Turning Point in Pacific Warfare." Joseph C. Harsch.

———, Dec. 22, 1942. "How Cruiser *San Francisco* Sank Japanese Battleship."

Citrus County (Fla.) *Chronicle*, Feb. 18, 1987. "A Tale of Courage, Allen Heyn Vividly Recalls His Struggle for Survival." Esther Duncan.

Darien (Conn.) *News-Review*, Mar. 3, 1983. "Joe Rogers Remembers the 'USS Juneau.'" William Cummings.

Des Moines Register, Nov. 11, 1988. "Waterloo Pays Homage to Own Special Heroes." Jack Hovelson.

———, Jan. 17, 1942. "Lost 5 Sons, 'Carries On.'" George Shane.

Eatontown (N.J.) *Daily Standard*, Apr. 12, 1943. "Hero of *Juneau* Returns" (Frank Holmgren). Nat Snyderman.

———, Jan. 12, 1943. "Navy Men Missing, Frank Holmgren, Charles Hayes, in Navy, 'Lost.'"

Fredericksburg (Ia.) *Review*, Dec. 3, 1987. "Americans Remember Pearl Harbor and 'a Day That Will Live in Infamy.'" (Bill Ball).

Guadalcanal Echoes, July 1991. "Twin Sister, USS *Atlanta* CL51 & USS *Juneau* CL-52, Die Within Hours of Each Other on Friday the Thirteenth November 1942."

———, Apr. 1991. "Jap Sub Off Guadalcanal."

Hartford (Conn.) *Courant Magazine*, Nov. 13, 1985. "The Sinking of the USS *Juneau*." Chuck Kleeschulte.

———, Mar. 7, 1943. "The 'Juneau' Fights to the End!" (Victor J. Fitzgerald). Robert Ensworth.

Juneau (Alaska) *Empire*, July 6, 1987. "USS *Juneau* Remembered, After 45 Years." Leslie Murray.

Kansas City Star, Jan. 24, 1943. "Five Sons Her Sacrifice." E. B. Garnett.

Navy Times, Nov. 14, 1988. "Hometown Hurrah Set for Waterloo's Sullivan Brothers." Brian Mitchell.

———, Sept. 24, 1975. "Sharks: What We Don't Yet Know Definitely Can Hurt Us." Gregory Simpkins.

New Britain (Conn.) *Daily Herald*, July 30, 1946. "Hartney Closes Career in Navy."

———, Oct. 20, 1943. "Hero of Sea Battle in Pacific Receives Legion of Merit Medal."

———, October 19, 1943. "Recipient of Legion of Merit, Happy Wife and Their Baby."

New York Daily Mirror, Oct. 20, 1943. "Explosion Blew Sailor out of His Ship, Shirt, Shoes."

New York Sun, Oct. 19, 1943. "Sailor Escaped Sharks' Teeth."

New York Times, Jan. 9, 1980. "Adm. Gilbert Hoover, Won 3 Navy Crosses in the 2 World Wars." Wolfgang Saxon.

———, Aug. 9, 1950. "5 Sullivans' Parents Get Belated U.S. Aid."

———, June 13, 1943. "Parents of '5 Sullivans' Hailed."

———, Apr. 5, 1943. "Mother's Tears for Her Five Heroic Sons Christen New Destroyer 'The Sullivans.' "

———, Feb. 10, 1943. "Name 'The Sullivans' Set for Destroyer."

———, Feb. 9, 1943. "Speed Up Production, the Sullivans Plead."

———, Feb. 6, 1943. "Sullivans Urge Need of More Planes, Ships."

———, Feb. 3, 1943. "Sullivans to Tour War Work Plants."

———, Jan. 13, 1943. "Five Iowa Brothers Lost in Pacific Battle; Joined the Navy Together to Avenge a Friend."

New York World-Telegram, Oct. 19, 1943. "Sailor Who Fought Them 7 Days Declares Sharks Are Cowards."

Passaic (N.J.) Herald-News, Oct. 20, 1943. "Juneau Hero, Pal of Lost Passaic Boys, Tells of '7 Terrible Days.' "

Pittsburgh (Pa.) Post-Gazette, July 4, 1987. "He Still Has Nightmares" (Wyatt Butterfield). Vince Leonard.

———, Nov. 15, 1986. "Wyatt Butterfield: At the Mercy of a Merciless Ocean—Letter from a Survivor."

Providence (R.I.) Journal, Jan. 9, 1980. "Rear Adm. Gilbert Hoover; on 1st Federal Nuclear Panel" (obituary).

Salt Lake City Tribune, Feb. 15, 1942. "New Cruiser USS Juneau Joins Service."

San Francisco Chronicle, Dec. 16, 1945. "Ten Sailors Lived—Their Story."

San Francisco Examiner, Apr. 4, 1943. "Juneau's Last Fight Related."

———, Apr. 4, 1943. "Mother of Heroes Christens Warship."

Santa Cruz Sentinel, Jan. 12, 1982. "Joseph P. F. Hartney" (obituary).

Stratford (Conn.) News, Mar. 31, 1988. "From Guadalcanal to the Boxing Ring; This Stratford Resident Fought in Both." Paul Miller.

The Times (London), Feb. 8, 1991. "The Families That Fight Together." Susan Ellicott.

Veterans of Foreign Wars Post 1623, June 1984. "Sullivan Tragedy Was 20 Years Old."

Washington Star, Feb. 24, 1991. "Tragic Legacy Drives Only Son, Legislation." Pat Kinney.

———, Feb. 3, 1943. "Sullivans Assure Wallace They Will Carry On for Sons."

———, Jan. 17, 1943. "Mother of 5 Boys Lost in War Still Hopes It's a Mistake."

Waterloo Courier, Feb. 21, 1991. "Sullivan Offspring Being Heard." Larry Ballard.

———, May 29, 1989. "Relative: Sullivan Family Coped Well With Tragedy."

———, Nov. 13, 1988. "Convention Center Renaming Brings Emotion, Reflection." Pat Kinney.

———, Nov. 10, 1988. "Survivors Describe Horror of Sinking of the *Juneau*." Pat Kinney.

———, Nov. 4, 1988. "Sullivan Brothers: Community Recognizes Sacrifice." Pat Kinney.

———, July 19, 1977. "The Sullivans Dedicated in Buffalo Park."

———, Apr. 25, 1972. "Mrs. Sullivan Is Lauded as Patriot." Elaine Brown.

———, Apr. 22, 1972. "Mother of City's Famous Sullivan Brothers Dies."

———, Mar. 18, 1968. "Sullivan in Navy Tradition Renewed."

———, Mar. 2, 1965. "Five Sullivans' Father Is Dead."

———, Nov. 11, 1962. "Sullivan Tragedy Was 20 Years Ago." Patty Johnson.

———, Oct. 7, 1958. "A Sullivan Carries on Tradition."

———, June 18, 1952. "Dedication . . . and Some Disturbing Thoughts." Allen Drury.

———, Oct. 24, 1943. "Young Widow of Sullivan Brother Will Take Job in War Plant to 'Carry On.' "

———, Jan. 17, 1943. "Sullivan Boy's Romance Told."

———, Jan. 17, 1943. "Sullivans Given Two Tributes in Congress Record."

———, Jan. 15, 1943. "Five Sullivans Dead, 'Shipmate' Writes Parents."

———, Jan. 13, 1943. "They're Fighting Irish Clan, the Sullivan Family." Kenneth Murphy.

———, Jan. 12, 1943. "Five Sullivans Missing." J. L. (Dixie) Smith.

Documents

Alaska Congressional Delegation. Resolution honoring Lt. Lawrence Williamson and his crew for rescuing *Juneau* survivors. 1987.

Alaska Legislature. Certificate honoring Capt. Lyman K. Swenson. May 15, 1987.

Andereggen, Steve. "The History of USS *Juneau* CLAA-52, WWII Cruiser."

Arison, Rae E. Report to commander in chief, U.S. Fleet, on operations of Nov. 12–13, 1942, Oct. 7, 1943.

Butterfield, Wyatt. Manuscript: "Seven Days in Hell."

Callaghan, Daniel J. Biographical sketch by Navy Department.

Chew, John L. Reminiscences. Oral History Office, U.S. Naval Institute, Annapolis, Md.

Coward, J. G. Report to commander in chief, U.S. Pacific Fleet, on sinking of the USS *Juneau* as seen from USS *Sterett*. Nov. 22, 1942.

Eleventh Bombardment Group, Headquarters. Daily report on operations. Nov. 13, 14, 15, 18, 1942.

———. Report on operations in Solomon Islands, July 31, 1942–Nov. 30, 1942. Dec. 3, 1942.

Emory, C. D. Report to commanding officer, USS *Atlanta*, on action with enemy on Nov. 13, 1942, and loss of *Atlanta*. Nov. 15, 1942.

Entrikin, William R. Letter to author concerning sighting of *Juneau* survivors. May 14, 1991.

———. Individual Flight Record, Nov. 1942–Feb. 1943.

Forrestal, James, Secretary of the Navy. Citation, Bronze Star Medal to Wyatt Butterfield.

Friend, Arthur. Letter to author. Aug. 4, 1991.

Gilbert, Victor. Unpublished manuscript on war experiences aboard USS *San Francisco*.

Gill, Robert L. Letter to author concerning sighting of *Juneau* survivors. June 20, 1991.

BIBLIOGRAPHY

————. Career sketch.

————. Report to Headquarters, Eleventh Bombardment Group, on sightings of *Juneau* survivors. n.d.

Hall, Perry, ed. "The Sterett Story." 1977.

Halsey, William F. Letter to Allen Heyn. Sept. 22, 1954.

————. Report to commander in chief, U.S. Pacific Fleet, on the circumstances of the loss of the *Juneau* and the relief of Capt. Gilbert Hoover from his command. Nov. 21, 1942.

————. Radio message to Adm. Aubrey Fitch ordering additional air search for *Juneau* survivors. Nov. 18, 1942.

Harding, President Warren G., Letter to Gilbert Hoover, commander of USS *California*, commending him for his gunnery and engineering performances for year ending June 30, 1922. Aug. 8, 1922.

Hartney, Joseph. Narrative, experience of *Juneau* survivors, recorded by Navy Department. Jan. 8, 1943.

Hein, S. F., Commander, Squadron 33. Letter to Commander Destroyers, Atlantic Squadron, commending work of Captain Swenson. Oct. 17, 1940.

Heyn, Allen. Narrative, experience of *Juneau* survivors, recorded by Navy Department. Sept. 23, 1944.

Heyn, Maud. Letters to her son Allen. Jan. 26, Feb. 5 and 7, 1943.

Hoover, Gilbert. Report to commander in chief, U.S. Pacific Fleet, on battle of Nov. 13, 1942. Nov. 15, 1942.

————. Report to Adm. Chester W. Nimitz on the submarine torpedo attack on task unit and sinking of USS *Juneau*. Nov. 14, 1942.

————. Report to commander in chief, U.S. Pacific Fleet, on submarine attack on task unit and sinking of USS *Juneau*. Nov. 14, 1942.

Hoover, Gilbert, Jr. Obituary for his father. Jan. 8, 1980.

Imperato, Beatrice. Notes on relationship with Madison Sullivan.

Jenkins, S. P. Report to commander in chief, U.S. Pacific Fleet, on torpedo plane attack of Nov. 12, 1942, off Guadalcanal. Nov. 26, 1942.

————. Report to commander in chief, U.S. Pacific Fleet, on

battle of Nov. 12–13, 1942, and loss of USS *Atlanta*. Nov. 20, 1942.

Knox, Frank. Citation, Navy Cross Medal award to Capt. Lyman K. Swenson.

Lamb, Raymond S. Radio message to Admiral Halsey reporting failure to find *Juneau* survivors. Nov. 17, 1942.

Leslie, Raymond F. Report to USS *Atlanta/Juneau* Reunion Association concerning the battle of Nov. 12–13. June 12, 1991.

Mantere, George. Narrative, experience of *Juneau* survivors, recorded by Navy Department.

McCandless, Bruce. Blinker signal to Captain Hoover reporting death of Admiral Callaghan and aides. Nov. 13, 1942.

McCombs, Charles E. Report to commander in chief, U.S. Pacific Fleet, on role of USS *Monssen* in battle of Nov. 13, 1942. Nov. 16, 1942.

McWilliams (Lt). Note dropped to survivors promising rescue.

Mott, William C. Letter to Mrs. H. E. Schonland regarding the award of the Congressional Medal of Honor to her husband for his role aboard the USS *San Francisco* in the Battle of Guadalcanal. Nov. 30, 1984.

Navy Department, Office of the Chief of Naval Operations, Division of Naval History. Biographical sketch of Lyman K. Swenson.

———. History of Enlisted Personnel Distribution, Section on Family Groups. Jan. 18, 1946.

———. History of Ships Named *Helena*.

———. History of Ships Named *Juneau*.

———. History of USS *Atlanta* (CL 51).

———. History of USS *Fletcher* (DD 445).

———. History of the USS *Helena* (CL 50).

———. History of USS *Lyman K. Swenson* (DD-729).

———. History of USS *San Francisco* (CA 38).

———. History of USS Sterett (DD 407).

———. Press release, "United States Ship *Helena* Receives First Navy Unit Citation." March 11, 1945.

———. Memorandum to the press, battle record of USS *Juneau*. Oct. 26, 1944.

———. Press release, "The Life and Death of the USS *Helena*." Sept. 5, 1943.

———. Telegram to Floyd Holmgren erroneously informing him that his son was missing in action. Jan. 11, 1943.

Nimitz, Chester W. Letter to Mr. and Mrs. Thomas Sullivan. June 2, 1952.

———. Preliminary report of action, Nov. 12–13, 1942. Dec. 26, 1942.

———. Report to commander in chief, U.S. Fleet, on circumstances of loss of *Juneau* and recommendation that Capt. Gilbert Hoover be sent back to sea. Dec. 4, 1942.

———. Communications to Frank Knox and other exchanges involving William F. Halsey, Richmond Kelly Turner, and Gilbert Hoover in regard to the battle of Nov. 13, 1942 and the sinking of the USS *Juneau*. Nov. 14, 1942–Nov. 27, 1942.

O'Neil, Roger. Narrative, experience aboard *Juneau* and account of sinking, recorded by Navy Department. Jan. 23, 1943.

Parker, Edward N. Oral history of USS *Cushing*'s role in battle of Guadalcanal, recorded by U.S. Naval Institute.

———. Report of engagement off Savo Island on Nov. 13, 1942, and destruction of the USS *Cushing*. Nov. 16, 1942.

Pfizenmeir, John. Role of USS *O'Bannon* in battle of Nov. 13, 1942. History of USS *O'Bannon* (DDE-450).

Rogers, Joseph. Manuscript: "This Is My Story."

Roosevelt, President Franklin D. Letter to Mr. and Mrs. T. F. Sullivan. Feb. 1, 1943.

Schonland, H. E. Action report to commander in chief, U.S. Pacific Fleet, on air attack of Nov. 12, 1942. Nov. 16, 1942.

———. Action report to commander in chief, U.S. Pacific Fleet, on loss of USS *Juneau*. Nov. 15, 1942.

Siciliano, Sam P., Navy correspondent. Press release, "War Record of the USS *San Francisco*."

Stanton, Diane, Grout Museum of History and Science, Waterloo, Ia. "The Sullivan Family: Fact Sheet." Oct. 1986.

Stokes, Murray. Engagement with Japanese surface units off Savo Island, about 0200, Nov. 13, 1942. Nov. 15, 1942.

Sullivan, Genevieve. Letter to her brother Joseph (Red). Nov. 23, 1942.

Swenson, Lyman K. Blinker signal to Hoover asking him to call for air coverage. Nov. 13, 1942.

BIBLIOGRAPHY

————. Blinker signal to Hoover describing damage to *Juneau*. Nov. 13, 1942.

————. Battle Bill and Emergency Procedures, USS *Juneau*. May 26, 1942.

————. Letters to family and friends. Oct. 1940–Apr. 1942.

Swenson, Russell (captain's nephew). Notes on naval career and events in the life of Lyman Knut Swenson.

Turner, Richmond K. Radio message to Halsey regarding *Juneau* sinking. Nov. 15, 1942.

United States Fleet, Headquarters of Commander-in-Chief. *Secret Information Bulletin,* no. 4, "Battle Experience, Solomon Islands Actions." Nov. 1942.

Veterans of Foreign Wars of the United States, Belmar-Wall Juneau Post 2620. History of USS *Juneau CL-52.*

Walker, George. Diary, operations of his B-17. Nov. 13–17, 1942.

Wang, Charles. Tape of experience in the water.

————. Letter to Mrs. Thomas Oberrender, widow of officer who went down with USS *Juneau.*

————. Narrative, experience of *Juneau* survivors, recorded by Navy Department. Feb. 10, 1945.

————. Letter to mother. Dec. 11, 1942.

————. Telegrams to mother, Dec. 9, 1942; Jan. 31, Mar. 30, 1943.

Wang, Richard. Biographical sketch of Charles Wang.

War Diary, *Juneau (CL-52).* Mar. 22, 1942–Oct. 31, 1942.

Williamson, Lawrence B. Letter to author concerning rescue of *Juneau* survivors. Oct. 8, 1991.

Wylie, J. C. Unpublished magazine manuscript, "The Loss of the *Juneau.*"

Zook, Lester. Narrative, experience of *Juneau* survivors, recorded by Navy Department. May 27, 1943.

————. Letter to Mr. and Mrs. Thomas Sullivan. Received Jan. 14, 1942.

Appendix

Last Muster Roll of the Crew of the USS *Juneau*

Enlisted Men

ABBOTT, Victor Harold	CMM(AA)
ACHESON, John Matthew	F3c V-6
AITCHISON, James Thomas	Sea2c V-6
ALLAN, Murray Glen	F1c
ALLEY, Harold Ivan	CTC(AA)
ALMON, Glen Foust	Sea2c
ANDERSON, Chester William	Sea2c
ANDERSON, Leonard Davis	EM2c V-6
APGAR, Robert David	Sea2c
AQUINO, James Nick	Sea1c
ARMITAGE, Bernard Francis	Sea2c V-6
ARMSTRONG, Wesley	CRM(AA)
ARNETT, Otis John, Jr.	F2c
ASTI, Alexander Patrick	Sea2c V-6
AUTERY, Willie, Jr.	GM3c
BAILEY, Charles William, Jr.	Sea1c

BAILEY, Walter Grover	Cox
BAINBRIDGE, George Frederick	Sea2c V-6
BAKER, John Clark	Cox
BAKOWSKI, John Joseph	GM3c O-1
BANKOWSKI, John Walter	CSF(AA)
BARBOUR, William Kyle	GM3c
BARDEN, Wilbur Duane	Cox
BARKER, Alfred Kinnio, 3rd.	Sea2c
BARMORE, Marvin Leroy	EM3c O-1
BASS, Edward Arthur	Sea2c
BATEMAN, Bosie Adylett	Sea1c
BATES, Wallace Julius	Sea2c
BATTAGLIA, Joseph Nicholos	SM1c
BAUBLITZ, Glenn Leroy	Sea1c
BAUCOM, Joseph Lamont	Sea1c V-6
BAUER, Robert Clayton	GM3c O-1
BEAMAN, George Jenks	Sea2c V-6
BEATY, Robert Woodruff	Sea2c V-6
BEAUMONT, William Howard	Sea1c
BEERS, Thomas Eugene	BM2c
BELISLE, Raymond Rene	Sea2c
BENNETT, Donald	EM3c
BERESFORD, John Anthony	CM3c
BERG, Stanley Paul	Sea1c
BERMAN, Alvin Seymour	Sea2c
BERNAT, Martin George, Jr.	Sea1c
BERNHARDT, Gust	Sea1c
BERRY, Ralph Herbert	CEM(PA)
BERTOCCI, Charles	Sea2c
BERTOLET, Harry Benjamin, Jr.	RM3c
BICKERT, Elwood Oscar	Sea2c
BIECHMAN, John Charles	Sea2c
BIRCH, Edward David	Aerog2c
BLACKWELL, Joseph Warren	F1c
BLATTENBERGER, Cletus Clair	F3c V-6
BLAU, Donald John	Sea1c
BLOCK, Donald	Sea1c
BLOH, John Franklin	Sea2c
BOATRIGHT, Jack Robert	GM2c
BOLTER, Clinton Francis	RM2c
BORDEN, James Alexander	Sea2c
BOSTROM, William Otto	SK2c V-6
BOTHNER, Albert Robert	F3c
BOUDREAU, John Donald	Sea1c
BOWLIN, Garnet Houston	Sea1c
BRAA, Fredrick William	MM1c

APPENDIX

BRADLE, John	Sea1c
BRADSHAW, Martin Joseph	Sea2c
BRADSHAW, Willis Tom	Sea2c
BRAY, Dempster Shell	MM1c
BRENNAN, John Joseph	Sea2c
BRENNER, Jack	Sea2c
BROWN, Aaron	MAtt2c
BROWN, Frederick Ervin	CEM(PA)
BROWN, Jack Cone	Sea1c
BROWN, James Arnold	Ptr3c
BRUNEAU, Howard Alexander	Sea1c
BRYAN, Kensey Newton	Sea1c
BRYSON, Clarence Willard	Sea2c
BUBB, Ralph Charles	Sc3c
BUMBALL, Stephen, Jr.	Y3c V-6
BURDI, Frank Joseph	F3c V-6
BURKETT, Charles Raymond	Sea2c
BURNS, Raymond Francis	Sea1c
BUTTERFIELD, Fred Currier	Sea2c
BUTTERFIELD, Wyatt Bertram	Sea2c
BYERS, Hume McNeal, Jr.	Sea2c
BYINGTON, Charles Norman	Sea2c
BYRD, Earl	Sea1c
BYRON, Thomas Clarence	BM1c
CADBY, Robert Andrews, Jr.	Sea2c
CAHILL, Adrian Joseph	Sea2c
CAHILL, William Matthew	Sea2c
CALDARA, William Fred	F2c V-6
CAMPBELL, Colin Hugh	Sea2c
CAMPBELL, Gordon Malcom	F1c
CANNON, James William	SC2c V-6
CARACCIOLO, Anthony Bernard	F1c
CARPENTER, George Raymond	Sea2c V-2
CARR, Clifford James	Sea2c
CASTRO, Clement	Y2c
CAULK, Charles Leonard, Jr.	Sea2c V-6
CAULK, Howard Wright, Jr.	Sea2c V-6
CAVA, John	Sea2c
CECIL, Orrel Glenn	PhM2c
CERANIC, Thomas Nickales Paul	Sea1c
CHEGUS, Steve	Sea2c
CHERMACK, John Adolph	Sea2c
CHMIEL, John Peter	Sea2c
CHRISTMAN, Otto	CTM(PA)
CLASS, Francis Edgar	Sea2c
CLYDE, Emmette Ham	Bkr3c

COATES, Charles	CM1c
COHILL, Joseph Edward	Sea2c
COOMBS, Charles Kenneth	Sea2c
COOMBS, Russell Arnold	BM1c
CONNOLLY, Charles Francis	Cox
CONNOLLY, John William	Y3c V-6
CONNOLLY, Robert Francis	Sea1c V-6
COOK, Winston Fenton	TC1c
COOKE, Charlie Alton	EM1c
COULTER, Joseph May	Sea2c V-6
COWARD, Edward Cott, Jr.	FC3c
COX, Louis Edward	CBM(AA)
COX, Roy Theodore, Jr.	CM3c V-6
COYNE, William Michael	Sea2c V-6
CRAWFORD, William Victor	F1c V-6
CRAWLEY, Clifford Lee	CEM(AA)
CRITCHLEY, Edward Moses	Sea2c V-6
CROOK, Warren Holman	SM3c
CRUM, Orrin Lewis, Jr.	SK2c V-6
CURTIS, Chappell Howard	Cox
CURTIS, Relis	OC3c
CWYNAR, Walter John	GM2c
D'AGOSTINO, Paul David	SM2c
DALLISSIO, James William	Sea2c
DAMON, Curtis Wheeler	Sea1c
DAMON, Donald David	Sea2c V-6
DANIELLO, Frank Anthony	Sea2c
DAVIDSON, William Simpson, Jr.	Sea1c
DAVIS, George Harry	Sea2c
DAVIS, James Buchanon	Sea2c
DAVIS, Silas Jasper, Jr.	Sea2c
DAWSON, Claude Van	BM2c
DAY, Donald Stewart	Sea2c
DAY, Richard Edward	F2c V-6
DAYBILL, Mark Robert	CTC (PA)
DEGRAZIA, Albert Peter	Sea2c
DEGROAT, Carl Otto	Cox
DEL GIUDICK, Peter Paul	Sea1c
DE MARCO, Louis Wilson	Sea2c
DENIS, John William	Sea2c V-6
DENNIS, Dicky Henry	Sea1c
DENNIS, Jeremiah Daniel	MM2c
DEPEW, George	Sea2c
DEYO, Raymond Dean	Sea2c V-6
DIAL, George Lawrence	F3c
DICKSTEIN, David	CRM(PA)

APPENDIX

DIEDERICH, Heinz Gunter	MM2c
DONNELLY, Roger Henry	Sea2c V-6
DOUGHERTY, Edward Aloysius, Jr.	WT1c
DOYLE, William Daniel	Sea2c
DRAPER, Donald Leonard	Sea1c
DRUMHELLER, Ned Blabern	Sea2c
DUDKO, Dimitro	Sea1c V-6
DUL, Joseph John	Sea1c V-6
DUMAIS, Armand Emilien	Sea2c
DUMPER, Lawrence Hunt	Sea1c
DUXBURY, John Joseph	Sea2c V-6
ECKERT, William Albert	Sea1c V-2
EDGAR, Maynard Harley	EM2c
EDINGTON, Glenn Spencer	EM2c V-6
EDSALL, Robert Eric	Sea2c
EDWARDS, Edward David	BM2c
ELLIOTT, Emanuel	RM2c V-6
ELSESSER, Robert August	Sea1c
EMRICH, Harold Vincent	Sea2c
ENGBERG, Gordon Edward	SM2c V-6
ENYART, Owen Benjamin	FC3c V-6
EUSTACE, Edward Joseph	Sea2c V-6
EUSTACE, Edwin James	Sea2c V-6
EVANS, Cleo William	Sea1c
FACINOLI, Frank John	GM3c
FAGAN, John Joseph	CGM(AA)
FALTYSEK, Edward Jerome	Sea1c O-1
FANT, Russell Joseph	BM1c
FARMER, James Murray	Sea2c V-6
FELL, Stanley Allen	F1c
FERGUSON, John Baptist	MM2c V-6
FERNANDEZ, Casper Peter	Sea2c V-2
FERRUGGIARO, Alfred James	Sea1c V-6
FIECHTL, Benedict Lyman	EM1c
FINK, Glenn Russell	F1c
FITZGERALD, Victor James	Sea2c V-6
FLANDERS, Harold Arthur	BM1c
FLEMING, Robert Alexander	F2c
FLINT, William Carl	Sea2c V-6
FLOYD, Robert McKenney	Sea1c
FOLEY, William James	Sea2c V-6
FOLK, Donald Eugene	EM1c
FONTONELLA, Joseph	Sea1c V-6
FRANKFORT, Lloyd Shue	Sea2c V-6
FRANKLIN, Howard	Sea1c
FRASCA, Anthony Vincent	Sea2c

FREEHAN, Paul Webster	Sea2c
FRENCH, Jerome Edward	Sea1c
FRIEND, Arthur Theodore	Sea1c
FROST, Kenneth Thomas	Sea1c V-6
FUTERKO, Michael	Sea2c
GALLAGHER, Daniel Vincent	Sea2c
GALLAGHER, George Arthur	Sea2c
GALUSKI, Henry	Sea2c
GARDNER, Henry Jordan	MM2c
GATTIS, Marvin Lee	GM3c V-6
GAYLE, Robert Curtis	Cox
GERTZ, John Herman	Sea1c V-6
GESSINGER, Robert Ray	Sea2c V-6
GEST, Francis Joseph	Sea2c
GIESEN, Leo Sigmund	Em3c V-6
GILBRIDE, Andrew Leo	CMM(AA)
GILLEN, Joseph Thomas	Sea2c V-6
GOGGLIN, Albert	Sea2c V-6
GRADY, Richard Joseph	Sea2c
GRAHAM, Alden Douglas	Sea1c
GRANT, Charles Carl	CCSTD(PA)
GRAVES, Oscar Romeo	Sea1c V-6
GRAY, Robert Francis	Sea2c
GRAY, William Everett	GM3c
GREENLEE, Galen	MM2c
GREER, Herbert Austin	TM3c
GRUBB, William Osbourne	Sea2c V-6
GRYCKY, John Andrew	Sea2c V-6
GUARENTE, Gustave Raymond	MM2c
GUIDA, Bernard Michael	Sea2c V-6
GUTHIEL, William Frederick	Cox
HAFNER, Jack	Sea1c
HAGELGANS, Walter LaVelle	Sea2c V-6
HALE, Tom McMoy	Sea2c V-3
HALEY, Frank John	Sea2c V-6
HALL, Earl Aloysius, Jr.	Sea2c
HALLGREN, Edwin Harold	Sea2c
HAMILTON, Lane, Jr.	Cox
HAMMEAL, Earl Theodore	Sea1c
HAMMOND, Oscar Hunter	CWT(AA)
HANCOCK, John Thomas	F1c
HANSEN, Quentin Wilbur	F1c
HARBOLD, Lewis Henry	F3c
HARDWICK, Timothy Dwight	F3c V-6
HARRINGTON, John Leslie	Sea2c V-6
HARRINGTON, Joseph Henry	Sea2c

APPENDIX

HARRIS, Robert Claude	MM1c
HARRISON, Fred Dryden	Sea1c
HARRISON, George Perry	Sea1c
HART, Daniel John	Sea2c V-6
HARTLINE, Robert Roy	F3c V-6
HARTNETT, Emmett Eugene	F1c V-6
HARTNEY, Joseph Patrick Francis	SM2c
HARVEY, James Robert	GH3c
HARVEY, Ralph Elmer	Sea2c
HASCHAK, Michael	Sea2c V-6
HATEM, Albert Anthony	F2c
HAUSZ, Joseph, Jr.	Sea2c V-6
HAWTHORNE, Walter Francis	Sea1c V-6
HAYES, Charles Stanley	Sea2c
HAYES, William Patrick	Sea2c
HAYLES, John Thomas, Jr.	F1c
HAYS, Richard Shevlin, Jr.	Sea2c V-3
HEADINGTON, James Benjamin	F2c V-6
HEATH, Charles Lawrence	Sea2c
HECKEL, John Francis	F2c
HEINZINGER, Edward James	Sea1c V-6
HELT, Jay William	F2c V-6
HENDRIX, Simon Thomas	F1c V-6
HENNESSEY, James Joseph	Sea2c V-6
HENNESSY, Robert Patrick	Sea2c V-6
HENNING, Daniel Valentine	MM1c
HENNINGTON, Richard Joseph	SC2c
HERBERT, Sidney Hurell	Sea2c
HERMANNS, John Walter	Sea2c V-6
HERR, Charles Edmund	Sea2c
HERSHEY, Lavern Eugene	Sea2c V-6
HEYN, Allen Clifton	Sea2c
HICKEY, Joseph James	Sea2c V-6
HICKEY, Joseph Thomas	F3c V-6
HICKS, Ellsworth John	WT1c
HICKS, George Henry	Sea2c V-6
HIGGINS, Robert Harold	Sea2c V-6
HIGHT, Wilfred Holden	Sea2c V-6
HILL, Richard	Sea2c
HILL, Thomas Elija	SF3c
HINSON, Clarence	Sea1c V-6
HISSEM, Herbert Lewis, Jr.	F3c V-6
HODGE, Burnell Bonner	SF3c V-6
HOFFMAN, Conway	Sea2c V-6
HOFFMAN, Henry Reubin	Sea2c V-6
HOLBROOK, Ernest, Jr.	Sea2c

HOLLAND, George Robert	Sea2c
HOLLAND, Roy Curtis	Sea2c
HOLMGREN, Frank Alfred	Sea2c
HUNT, Bernard John	Sea2c
HURBAN, Frank Joseph	Sea2c
HYNARD, Emery Charles	F2c V-6
INGRAM, Frank	Sea2c V-6
IRWIN, George Edward	EM2c
JACKSON, Aubrey Stancil	RM3c
JACKSON, Herbert Edward	Sea2c
JACKSON, Sidney LaVerne	Sea1c V-6
JAMES, Arthur	MAtt2c
JAMIESON, Francis Roland	F1c
JAMROS, Joseph John	Sea2c V-6
JEFFERSON, Benjamin Franklin	MAtt2c
JENKINS, Carl Melvin	Cox
JOHNSON, Ned Burton	Sea1c
JOHNSON, Richard Willis	QM2c
JOHNSTON, Gerald Clyde	Sea2c
JONES, Bart, Jr.	Sea1c
JONES, Marvin Randolph	MAtt3c
JONES, Walter Thomas	Y3c
JONES, Winfield Scott, Jr.	F1c V-6
JORDAN, Mitchell Leland	EM3c
JOSEFICK, Stephen George	Sea2c V-6
JUNOT, John Edward	Sea2c V-6
JUSCZYK, Sylvester Jacob	RM3c
KALINICH, Charles, Jr.	Sea1c
KANE, Thomas, Jr.	F3c V-6
KEEN, John Samuel	Em1c
KELLEHER, Daniel William, Jr.	Sea2c V-6
KELLS, Hugh Andrew, Jr.	Sea2c V-6
KENNEDY, Marion Kenneth	Sea2c
KEPPLE, Robert Craig	Sea2c
KERMIN, Milo	Sea2c
KIENZLE, George Henry, Jr.	Sea2c
KIJEX, Benjamin Stanley	Sea1c
KILE, Wayne Dale	GM2c V-6
KILLIAN, Harvey	F2c V-6
KINGDON, Wilmer	F2c V-6
KISTLER, Edward Glen	Sea2c V-6
KLISHON, Peter Stanley	Sea2c
KLUS, Stanley Joseph	Sea2c V-6
KNAPP, Robert Thomas	QM1c
KOEPER, Edward Louis	Sea2c
KOKOSKA, Stanley	Sea2c V-6

APPENDIX

KOLSCHOWSEY, Donald John	Sea2c V-6
KOWALSKI, Walter	MM1c
KRAKOWER, Robert Norton	F2c V-3
KRALL, Albert Joseph	Sea1c V-6
KRALL, Michael Thomas	Sea1c V-6
KUNKA, Steve	Sea1c V-6
LAMBERT, Cecil Grant	SC3c V-6
LANDIS, Edward Ritter	Sea2c
LANIER, Roy	CTC(PA)
LARSON, Laurence Everett	Msmth1c
LAUXMAN, Herbert John	RM3c
LAVALLEE, Joseph Arthur	Sea2c V-6
LAVEY, Lawrence John	Cox
LAWRENCE, Anthony James	Sea2c
LAYMON, Cecil Herbert	CWT(PA)
LEDDY, Paul James	Sea1c
LEE, James Walter	Sea2c
LEE, Robert Edward	Sea2c
LEIMAN, Elliot	Sea1c
LENNARTZ, Carl Michael	Sea2c
LEWIS, Julian Harding	F1c
LIGAMMARI, Anthony Bernard	MM1c
LIPOWSKI, Benjamin	Sea1c
LIPSCOMB, Delmar Church	PhM2c
LISTER, Walter Olan	RM3c
LOKEY, Allen Zane, Jr.	Bmkr2c
LONG, Harvey William	Sea2c V-6
LONG, Montie Oliver	GM3c O-1
LONG, William Francis	Sea2c V-6
LONG, William John	Sea2c V-6
LOUGHNANE, John Joseph	Sea2c V-6
LUETH, Walter	CMM(PA)
LUSA, Peter Paul	EM3c V-6
LYON, Edward Allen	FC1c
MacDOUGALL, James Albert, Jr.	Cox M-1
McCANN, Robert Frederick	GM2c V-6
McCARTHY, Francis Xavier	Sea1c
McCARTHY, John Joseph, Jr.	Sea2c V-6
McCONNELL, Joseph Richard	Sea2c V-6
McCORMACK, Robert William	Sea2c
McCORMICK, Robert William	Sea2c V-6
McCRACKEN, Ralph Eugene	TM2c
McCRORY, Hubert Lee	SC3c V-6
McDONALD, Francis Xavier	Sea2c
McDONOUGH, Leo Anthony	SF1c
McDONOUGH, Martin Francis	Sea2c V-6

McEWAN, Earl Herbert	Sea2c V-6
McFADDEN, William Henry, 3rd	Sea2c V-6
McGINLEY, Francis Patrick	Sea2c V-6
McGINN, Charles William	Sea2c
McHUGH, Martin Patrick	Sea2c
McKEE, John Aloysius	GM1c
McLESKEY, Harry Neal	F2c V-6
McNALLY, Edward George	Sea2c V-6
McSPADDEN, John William	CM2c
MADDEN, Donald Thomas	Sea2c V-6
MAGILL, William Watson	Sea2c
MALKOWITZ, Michael	WT2c
MALLETT, James Edward	EM3c
MANTERE, George Ilmari	GM1c
MARKOVETZ, Francis	Bkr1c
MASON, Robert Walker	Sea1c V-6
MASSENGILL, Harold Willie	Sea1c
MASSEY, Russell Bruce	FC1c
MATTESON, Arthur Levi	Sea2c V-6
MEEKER, William George, Jr.	Sea2c V-6
MEKRUT, Fred Frank	Sea2c V-6
MENARD, Homer Paul	TC1c
MENTZER, John Hooper	Sea1c
MERCHANT, Robert Andrew	SC3c V-6
MERCHANT, Theodore Donald	PhM3c
MERCURIO, Dominic Benedict	Sea1c
MERKLE, Ferdinand Joseph	Sea1c
MERRIFIELD, Howard Henry	Sea2c
MICHAEL, Stanley Patrick	Sea1c
MICHAUX, Edward	Cox
MILLS, Howard Dolland	BM1c
MINER, Donald Norman	Sea1c
MINES, Wilbert Earl	OS2c
MOETZ, George	Sea1c V-6
MOGIELSKI, Frank Michael	Sea1c V-6
MOIR, John	OTC(AA)
MOONEY, James Henry	F2c V-6
MOORE, Clifford Carl	Sea1c
MOORE, Harold Raymond	Sea1c
MOORE, James Adolphus	GM1c
MOORE, James William	OC3c
MOORE, Raymond William	Sea2c
MORAN, Thomas Joseph	Sea1c
MORELLI, Patrick James	Sea1c
MORGAN, Jesse Jr.	Sea1c
MORO, George George	Sea2c V-6

APPENDIX

MORRIS, Carl Livingston	EM1c
MOSHER, Robert Arthur	Sea1c
MOZEVECH, Alphonse Martin	RM3c V-3
MOZGAWA, Edmund Joseph	Sea2c V-3
MULDOON, George Arthur	Sea2c
MULRY, John Edward	F3c V-6
MURPHY, Owen Sylvester, Jr.	FC3c
MURRAY, Albert Francis	F2c V-6
MURTAUGH, Edward	Sea2c V-6
MYERS, Glenn Owen	CQM(PA)
MYLER, Dave Thomas	SK2c
NAMEJANSKY, Edward Ernest	RM3c
NEIDER, Harold Paul	Sea2c
NELSON, Charlie	MAtt2c
NELSON, Daniel	F2c
NELSON, William Frederick	Sea2c V-6
NENNIG, Cyril Peter	Y2c
NETO, Modesto	OC1c FAD
NEWMAN, Alfred Henry	Sea2c
NICHOLS, Wade	F1c
NICHOLSON, Peter Albert	Sea2c V-6
NITZ, Theodore	SK1c
NOLL, Theodore	Sea2c V-6
NORELL, Dick Carter	EM2c
NORRIS, Joseph Edward	Bmkr2c
NOVOTNY, Frank Adolph	F1c
O'DONNELL, John Joseph	Sea2c V-6
OLDREAD, Edmond Joseph	WT1c
ORIAS, Michael	SC1c
OSTERGREN, Eric Gustaf	FC3c
PACHOLEK, Peter Joseph	Sea2c V-6
PAGE, John Walker, Jr.	Bakr1c
PAGNILLO, Peter	Sea2c V-6
PAINE, Winston Warren	EM3c
PALMER, Bruce Davis	Sea2c
PALMOS, Paul	EM2c V-6
PARKER, William Russell	F2c V-6
PARTEN, George Warren	PhM3c
PATPALAK, Andrew Thomas	Sea2c V-6
PATSEL, Arlie McKinley	Sea1c
PEACE, Alonzo Franklin	BM2c
PEACOCK, George Wilmer	Cox
PETERS, Harry Erwin	Sea2c V-6
PETERSON, Anthony James	Sea2c
PETERSON, Fred Eric	F1c
PHILLIPS, Raymond Joseph	Sea2c V-6

PHLEGAR, Philip Eldridge	FC2c V-6
PIERCE, Harry	Sea1c
PIERCE, Louis Lee	FC1c V-6
PIERCE, Theodore Glenn	Sea1c
POARCH, John Trammell	F1c V-6
POGUE, Freddie Wilson	GM3c
POHL, Lester	Sea2c
POISSANT, Duane Larson	Msmth1c
POLLEY, Arthur Henry	Sea2c V-6
POSEY, William Cullen	Sea1c
POWELL, Clarence Daniel	Cox
PRESLAK, Peter	Sea1c
PRICE, Charles Henry	MM1c
PRICE, Warren Clyde	Sea1c
PRITCHETT, Warren Neal	F1c V-6
PUSTELNY, Michael Joseph	F2c
QUINLAN, Philip Douglas	Sea1c
RABKIN, Israel	Sea2c V-6
RAY, Norbert Lorraine	WT2c
REAGAN, George Hubert	CWT(PA)
REDMON, Alexander	MM1c
REGEIC, Joseph Michael	Sea2c
REICHELT, Henry Neil	Sea2c V-6
REILLY, Jeremiah William	GM3c
REITMEYER, John Paul	SF2c V-6
RHODES, Robert Charles	Sea2c V-6
RICHARDS, John Anthony	Sea1c
RICHMOND, Glenn Francis	F2c V-6
RICIGLIANO, Frank John	Sea2c
RIKARD, John Everett	Sea1c
RIPLEY, James W.	Sea2c
RITCHEY, J. D.	Sea1c
ROBERSON, Leroy Raulston	SK1c
ROBINSON, Frederick Funston	BM2c
ROBINSON, Lester Cornell, Jr.	MM2c
ROBINSON, William Harve	CEC(AA)
ROE, George Daniel	SC2c V-6
ROGERS, Louis	Sea2c V-6
ROGERS, Mason Bacot	CM3c
ROGERS, Patrick Anthony	Sea2c V-6
ROHLOFF, William	Sea2c V-6
ROHRBACH, Melvin Frederick	Sea2c V-6
ROPER, Sydney Lee	Sea1c
ROSS, Arthur Ray	WT2c
ROSS, Robert Tillman	Sea1c V-6
ROSSI, Jean Elmore	Sea1c V-3

RUDDY, John Laurence	Sea2c V-6
RUDOLPH, John William	Sea1c
RUFF, Adam	Sea1c
SAAF, Courtland Philip	Sea2c V-2
SACCOMANNI, Patsy	Sea2c
SALLEE, Bruce Terry	FC3c
SAMPSON, George Richard, Jr.	MM2c V-6
SANDEL, Lloyd George	MM1c
SATTERFIELD, Kenneth Russell	Y1c
SAXER, Lawrence Edward	Sea1c V-6
SCULLY, Frederick John	Y2c
SEALEY, Carl Edward	MM1c
SELL, Frank Mitchell	Sea2c
SELOBYT, Stanley Steven	Sea2c V-6
SERAMBA, James Kendall	Sea1c
SHAFER, Carl George	SC3c
SHALITTA, Simon	Sea2c V-6
SHAMP, James Benjamin	Sea2c
SHEAHAN, Martin Albert	Sea2c V-6
SHEPPARD, William Morris	F1c V-6
SHERMAN, Robert Edward	Sea1c
SHOTT, Joseph Michael	MM1c
SIEGLE, Walter Orville	Sea2c V-6
SILVA, Robert Joseph	MM1c
SIMS, William Turner	PhM2c
SINK, Dwight Gray	Sea1c
SLAEY, Willard Bonita	MM2c
SMITH, Edward Allen	WT2c
SMITH, Fred Cecil	EM2c
SNEED, Thomas Paul	OC2c
SNESAR, Joseph Frank	Sea2c V-6
SNINCSAK, Theodore Michael	Sea2c
SNYDER, Christie John	Sea2c
SOLDMAN, Roy Frank	Sea1c
SOULE, LeRoy Walter	Sea2c
SPARKS, Calvin Coolidge	SC3c
SPECK, Charles John	Cox O-1
SPEENBURG, Clinton Andrew	WT2c
SPENCER, Harrison Leonard	Sea1c
STAHL, William Leland	Sea2c V-6
STALCUP, Merle Stanley	BM2c
ST. AMAND, Leo Roger	F2c
STEVES, Royal John	Sea2c V-6
STEWART, Arlie Boyd, Jr.	Sea2c
STEWART, Guy Alton	BM2c
STEWART, Ian Hamilton	Sea1c

STEWART, Stanley Vernon	SK3c V-6
STEWART, William	GM3c
STINSON, Walter Mason	CPhM(PA)
STRAUB, Eugene Neter	GH2c
STROUP, Merle John	Sea2c V-6
STULL, Robert Neal	Sea2c
SULLIVAN, Albert Leo	Sea2c V-6
SULLIVAN, Francis Henry	Cox V-6
SULLIVAN, George Thomas	GM2c V-6
SULLIVAN, Joseph Eugene	Sea2c V-6
SULLIVAN, Madison Abel	Sea2c V-6
TAULBEE, Arnold	WT1c
TAYLOR, Douglas Shelbert	BM2c V-6
TAYLOR, Roy Edwin	Sea2c
TEICHMAN, Robert Thomas	Sea2c
TERLUK, John Joseph	Sea2c V-6
TESLA, Joseph Francis	Sea2c V-2
TEUFEL, William Raymond	Sea2c
THOMAS, Edward	FC2c
THOMAS, Theodore Roosevelt	Sea2c
THOMPKINS, Wilbur John	Sea2c V-6
THOMPSON, Elza Laymond	MoMM2c V-6
TICE, Thomas Green	Sea2c
TIERNEY, John Joseph	Sea2c V-6
TORJUSEN, Edmund John	Msmth2c
TOWNER, Cornelius Orville, Jr.	Sea1c
TRAVIS, Elmer James, Jr.	Sea2c
TRAVIS, Wayne Inglis	Bkr2c
TREST, Guy Colon	GM1c
TUCK, George Thomas	GM2c
TURNER, William John	MM1c
TUTERA, John	Sea2c V-6
TUTTLE, Fred	Sea2c V-6
URBON, Stanley Edward	Sea2c V-6
VANDE WALLE, Frank, Jr.	GM3c
VANDRILLA, Steven Roland	Sea2c V-6
VAN GEEM, Carl Edward	GM3c
VAN HASSEL, Harold William	Sea2c V-6
VANN, Robert Rager	Bmkr2c
VELLA, Tom	SC3c
VICTORY, Roy	MAtt1c
VINTON, Donald Edward	QM3c

APPENDIX

VIRCHOW, LeRoy Frank	BM1c
WALLACE, George Albert	F2c
WALLACE, John	Sea2c
WALLEN, Pershing George	CM3c
WALSH, Francis Michael	Sea2c V-6
WALTERS, Thomas James	GM3c
WALTMAN, Jesse Baker	WT2c
WARBURTON, Robert Henry	Sea2c V-6
WASHINGTON, James Decordell	MAtt2c V-6
WASHURNE, Herbert Russell	Sea2c V-6
WATFORD, Samuel Lee	OS1c
WATSON, Daniel McKay, Jr.	MM2c
WAWRZYNOWICZ, Andrew Joseph	Sea2c V-6
WEAVER, Norman Edgar	CRM(AA)
WEBER, George Henry	WT1c
WEEKS, Harold Francis	Sea2c V-6
WEEKS, William James	Sea2c V-6
WEINBERGER, Russell Victor	Sea2c
WEITOWIC, Philip	F3c
WENTWORTH, Vern LeRoy	FC3c
WERLY, William Gustav	GM3c O-1
WHEATLEY, Booker Taliaferro	MAtt1c
WHITE, George Linwood, Jr.	Sea1c
WHITE, Richard Melvin	Sea1c
WHITE, Russell Perry	Sea1c
WILLIAMS, James Dixon	EM1c
WILLIAMS, Robert Raymond	MM2c
WILLIAMS, Russell Earl	Sea2c V-6
WILLOUGHBY, George Arthur	Sea1c V-6
WILSON, Alfred David	Sea1c V-6
WINKELRIED, George David	Sea1c
WINTLE, William	Sea1c V-6
WISEGARVER, William Howard	MM2c
WOLFE, Donald Paul	MM2c
WOOD, Roosevelt	MAtt3c
WOOD, Wilbur Irwin	Sea2c V-6
WOOLLEY, Ernest	Sea2c
WRIGHT, Grover Rodeheaver	GM2c
WRIGHT, Harry	Sea2c V-6
WYLES, Willie	MAtt3c
YADDOW, Wayne John	Sea2c V-6
YAROSZ, Stanley Peter, Jr.	Sea2c V-6

YOSCO, Albert Anthony	Sea2c V-6
YOUNG, Clayton Wolf	F1c
YOUNG, Major Eliga	MAtt2c V-6
ZAK, Adam Valentine	F2c V-6
ZENKER, Julius	Sea1c
ZGLISZEWSKI, Clements	F2c V-6
ZIANA, Albert William	Sea2c
ZOOK, Lester Eugene	SM1c
ZUBOS, Walter	CY(PA)

Officers

BAUMBACH, E. O.	Lt.
BLODGETT, J. T.	Lt. (jg)
BLUE, J. S.	Lt. Comdr.
COX, R. M., Jr.	Ens.
DOUDIET, N. W.	Lt.
FARMER, W. H.	Lt. Comdr.
FETCHER, W. M.	Lt. (jg)
FISHER, H. E.	Ens.
FODALE, C. B.	Ens.
FRIEDEN, D. L.	Ens.
FULLER, G. S.	Lt.
GEARING, H. C. III	Lt.
GLENN, R. C.	Lt. (jg)
GRAF, W. F.	Lt. Comdr.
GRAHAM, F. C.	Lt.
GRANT, C. S.	Lt.
HOBBY, W. M., Jr.	Comdr.
JONES, Q. B.	Lt.
KLOTER, J. A.	Ens.
LYSTER, T. C., Jr.	Lt.
MAIN, M. G.	Ens.
NASON, B. C.	Ens.
NEFF, J. G.	Lt. Comdr.
OBERRENDER, T. O.	Lt. Comdr.
O'NEIL, R. W.	Lt.
OSBORN, W. G.	Lt.
PITNEY, J. W.	Ens.
RODDY, T. M.	Lt. (jg)
SALVAGE, J. W.	Lt.

APPENDIX

SUTTON, S. B.	Ens.
SWENSON, L. K.	Capt.
THOM, H.	Ens.
TRAXLER, V. H., Jr.	Ens.
WANG, C. N.	Lt. (jg)
WHEELER, C. L.	Lt.
WILLIAMS, K.	Lt. Comdr.
WILLIAMS, T. H., Jr.	Lt. (jg)

Index

A

Aaron Ward, USS, 102, 122, 133
Abe, Vice Admiral Hiroaki, 103,
    112, 114, 133
  horseshoe battle formation of,
    103–04, 106, 117
  orders 180-degree turn, 104–05,
    121
  pessimism about Yamamoto's
    battle plan, 91–93
  retired in disgrace, 134
Abel, George W., 13
Abel, May, 13–14, 247–48
Akatsuki, 131
Amatsukaze, 75, 89, 104, 112,
    121, 131–32, 134
Analects (Sun-tze), 76
Anderson, William, 224, 226,
    231–32
Arizona, USS, 11, 24
Atlanta, USS, 36, 62, 94, 102, 107,
    111, 116–19, 121, 133

Australia, 50, 64, 89
  Japanese submarine operations
    off coast of, 45

B

B-17. *See* Gill, First Lieutenant
    Robert L.
Balboa, Panama Canal Zone, 45,
    49–50, 62
Bali, 114
Ball, Bill, 11–12, 17, 24
Ball, Masten, 11
Ballard, USS, 223, 225, 233, 234
Barton, USS, 102, 122, 133
battle formation
  Japanese, 103–04, 106, 114
  U.S., 102, 116
Berman, Alvin, 188
Blodgett, Lieutenant John
  death of, 213
  survival after sinking, 169, 183–
    84, 199, 204, 206

DAN KURZMAN, a former foreign correspondent for *The Washington Post*, is the author of eleven previous books and the winner of five major literary and journalistic awards. He won the Overseas Press Club's Cornelius Ryan Award for the best book on foreign affairs for *Miracle of November: Madrid's Epic Stand 1936* and for *Subversion of the Innocents*; the George Polk Memorial Award for articles that formed the basis for his book *Santo Domingo: Revolt of the Damned*; the National Jewish Book Award for *Ben-Gurion: Prophet of Fire*; and the Newspaper Guild's Front Page Award for dispatches he wrote from Cuba.

Mr. Kurzman has written or broadcast from almost every country in Europe, Asia, Africa, the Middle East, and Latin America. Before joining *The Washington Post*, he served as Paris correspondent for the International News Service, as Jerusalem correspondent for NBC News, and as Tokyo bureau chief of the McGraw-Hill News Service.